THE GENEALOGICAL SUBLIME

A VOLUME IN THE SERIES
Public History in Historical Perspective

Edited by
Marla R. Miller

THE
GENEALOGICAL
SUBLIME

JULIA
CREET

University of Massachusetts Press
Amherst & Boston

Copyright © 2020 by University of Massachusetts Press
All rights reserved
Printed in the United States of America

ISBN 978-1-62534-480-9 (paper); 479-3 (hardcover)

Designed by Jen Jackowitz
Set in Monotype Dante & Trade Gothic
Printed and bound by Maple Press, Inc.

Cover design Frank Gutbrod
Cover art by Elias Sch./Pixabay.com, Creative Commons

Library of Congress Cataloging-in-Publication Data
A catalog record for this book is available from the Library of Congress

British Library Cataloguing-in-Publication Data
A catalog record for this book is available from the British Library.

CONTENTS

ACKNOWLEDGMENTS

Much of the primary research for this book was conducted in the process of making my documentary about the industry of family history, *Data Mining the Deceased: Ancestry and the Business of Family* (2017). To my camera crew and editors (and dear friends) Wrik Mead, Andrew Nisker, Almerinda Travassos, Ryan Randall, Zab Hobart, Mary Daniels, and Dennis Day, and to Linda Fong at TVO, you were invaluable in capturing and shaping the stories that became the documentary and now this book.

People gave generously of their time in discussions and interviews, not all of which are referenced in this book, but whose influence and voices shaped my thinking throughout. First, to Henry Blumberg, president of the Latvian Special Interest Group of the Jewish Genealogical Society of Canada, I owe a special debt. An orphan with no known relatives, Mr. Blumberg managed to reconstruct a family line with over 1,000 members; yet, at the same time, as a lawyer, he was concerned about privacy law and lectured to genealogical groups about the details of user agreements and the ownership of information. Henry and his wife, Marcia, have supported this project from day one, as did Amira and Michael Dan.

I would have never been able to organize interviews in Salt Lake City and Provo, Utah, with Church of Jesus Christ Latter-day Saints executives and family historians without the help of my then-research assistant, Leah Schneider. Thank you to Gary Carter, professors of genealogy at Brigham Young University, Roger Minert and Kip Sperry; former and current executives of FamilySearch, the public online database of the LDS Family History Library, Jay Verkler, Shipley Munson, Paul Nauta, and Don Casias. Thanks also to Kory Meyerink of ProGenealogists, Dan

Taggart and Paul B. Allen, the cofounders of Ancestry.com, and Gary Mokotoff, founder of the American Jewish Genealogical Society.

Archivists and academics with an intimate knowledge of the subject were invaluable to my early thinking. Ian E. Wilson, the former director of Library and Archives Canada, had a great deal to say about the digitization agreements that archives worldwide are signing with commercial databases. Susan Tucker's work helped shape my thinking about the role of traditional archives and archivists in relation to genealogists. Catherine Nash's research on the drives and delusions of genealogy and geography, and Anne-Marie Kramer's on the dangers of exposing family secrets helped me see that I was on the right track. In Boston, interviews with cognitive psychologist Steven Pinker and Brenton Simons and Ryan Woods at the New England Historical and Genealogical Society offered psychological and historical depth. In Iceland, Gunnar Viking Olafsson, Friðrik Skúlason, and Anna K. Kristjánsdóttir gave me a window into the genealogical pasts and futures of their remarkable country.

As the project evolved, my questions about direct-to-consumer DNA testing for ancestry became ever more central. I arranged to help Kevin Winston, an African American, and his wife, Lisa, explore his family history and genetic genealogy so that we could trace a process of discovery from beginning to end (so-to-speak). Sorenson Genetics provided the test as well as an interview with CEO Scott Woodward. Alondra Nelson, at Columbia University, brought me into a discussion of genealogy, race, and genetics, and Wendy Roth, Hendrik Poinar, Susan Young, Françoise Baylis, Darryl Leroux, and Keiran McDoughty, panelists at the Genealogy and Genetics Workshop at York University in September 2018, clarified many issues of this complicated crossover.

None of this research would have happened without the support of the Social Sciences and Humanities Council of Canada and that of François Cadieux, manager of the Contributions Program, Office of the Privacy Commission of Canada. Thank you to my colleagues and staff at York University who have been so supportive over so many years, Thomas Loebel, Rose Crawford, Kim Michasiw, Lily Cho, Janet Friskney, Janet Newton, and Celia Haig-Brown.

Without Matt Becker, acquisitions editor at University of Massachusetts Press, *The Genealogical Sublime* might still be on the back burner. Marla

Miller, Public History in Historical Perspective series editor pushed the book to a higher standard, and Mary Dougherty, Rachael DeShano, Courtney Andree, and Annette Wenda pushed it out the door. Thank you in particular to the reviewers, and Jerome De Groot, for making the manuscript immeasurably stronger. Thanks also to Sally Keefe-Cohen for being a publishing mentor and to JoAnne Fishburn for helping me reach an audience.

My sister Francesca and Bill Mitchell read the book in draft to make sure that it was accessible to a general audience; it would have been much less elegant without them. My brothers Simon and Stephen encouraged and challenged me in equal parts. Sabrina, Oscar, Rebecca, Megan, Jovanna, Nicholas, Vicky, Patty, and Carla (and Indy), thank you for being part of the loving, fractious family that we are.

THE GENEALOGICAL SUBLIME

INTRODUCTION

AN UNCANNY ORIGIN STORY

The Genealogical Sublime arose out of a very personal turn into the world of family history, origins, and "archive fever."[1] My search involved all the things that genealogists and family historians say motivate them: a family secret, the hunt, the feeling that the past will explain something about who we are in the present, and the need to fill in the gaps in family narratives, repair traumas, search for relatives, living and dead, and, ultimately, find or tell one's origins. I found the search consuming.

By the mid-2000s, after a decade of digging, I realized that my sojourn back into my own past could go on forever—and that I was not alone. In that short time, genealogy had become a lucrative business, an accelerating online industry, a massive data-mining project, and the existential stuff of reality TV. I was part of a zeitgeist—the genealogical spirit of my time. I began to sense other underlying drives that seemed less personal. Curious about the larger phenomenon, I wondered how this genealogical zeitgeist might have affected what I felt as a profoundly personal journey.

As I was trying to understand the uncanny pull of family history—revealing things both deeply familiar and unfamiliar to me at the same time—and wondering whether I would ever stop, I came across an unsettling story, "The Encyclopedia of the Dead (a Whole Life)," by Yugoslavian writer Danilo Kiš.[2] The story is the account of one night in the narrator's life. Having gone to Sweden for research and, in large part, to escape the grief of her father's death two months earlier (as if, she says, "we did not bear our grief *within* ourselves"), she is taken to the Royal Library after hours and delivered into the care of a guard who escorts her to a vault in which she is left and locked. Here, to set the scene, fill in every trope of the Gothic: the guard resembles Cerberus, the three-headed guard dog of Hades, and the library a dungeon, and our narrator is buried alive in this dimly lit, drafty, cobwebby, womblike tomb of tomes hewn from stone. A series of sudden realizations and moments of frightening recognition swiftly move the story from realism to magic realism (in the mode of Gabriel García Márquez and Jorge Luis Borges). Each room, our narrator realizes, houses one letter of the alphabet. Driven by premonition before she has fully comprehended the significance of this recognition, she runs to the room housing the letter M. By the time she gets there, she is sure that this is the rumored, celebrated, and carefully guarded *Encyclopedia of the Dead.*

She finds herself cradling the tome that contains her father's entry, already written before he had died. "The thick layer of dust that had gathered along their edges and the dangling cobwebs bore clear witness to the fact that no one had handled the volumes in a long time. They were fettered to one another like galley slaves, but their chains had no locks."[3] The volumes were under "house arrest," as Jacques Derrida would put it, chained forever to their archival domicile. Our narrator reads, oblivious of time, until, like every figure that enters the underworld, she begins to worry that she has overstayed her welcome.

The authors of Kiš's not-so-imaginary encyclopedia are an "odd caste of erudites" who "believe in the miracle of biblical resurrection, and they complete their vast catalogue in preparation for that moment." The entries allow everyone to find "not only his fellow men but also—and more important—his own forgotten past."[4] Rather than acquiesce to the loss of memory that accompanies that death—and rather than accept the incompleteness of the historical record—the encyclopedia instead fills in *all* the gaps, exhuming the uncanny nightmare of the living who both fear and long for a complete record of the dead. We read over the shoulder of our narrator fragments of what she has managed to copy down, which we then, with little difficulty, expand again to sustain the fantasy of a completely recorded life.

The story ends with our narrator waking from her archival nightmare to the truth of an unfamiliar image in the last pages of her father's entry. He had taken to drawing and painting floral patterns on everything in the last years of his life. In the encyclopedia she finds an illustration of

dichotomy of genealogical research

his basic floral pattern that doesn't resemble his obsessive artwork. "Yes, I said to myself, even *they* can make a mistake. And then, after copying the gigantic peeled orange into my notebook, I read the concluding paragraph and let out a scream. I awoke drenched in sweat."[5] Her father's doctor confirms that the drawing looks exactly like the cancer in her father's intestines that killed him. Our narrator's desire to know everything about her father produces a nightmare of knowing too much, of seeing her father's death inside him at the cellular level.

In the story's last publication, a long postscript followed, itself a story of a disturbingly familiar and unfamiliar coincidence. Kiš's imaginary caste of historians and their encyclopedic archive, collected in the name of resurrection, were not imaginary at all. Shortly after Kiš's story first appeared in print in 1981, a Yugoslav magazine published the following item under the title "Archives." "East of Salt Lake City . . . deep in the Rockies' granite bowels, lies one of the most unusual archives in all the United States."[6] A labyrinth of tunnels and rooms blasted into the rock leads to six immense halls lined with a double layer of concrete, temperature and humidity controlled, with constantly circulating purified air, cooled by a natural spring flowing under the archive. All entrances to the vault are guarded with iron vault doors, and access is limited to a highly selected staff. Compiled by the Genealogical Society of the Church of Jesus Christ of Latter-day Saints, the vault houses the names of eighteen billion people, living and dead, "as much information as is contained in six million books of three thousand pages each." It contains 1.25 million microfilms, records photographed all over the world, amassed toward the ultimate goal of recording the whole of mankind, past, present, and future, in the name of retroactive baptism for ancestors "unfortunate enough to have missed the 'Mormon revelation.'"

"The Encyclopedia of the Dead (a Whole Life)" and its footnote (included in a collection of Kiš's stories under the same title) were my introduction to the Granite Mountain Records Vault that the Mormon Church carved out of Little Cottonwood Canyon in the 1960s, a vast underground vault that now stores the world's largest genealogical archive, one quarter (and counting) of the world's vital records. My experience in the family history archive had been compulsive and compelling, but, clearly, I was only one family historian in an uncanny enterprise that promised the dead a path to heaven and resurrection and the living an eternal place in a cave hidden underground.

My fascination with the Mormon project would launch my research into the industry of family history. As I would find out, the mid-1800s Mormon doctrinal imperative to baptize the world had fostered our genealogical zeitgeist and the commercial databases that were to follow in the 1990s. I became intrigued by the databases as digital manifestations of paper and family archives of infinitely linked pedigree charts, of places where we seek the secrets of the self. Did the uncanny qualities of Kiš's story, our drive to capture every detail of the past and everyone in it, resonate in the databases ever more so? What kind of a story can you tell about genealogical databases, I wondered? A sublime one, it turns out.

The Genealogical Sublime traces the histories of the longest (Confucius), largest (the Church of Jesus Christ of Latter-day Saints), most complete (Iceland), most lucrative (Ancestry.com), and most rapidly growing (genetic) genealogical databases in the world, all of which aspire to an uncanny completeness. Genealogy lends itself to obsessive pursuits, and new technologies allow us to indulge these obsessions as never before. In the light of database and DNA technologies built out of finding family— the most innate of impulses—something else emerges: a sublime desire to gather all of the world's genealogical records. Borrowing from Immanuel Kant's "mathematical sublime" and David Nye's "technological sublime,"[7] these databases manifest a drive I call "the genealogical sublime," most powerfully revealed in the idea that DNA databases will both prove the relationships of everyone in the world and secure our individuality at the same time. In its broadest definition, the sublime is that feeling of awe, of pleasure and displeasure. In this case, we find awe and pleasure in being connected to other people, externally and internally, and the displeasures in the revelations of unexpected genetic contributions of being connected in numbers that are unfathomable. Recognizing "awe" at the level of the individual family historian, I wondered if the databases manifested something similar on a much larger scale, magnifying the sublime dimensions of the genealogy.

The industry thrives on promoting an unanswerable question, "Who do you think you are?" This is a question that is both pressing and pernicious. Inflected in that question is a metaphysical yearning and a spiritual need to know ourselves. It provokes an existential anxiety and promises

paradox/dichotomy

to solve it. Reconsidered in the light of database and DNA technologies that lust for completion, from this innate need for origins and relations exploited by the industry, something else emerges—a web of ancestors beyond what we mathematically comprehend revealed in origins and secrets embedded in almost immeasurable parts of our genome. We find ourselves as smaller and smaller data points in larger and larger data sets in the face of which we spin meaningful narratives. Kant's notion of the mathematical sublime is exactly that: the mathematical concept or set that overwhelms us and against which we erect a narrative bulwark. For Kant, the sublime is a *boundless* object, one that is attractive to the mind "but is ever being alternately repelled." The object is not really an object at all, not a thing we can observe, not a quality, but a quantity.

At 118 generations, the Confucius pedigree is the oldest written genealogy in the world. As China softens its image in the world, Confucius—reviled by Chairman Mao as a "stinking corpse"—and his moral philosophy have been resurrected, along with his genealogy, which ballooned from six hundred thousand to more than three million once it was digitized, admitting women for the first time. Far beyond only illuminating familial relationships, genealogy has profound moral and political uses. FamilySearch, the database of the Church of Jesus Christ of Latter-day Saints, is the largest genealogical archive in the world—and strives to capture *all* the genealogical records of the world in the interest of posthumous baptism and other religious ordinances. As of the second decade of the twentieth century, the church has amassed in the neighborhood of four billion genealogical images, approximately one-quarter of the world's records. The genealogical project of the church fostered the conditions for the emergence of the industry of genealogy as a republican enterprise that disguises its moral roots. At last count, Ancestry.com, the most lucrative database, and its ambitions outstrip the moral intimacies of families. The largest private genetic database in the world, with ten million customers, it boasts eleven billion "connections." Íslendingabók, the "Book of Icelanders," is the most complete of any nation, amassed to fend off inherited diseases. The Iceland database was paid for by deCODE Genetics, a company designed to exploit the genealogical riches of Iceland. Reaching back to the ninth-century sagas, combined with genetic homogeneity, it provides the first braided genetic genealogy database and sets the example for what has become the dominant mode of genealogy.

The technologies driving this new kind of genealogy serve not only the family historian and the genealogist but also a host of religious, moral, racial, political, corporate, scientific, and surveillance interests. Their ambitions have very worldly pursuits at the same time that they traffic in sublime desires. In each case, these databases have all been developed for something beyond the search for ancestors. Behind the face of the pitch of *extended extended* family is the reality that all of the information is now being sold to pharmaceutical companies, the most profitable arm of the biggest genealogical companies. Hence, the argument of this book hinges on a very particular genealogy of genealogy: the emergent lust for sublime genealogical completeness and individuation fostered by new twentieth- and twenty-first-century technologies. We can see the technological nature and vested interests of what we think is the most innate of impulses—finding family.

The dream of complete connection was there from the advent of the online bases. Timothy Sullivan, chief executive officer (CEO) of the Generations Network, Inc., the umbrella company of all the Ancestry.com databases around the world, presciently declared in 2009, "Our very clear goal is to build the world's largest database of genetic genealogy results." Ancestry.com reported a record number of DNA kits sold between Black Friday and Cyber Monday 2017. By 2018 it accomplished its goal, surpassing ten million samples, more than half of the consumer tests. A competitor, Family Genetics, already claimed to possess "the world's largest genetically beaded genealogical database," and David Sacks, CEO of Geni.com and former CEO of PayPal, trumpeted an even grander ambition: "Geni is creating a family tree of the whole world, and layering in a family social network and family wiki on top of that. We want to become a place to connect and preserve the family."[8] As of 2019, twenty-six million people have sent in DNA samples to genetic genealogy testing companies. Of these, millions have then uploaded their results to public databases. Recent estimates are that the DNA of 60 percent of Americans of European decent can now be identified by information in public databases. The mathematical sublime characterizes the overwhelming nature of these digital networks of intimate relations, the religious sublime our feelings about the moral good we will find there, and the technological sublime their manifestations in commercial culture.

The single largest study to date amassed all publicly available population-scale family trees, including a single pedigree of thirteen million people, in search of the holy grail of genetic genealogy—the markers of longevity. The study illustrated the paradox of the genealogical sublime: that we are amassing the records of the dead in order to forestall death itself, physical and metaphysical. The scientists and statisticians had to admit in the end that previous studies had likely "overestimated the heritability of longevity," yet the drive to survive now drives the industry itself, behind the facade of the benign narrative of finding family. The genealogical sublime strives, as every case study shows, to achieve completeness in the interests of life beyond death—a sublime effort that engages Kant's central idea of infinity, a concept that cannot be measured. To understand the relationship between the metaphysics of hidden selves, genealogical connectedness, and differentiation, this book focuses on the material histories of databases that come closest to those ambitions. "New sources of popular wonder and amazement" become the genealogical version of the technological sublime, which merges, in David Nye's words, "natural, technological, classical, and religious elements into a single aesthetic," even as we contemplate our own insignificance in them.

THE GENEALOGICAL SUBLIME

I can't quite contain it . . . and you never get it done.

—Elizabeth Yakel, "Seeking Information, Seeking Connections,
Seeking Meaning: Genealogists and Family Historians," *Information
Research* (2004)

Everybody knows that there are too many ancestors for any one person or any one group to try and track them all down. Mathematicians can tell you if you 2 to the nth power, then you'll certainly have more ancestors than you can deal with.

—Kory Meyerink, ProGenealogists

Immanuel Kant's "mathematical sublime" and David Nye's "technological sublime" updated in the context of genealogical infinity produce "the genealogical sublime," that unsettling feeling of locating ourselves in

ever-growing databases of ancestors, databases that thrive on the technological and mythical fantasy of completeness in the world, which we
in turn locate within ourselves, finding and drawing together the hidden
stories and percentages of us. How do we locate ourselves between the
need for origin stories and the mathematical expansion of relatives—and
the recession of origins—delivered to us by new genealogical technologies? How do we understand the incomprehensibly small parts of us,
our DNA, on which all those ancestors have left their mark? As I work
through the case studies, the genealogical sublime will reveal itself in the
awe and fear of being connected to a chain of being much larger than we
can comfortably imagine. The manifestation of that chain at the cellular
level, at the deepest level of self, we can know only through scientific magnification and probability and statistics. We negotiate in between the vastness of the database and the vastness of our genetic inheritance (vastness
outward and inward) through narratives of self. Storytelling about who
we are in the present is the necessary and pleasurable containment of the
fear wrought by the disintegration of the self in seemingly infinite data
and deep DNA time.[9] The chain has aesthetic beauty, the beauty of a historical object or document,[10] the confirmation of a relative, of a branch, of
a segment of DNA that proves a family legend; the completion of a chart
is deeply satisfying, even if its end points are somewhat arbitrary.

The genealogical sublime and the technological sublime (supported
by Fredric Jameson's "whole world system of a present-day multinational
capitalism")[11] are the theoretical threads that run through this book. Each
of the case studies, if you will, takes up the idea from a particular vantage
point. In so doing, the dimensions of the idea itself will become clearer as
the book goes on. But to set the stage for the emergence of the genealogical sublime, a quick overview (heresy) of the descent of the concept of the
sublime itself will help us understand its genealogical inhabitations.

The "sublime," in its earliest Western formulation, comes to us from
the Greek rhetorician Longinus in a first-century discourse titled "On
the Sublime." Longinus delineates the aesthetic power of great orators
and writers to move all listeners and readers. "Nothing is so conducive
to sublimity as an appropriate display of genuine passion, which bursts
out with a kind of 'fine madness' and divine inspiration, and falls on our
ears like the voice of a god." Longinus categorizes the qualities of rhetoric that reach godlike speech, from Zeus to Sappho to Homer to God's

sublime theory

proclamations of the beginning of the world in Genesis. Reading one of Sappho's odes on love, Longinus writes, "Observe too how her sensations contradict one another—she freezes, she burns, she raves, she reasons, and all at the same instant. And this description is designed to show that she is assailed, not by any particular emotion, but by a tumult of different emotions." Pleasure and displeasure combined are the hallmarks of the sublime, the sense of being consumed by something larger than ourselves, at once moved by it and frightened by it, grasping it and in its grasp. Classics professor Casper C. de Jonge underlines the "importance of the divine to the concept of the sublime,"[12] something superhuman and supernatural often framed in religious terms. The relationship between beauty and fear, belonging and awe, will occupy writers on the sublime for centuries to come, but this tumult of different emotions comes to be marked by fear and the imagination, along with the resonance of truth and beauty, feelings that traverse back and forth between the secular and the metaphysical.

Simplifying the infinite / under tending

For our purposes, Immanuel Kant's "mathematical sublime" from his *Critique of Judgement* (1790) is the foundation on which we can build a description and an understanding of the genealogical sublime: an infinite quantity, the representation of which produces a state of mind. "Nature is therefore sublime in those of its phenomena, whose intuition brings with it the Idea of their infinity." We achieve great pleasure through the contemplation of the finality of nature, says Kant, wresting all its "secrets" from it, in order to simplify the heterogeneity of its laws. "But still we listen more gladly to others who hold out to us the hope that the more intimately we come to know the secrets of nature . . . the more harmonious shall we find it in the apparent heterogeneity of its empirical laws." The pleasure we feel contemplating completeness or finality "is an aesthetic representation of the finality. The only question is whether such a representation of finality exists at all."[13] Our cognitive pleasures of aesthetic judgment produce the representation of completeness where such a figure does not exist at all in nature. We triumph over feeling insignificant in the face of numerical awe by finding superiority in our own judgment.

Genealogy, in the broadest sense, probes the secrets of history and human reproduction playing on the displeasures of lack and misrecognition ("Who do you think you are?"), while promising personal wholeness and world connection. We are compelled by the idea of that we will discover the secrets of our origins in the DNA and the databases of the world, but it is a figure that recedes from us. Nothing is more natural than human reproduction (even as fertility treatments make it more technological than ever before). To state the obvious, none of us would be here without it. But the idea of ancestry and its current computational obsessions extends the genealogical imagination technologically (even as it is mythical) toward the infinite, into which we, as individuals, disappear. This greatness beyond all standards of sense, as Kant phrases it, makes us "judge as *sublime,* not so much the object, as our own state of mind in the estimation of it." So how do we then use Kant's notion of the mathematical sublime, an imaginative encounter with infinity that frightens us, to understand the genealogical sublime?

David Nye, in his influential 1994 book, *The American Technological Sublime,* explains that the sublime "taps into fundamental hopes and fears," an "essentially religious feeling, aroused by the confrontation with impressive objects."[14] He argues that the nature of what we consider sublime has shifted from an aesthetic feeling about overwhelming natural phenomena in nineteenth- and twentieth-century philosophy to the overwhelming nature of technology in the twenty-first, technology imbued with moral values. In the American context, the context for most of the examples here as well, that feeling in the face of technological wonders—bridges and skyscrapers, electricity, the atomic bomb, the first manned flight to the moon—functions as a mode of social cohesion, a shared emotion beyond words, something no single religion could accomplish, given the plurality of American culture. Breaking away from a history of the sublime as a purely aesthetic experience in relation to works of literature and art, natural wonders, and frightening encounters, Nye situates the emergence of new forms of the sublime feelings not as absolute but as contingent, responding to contemporary social and political systems.

For my purposes, Jos de Mul's "(bio)technical sublime" comes even closer to the genealogical phenomena that I describe here. De Mul provides a good gloss of the history of the sublime, as does Nye, from the Greek version of Longinus to Longinus's centrality in the early modern revival of the sublime as aesthetic pleasure and fear, from "a delightful horror" (Burke). Immanuel Kant's romantic sublime is more troubled, things that "surpass," as de Mul writes, "our understanding and our imagination due to their unbounded, excessive or chaotic character." Though the phenomena that we consider sublime have changed, the affect is predominantly consistent: a mixture of awe and fear, of nature (God) and human, of grandeur and vulnerability, a combination of feelings that leave us in an ambiguous place. "Over the nineteenth and twentieth centuries, the main site for the ambiguous experience of the sublime has gradually shifted from *nature to technology*."[15] De Mul borrows his idea of the technological sublime from Nye, updating the terms from the awe inspired by great feats of engineering like the Golden Gate Bridge and the jumble of urbanity to computers—and databases, in particular. Computers have become our "ontological machines" and databases our dominant cultural form, transforming our experience of the sublime.

In Jorge Luis Borges's story "The Library of Babel," de Mul finds a compelling fictional version of the mathematical sublime, much like I found the fantasy of completeness in Kiš's "Encyclopedia of the Dead," the writer who sent me down this database rabbit hole. Borges was Kiš's mentor, and de Mul's reading of the Borges story in the context of the technological sublime points exactly to the combination of statistics, genealogical imagination, bio identity, and databases that moves toward the unsettling nature of the genealogical sublime that I experienced in Kiš's Gothic tale:[16]

In the case of Borges' *Library of Babel*, we can still comfort ourselves with the idea that this story is part of his *Collected Fictions*. After all, the Library of Babel is only a product of artistic imagination. However, in the domain of biotechnologies we confront databases that are even more astonishing, both in magnitude and in scope. If we take into account that the human genome alone consists of roughly three billion nucleotides, written in a four-letter language, we realize that the number of possible (re)combinations ($4^{3,000,000,000}$) of the human genome is even more sublime than the number of books in Borges' Library.[17]

The pursuit of ancestry negotiates between two kinds of forces: endogenous, part of the organism's natural functions, and entrained, adapted to synch with environmental oscillations. Human reproduction, for example, is endogenous; we can't live without it. Systems of kinship and the ancestral imagination, I think we can safely argue, are entrained, products in environmental and cultural oscillations. The more we pursue the gratifying objects of family history—the names, the dates, the documents, the

stories, the DNA—the more likely we are, at some point, to encounter
the overwhelming idea of the statistical computations of the genealogical
sublime, against which stories and verified ancestors act as a kind of buffer. The concreteness of the research and science of DNA is a defense (but
also an invocation) of the limitlessness of descent, an overwhelming idea
against which we erect all kinds of narrative bulwarks. It's worth a brief
overview of the roots of Western origin stories in order to orient ourselves
in those of the early twenty-first century.

(margin annotation: What genealogical research served as)

A VERY BRIEF GENEALOGY OF GENEALOGY

Our belief in scientific and historically verifiable genealogy as a source
of identity has its roots in far older traditions of what we might call the
Western mystical genealogical traditions that began the begats. The origin stories of ancient cultures created genealogies of the gods, sometimes
linking gods and man by blood, often in narrative form. Hesiod's epic
poem *Theogony*, "the birth of the gods," composed circa 700 BC, delineated
a genealogy of the pantheon of Greek mythology. The later addition of the
Catalogue of Women, also attributed to Hesiod or to his school, provides the
genealogical link between the gods and mortals. This origin story and the
genealogies that flow from it are thought to be modeled on earlier Near
Eastern myths from Mesopotamia, in particular the Babylonian Creation
story of *Enuma elish,* where elements mated to give birth to gods. Both
of these origin stories were oral traditions, written down centuries after
their invention, common to almost every culture.

For our purposes, the most relevant story, because it is currently the
most influential origin story in the global North and the most intense
site of genealogical interest and activity, is the Judeo-Christian tradition,
the books of Genesis and Chronicles of the Hebrew Bible. Genealogy and
its association with trees begin with the tree of knowledge as the first
use of the metaphorical figure of the tree, one split from the tree of life.
Tasting of the tree of knowledge, the wrong tree, signifies the "renuncia-
tion of immortality, but also the origins of all systems of kinship." The
tree of knowledge is the first family tree not because the original parents
ate from it, "but because they began the project of propagation of the
human race in its shadow."[18] Our knowledge of mortality is the origin of

the me in book/ argument

genealogy, and, as I will argue throughout the book, genealogy returns again and again to the problem of mortality itself.

The first family tree is an interruption in the tree of man—an interruption that current genealogical pitches attempt to heal, that is, "we are all related." The genealogical tree in its first instance, then, records a site of destruction, a trauma, a mythical origin that can never be retrieved. It's telling that some of the largest genealogical projects in the world, the Mormon database and the National Geographic Genographic Project, seek exactly this confirmation of mythical origins—Adam and Eve figure in both—through the scientific pursuit of human descent. As Alex Shoumatoff, in *The Mountain of Names*, one of the early journalistic histories of the human family, points out, whether one thinks a theoretical first couple exists requires "a subjective judgment about when we became human."[19]

The Gospels of Matthew and Luke in the New Testament once again establish the origins of man (Adam) through long lines of genealogies that lead to Jesus. The Gospel according to Matthew, the first book of the New Testament, traces Jesus's genealogy back to Abraham, the father of the Jews, while Luke back to Adam; the two genealogies overlap between Abraham and King David, but otherwise disagree. Out of these genealogies, along with a passage from the book of Isaiah from the Hebrew Bible—"And there shall come forth a rod out of the stem of Jesse, and a branch shall grow out of his roots"—the earliest family tree iconography, visual genealogies of Jesus, emerged in the eleventh century. Typically, Jesse (Yishal), the father of David, lies prone at the bottom of the Tree of Jesse, a stem or a "rod" emerging from his side or his navel from which flower the ancestors of Christ. The image became more and more popular in the Middle Ages, spreading from religious iconography to the pedigrees of nobility as early as the twelfth century, inverting the tree in the process.[20]

A breadth of approaches in Renaissance studies, historiography, art history, and cultural anthropology attests to the cultural ascension of the tree and the depth of our attachment to the image.[21] The argument, broadly, is that the iconography of the tree is not simply a useful image or metaphor; rather, its logic produces genealogical knowledge in its own image. The tree as a logic and an icon sets up a figure that defines us and our relationship to it even as we discern its shape. Sigrid Weigel's definition is very clear: "Genealogy *is* the history of the symbolic, iconographic and rhetorical practices, the systems for recording and the techniques of culture through and in which the knowledge of families, races and species or of the succession of life within time is handed down." As Weigel puts it, "genealogical *topoi*," commonplace ideas about ancestry, operate on and simultaneously organize "the threshold between nature and culture."[22]

The tree as we know it cohered in the fifteenth century and assumed its canonical status and came into vogue in the sixteenth century among European elites.[23] The advent of parish records in England in the 1530s ushers in an era of intense genealogical interest, melding religious iconography with secular inheritance and tax records. Research about the centrality of genealogy to general knowledge in early modern Europe is rapidly expanding. Eric Ketelaar argues that "from the fourteenth century on the genealogical gaze transfigured family archives into a cultural patrimony to be preserved, expanded and transferred to future generations," part of a general shift from imagined genealogies to evidence-based research.[24] But as Markus Friedrich cautions, in his introduction to *Genealogical Knowledge in the Making: Tools, Practices, and Evidence in Early Modern Europe* (much as I do in this book), "Rather than buying into (implicit) assumptions about the steady progress of genealogical knowledge-making towards a more factual outlook, our approach highlights that different concepts of what counted as proper genealogical knowledge existed, often clashed or tenuously co-existed throughout history."[25] Genealogical knowledge is always socially imbedded and produced. It is never "innocent."

The sacred and secular trees of the early moderns then generated the phylogenetic trees of the eighteenth century. Tracked through the nineteenth century, the tree of knowledge and the tree of life become explicitly overlaid in iconography that maps the ancestry of man onto a tree of knowledge, becoming the standard iconography for phylogeny (the history or evolution of a species). Twentieth-century anthropology, according to the cultural anthropologist Mary Bouquet in her lucid and illuminating discussion of the visual imperative of the genealogical diagram, reified this taxonomic device into an idea of kinship that illustrates relatedness based on a (European) naturalized iconography of the "tree imagery" as a "piece of visual equipment." In this uneasy relationship between synchronic (at the same time) and diachronic (over time) representation, between tableau and evolution, as Weigel puts it, "the latest members share a space and time with the earliest."[26] Here too we see the sublime desire to "step out of historical time into the eternal now."[27] That logic led to deadly histories.[28]

Ernst Haeckel's "Pedigree of Man" (1874) offers the clearest example of this kind of structuring principle, illustrating a natural philosophy that placed humans at the top of a hierarchical tree structure, as the pinnacle of a natural order of progression, with German Aryans at the zenith. Haeckel expanded this idea of natural pedigree into a religious and philosophical doctrine called "monism," the unity of man and nature, deeply opposed to the Judeo-Christian religious/philosophical tradition of the dualism of man and nature. As one of Germany's most honored thinkers, Haeckel's brand of social Darwinism was hugely influential in the early twentieth century, and he amassed a large following of monists who held that Jews were responsible for the introduction of dualism into the religions of the West. But beyond his philosophical distaste for dualism, Haeckel's *Pedigree of Man* set the quasi-scientific stage for racial eugenics. The importance of those genealogies and their origin stories have become ever more relevant rather than less, as we will see in the Mormon project and, oddly enough, in some of the most scientific narratives of genetic origins that evoke the evolutionary "Adam" and "Eve." Any genealogy of genealogy must deal with the its multiple lines of Western inheritance: mythic, biblical, noble, republican, biological, technological, scientific, and with the collapse of these in contemporary imagination, all part of how we have arrived at the genealogical sublime.

American genealogy, in keeping with its republican roots, begins anew on the shores of the New World. French historian François Weil's *Family Trees: A History of Genealogy in America* reveals how the idea of aristocratic pedigree was remade as a republican pursuit after the American Revolution, building on his earlier work on John Farmer (1789–1838), the first American "antiquarian."[29] With the advent of complete census records in the 1840s (African American families would only be added in 1865 after the Civil War), the Mormon mission, and multiple genealogical and historical societies, genealogy became an American pursuit, albeit one that was still marked by cultural capital, as Francesca Morgan observes about family research in antebellum New England.[30] Weil surveys the

genealogy simplifies complex contexts

development of new and successive meanings to genealogy, arguing that "family trees were a versatile means to cope with geographic, cultural and social mobility in a rapidly changing world." We will observe that genealogy still serves that purpose two hundred years later. Weil points out that although genealogy is an integral part of the American past and present, it "is arguably the element of contemporary American culture about which we know the least" and that the "history of genealogy remains largely to be written."[31] Weil asks for "a genealogy of genealogy," though in a strictly historical sense, as a history of family history in American culture, rather than appealing to Michel Foucault's genealogical method (which I will discuss shortly). The second chapter of this book discusses the development of American genealogy from the mid-1800s to the mid-1900s in the context of the development of the archival work of the Church of Jesus Christ of Latter-day Saints, but the turning point in the American genealogical interest came from one story in particular.

Most histories point to Alex Haley's phenomenally popular Pulitzer Prize–winning 1976 book and the blockbuster TV miniseries *Roots: The Saga of an American Family* as the story that fired the genealogical imagination in the latter half of the American twentieth century. Haley's story was novel but intensely researched, the tale of Haley's search for his African ancestor, a young man stolen from Gambia and enslaved in America.[32] That popular awakening provoked by *Roots* was paralleled by a growing awareness among librarians and archivists that frequent users of their collections were most interested in genealogy and heraldry. Haley claimed to have researched in "fifty-odd libraries, archives, and other repositories on three continents," and a large part of the appeal of Haley's journey was the research journey itself. Archives—government, church, newspaper, military, steamship lines, colonial records, and so on—from which the databases drew so many of their data sets were the places in which genealogy happened. Shortly after, the Afro-American Historical and Genealogical Society was founded by a group of historians and genealogists concerned that minority groups had been largely overlooked in the history of American genealogy.[33]

P. William Filby made the Peabody Library in Baltimore the most genealogy-friendly library in the United States, greatly increasing public access by compiling a bibliography of books on the subject, the "genealogy bible," which reached thirty-four thousand volumes by the time he stopped in 1986.[34] Archivists themselves began to notice some unusual desires manifesting in archives. Archivists and librarians had to embrace the genealogists, who, by the 1990s, accounted for 50 to 90 percent of all traffic in North American and British archives.[35] As the gatekeepers of access to historical information before the advent of the commercial databases, archivists of public archives were engaged early on in the mid-1980s in a very active conversation about genealogical demand and its impact on archival science and access.[36] Genealogists' demands, in turn, shaped institutional priorities, privacy law, and, later, digitization agreements.[37] As Gary Mokotoff, the editor of *Avotaynu*, an e-zine for Jewish genealogists, writes across the banner of every newsletter, "Genealogy preserves history; the history of a family. It cannot be done without access to records, just as historians cannot preserve a nation's history without access to records. It is a greater good than the right to privacy. It is a greater good than the risk of identity theft."[38] Tension between the right to privacy and the right to genealogical research and its spin-offs remains a constant consideration for governments, with genealogists advocating for ever-greater access, archives selling records in exchange for digitization, and industry claiming ever-greater proprietary rights. These privacy concerns seem almost quaint in the light of the revelation in 2018 that the police were using genetic genealogy databases to solve cold cases and that DNA databases could be used to identify almost 60 percent of white Americans, even though they held less than 2 percent of the national genome. I will explore this phenomenon in my conclusion, "The Genealogical Sublime: We Are All Related."[39]

A revealing moment in the origins of online genealogy was the crash of the United Kingdom 1901 census website just three days after its launch by the UK Public Record Office (PRO) on January 2, 2002. Advertised heavily in advance, thereby stoking unprecedented levels of interest in genealogy and UK ancestry around the world, the site, designed to handle 1.2 million inquires a day, attracted 32 million hits per day (roughly equivalent to the number of names in the census), immediately overwhelming the server. The PRO withdrew the site, relaunching it quietly seven months later.[40] In the first decade of the twenty-first century, genealogy became, according to urban legend as much as anything, a hobby second only to gardening and an online industry second only to pornography.[41] That oscillation between benign and voyeuristic pursuits very much characterizes the contemporary industry. In many respects, genealogists are no different from any other kind of "consumer tribe."[42] As the zeitgeist of family history burgeoned, more scholars became interested in the assumptions and motivations underpinning ideas of relatedness, technology, and archives.[43]

The literary theorist Jacque Derrida's hugely influential *Archive Fever* described the archive as an unreliable place in which we find the troubles of secrets, "always at the unstable limit between public and private, between the family, the society, the State, between the family and an intimacy even more private than the family, between oneself and oneself." He saw the compulsion to return to origins as a repetitive, irrepressible desire, "for the return to the most archaic place of absolute commencement," a fantasy with no end.[44] We use the records of the dead to cushion the idea of death itself. In a theme that we will see repeated, Derrida argues that archives are heavily guarded places and, much as I am doing here, that the structure of the archive itself produces as much as it records history. These vast new databases and their striving for ontological completeness have the potential to unravel the existing stories we tell ourselves.

Observations from the wider field support the idea that genealogy as an individual ontological project helps to construct a "complete" self. Jerome de Groot observes that local history and genealogy were the two "most important phenomena in 'public' history" of the late 1990s and the early 2000s. De Groot too sees completeness as the goal of the digitization of genealogy. "Cultural artefacts, in the form of historical knowledge and information, here become commodities in an economy in which the consumption of such goods is driven by a desire to understand the self and make complete." Similarly, in "Genealogical Tourism: A Phenomenological Examination," Carla Santos and Grace Yan surmise that a genealogical tourism is driven by a "sense of loss that under-pins modern society," becoming "a central component of the ontological project of the self." Anne-Marie Kramer, a British sociologist who studies the cultural practices and implications of genealogy, observes that people frequently don't know what they mean by "roots" or "origins": "Roots are seen to be something absolutely essential for life. What plant can grow without them? What human, then, could grow without roots? But what is rootedness? Is it rootedness to other people? Is it rootedness in time? Is it rootedness in place? To particular communities? To a landscape? To a particular place, a residence, let's say, where a family has lived? So there's

considerable uncertainty and everybody thinks that everybody needs to
have roots. Genealogists think that's really important, but they're not
quite sure what that means."[45] The human geographer Catherine Nash,
most recently in *Genetic Geographies: The Trouble with Ancestry* and in numerous previous articles and books on genealogy and kinship, has analyzed exactly that question of how genealogists produce personal and
political meaning in genetic accounts of origins, ancestry, relatedness,
and difference.[46] The cognitive sociologist Eviatar Zerubavel, having previously studied the sociology of time, turns his attention to genealogy in
Ancestors and Relatives: Genealogy, Identity, and Community, examining how
we "envision ancestry, descent, and other forms of relatedness" as part
of "the genealogical imagination." Zerubavel observes that the way we
think about ancestral deep time is a modern invention, entirely based on
the radical reconception of human time by the archaeological discoveries
of the mid-nineteenth century. The result is that "genealogical memory,
in other words, is, at least in theory, essentially boundless."[47]

Perhaps in order to contain the boundless nature of genealogical memory and its sublime discomforts, we still embrace the enduring idea and
icon of ancestral time—the tree and its associated aesthetic figures of
roots, branches, vines, and graphs (ascending and descending). The tree
is such a naturalized notion of genealogy that we are not likely to see it as
an icon at all, even in a hyperdigitized environment. As every Ancestry.
com ad suggests, each leaf is longingly attached to a robust branch that
leads out from a living trunk into which nutrients from earthbound roots
flow. Even though "tracing one's roots" has been made possible by the
migration of the genealogical research itself from churches and municipal
archives to the mass digitization of records accessed by powerful search
engines, the aesthetics and logics of tree, leaf, and root images and metaphors comfort us with the notion that we are engaged in the most natural
of pursuits. The tree reassures us of our place in time and space, even
our participation in a chain of mythic dimensions, reduced to the scale
of personal pedigree. Any number of critics have offered a reading of the
ideology of trees, or "arborescence," including Gilles Deleuze and Félix
Guattari, Pierre Bourdieu, Anne McClintock, and Marylin Strathern.[48]
The argument, roughly, is that the iconography of the tree is not simply a
useful image or metaphor but a structuring principle that embodies and
masks hierarchical relationships. While we might eschew the tree's easy

adding to increased drama of this manor research [handwritten margin note]

and misleading taxonomy, the popularity of the idea and the icon, combined with the arbitrariness of its sign, has never been more widespread. "The process whereby pedigree and genealogy have become common currency, both within commodity capitalism and anthropological discourse, tends to obscure the visual origins and representational weight of these graphic conventions."[49] Even more so, the contemporary expression of genealogical ideas fits David Nye's description of the technological sublime, which collapses the distinction between nature and culture.

The digital revolution is another turning point in the genealogy of the genealogical tree, where the flattening and shortening of time and space combined with mass migration, cultural mixing, and exponential advances in human genetic mapping have heightened our anxieties about our place on the family tree of man.

A METHOD

To help me understand the history of the databases and the genealogical meaning that we now derive from them, I turned to a second meaning of genealogy. There is a loose method to this book, what we might call

FIGURE I. Legacy Family Tree 7. © MyHeritage Ltd. Used by permission.

"a genealogy of genealogy."[50] It's a peculiar twist of a homonym, the two distinct—but related—meanings of genealogy. The first, and the most commonly used definition of genealogy, is that of constructing a family tree, the search for family history that assumes knowable sets of origins. The second meaning of genealogy is familiar to scholars in the humanities. We know it as a historical approach that Michel Foucault articulated, derived in part from Friedrich Nietzsche's polemical tract "On the Genealogy of Morals."

According to Foucault, three "postulates" (claims of truth) adhere to the metaphysics of origins: that things are most precious, essential, and perfect at the moment of their birth; that origins proceed a fall, giving rise to the idea that origins are divine; and that truth lies at the point of origin, a truth that has been obscured and lost. We will see how all three of these postulates support the metaphysical and historical intensity that characterizes the accumulation of records. However, the genealogist who undertakes genealogy as a critical method does exactly the opposite, where history is the necessary tool or antidote to the "chimeras of the origin."[51] We might add a fourth contemporary postulate that will become readily apparent: that without an origin story, we suffer a form of existential lack or absence, a lack that is perniciously exploited through that haunting question: "Who do you think you are?" Loss or lack sends us searching for origins and roots, even as we can't quite articulate what that means.

Foucault offers a differentiation of two of Nietzsche's terms *Herkunft* (descent) and *Entstehung* (emergence). "*Herkunft* is the equivalent of stock or descent; it is the ancient affiliation to a group, sustained by the bonds of blood, tradition, or social class. The analysis of *Herkunft* often involves a consideration of race or social type. . . . Far from being a category of resemblance, this origin allows the sorting out of different traits."[52]

Descent, Foucault continues, "attaches itself to the body." Genealogy as an analysis of descent is thus situated "within the articulation of the body and history." Ancestral identification is, of course, one of the strongest articulations of the body and history. Genetic genealogy has taken this combination of history and bios and turned it into the most potent form of continuity and descent, reading DNA as unbroken essence. Weigel is one of the few critics who has explicitly tied Foucault's method of genealogy to the history of genealogy as a pedigree practice by cogently arguing that genealogy is "the logic of the language of lineage."[53]

Nietzsche's essay is useful for us here because it makes a link between morality and genealogy, the last link in the genealogical sublime. Nietzsche begins his essay with the etymology of the word *good* in multiple languages—Greek, German, French, and Gaelic. In each language, *good* leads back to the idea of "noble" and "aristocratic," in the social sense of spiritually noble, high-minded, privileged, and, not coincidentally, lighter skinned. In contrast, *common, vulgar, low,* and *dark* are the conceptual descriptors of what is "bad." In Gaelic, Nietzsche finds what he also found in German: "the word *fin* (for example, in the name *Fin-Gal*), the term designating nobility and finally the good, noble, pure, originally referred to the blond-headed man in contrast to the dusk, dark-haired original inhabitants."[54] Retracing etymology to racial differences, Nietzsche finds a correlation between fair hair and skin and the notion of goodness and "dusky" or dark-haired people as symbolically and phylogenetically "bad."

Nietzsche's genealogy of morals is intertwined with a dubious genetic genealogy of "knightly superiority," but one that will become revealing as we flesh out (so to speak) the intersections of the philosophical investigations and the contemporary cultural commodification of genealogy. He then traces a second trajectory, that of the "priestly superiority." Nietzsche argues that "the concept of political superiority always resolves itself into the concept of spiritual superiority."[55] Nietzsche launches a diatribe against the Jews (that dark-haired, swarthy people), that priestly people, as the moral slaves who rebelled against their masters. The priests eschewed the very excesses that the aristocracy indulged, finding spiritual superiority in powerlessness. Subjugation became, in Nietzsche's tale of the emergence of morality, one of the accidents of history that produced morality. That morality was also a discourse of resentment (or *ressentiment*), which became the basis of (if in a convoluted logic) Christianity, the Protestant revolution, identity politics, and the virtue of the common man—the God-fearing over the godless, the morality of the oppressed over the immorality of the oppressors, no matter how "superior."

Resentment is thus, according to Nietzsche, the basis of moral thought. It is an action that is basically a reaction, a reaction against an "other" who is, to some extent, a projection. Nietzsche ascribes this kind of forgetting of the "origins" of morality to the democratic principles, that is, the French Revolution and the wave of republicanism that followed, where the common man was elevated to moral equality or greater with those who had inherited their pedigree and the spoils of conquer. Much of Nietzsche's argument is overblown and offensive, yet it contains a method that Foucault found attractive almost a century later in the sense that it tracked the development of competing discourses of morality and goodness, rather than assuming that these were traits inherent or inherited in humans or ones that had developed in linear fashion as a set of rewarded behaviors. Nietzsche's genealogy argued against the notion of historical descent, in favor of something more chaotic, emotional, biological, and counterintuitive.

Emergence is the second of Foucault's terms derived from Nietzsche. Foucault defines it as "the entry of forces . . . their eruption, the leap from the wings to centre stage, each in its youthful strength." Emergence describes the forceful and often conflicting discourses that can be historically located as a way of understanding the point at which we have arrived. Emergence is a creed of resistance, played out in forces that buffet the body. Both descent and emergence are observed and manifested physically. The second purpose of history, guided by genealogy, "is not to discover the roots of our identity but to commit itself to its dissipation. It does not seek to define our unique threshold of emergence, the homeland to which metaphysicians promise a return; it seeks to make visible all of those discontinuities that cross us."[56] The question that will arise during the course of this investigation is whether, in the pursuit of descent and homelands, the genealogist uncovers quite the opposite: the dilution and discontinuities of bloodlines, the migrations of homelands, where these metaphysical desires are met by dissipation rather than concentration. Querying his database of thirty-five thousand relatives, one of my interview subjects, Ron Raymer, discovered that his ancestors had come from twelve hundred places.

The recognition of this embodied locations keeps the historian from any metaphysical perspective or claim, yet, as I will argue, contemporary genealogy resurrects the promise of origins located inside the body. Foucault's genealogy posits the instinct for knowledge as "malicious" and risky, delighting in disturbing discoveries. Again, the search for hidden knowledge is a sublime desire. Discovery, the more delightfully disturbing the better, drives the industry. Some of the most affecting stories are of the reveals of genetic genealogy—the shock of "nonpaternity" events, the (not always) joyous reunions with adoptees in particular who have tracked biological parents through DNA searches. Secrets and hidden knowledge that lurk within the body are the most sublime of desires, frightening as they are in the moment, threatening to destroy the very subject who searches and those around her. As much as the mathematical sublime attracts the men who search, women—if I can make this crude division—are more likely to look for the traumatic break, the shame that produced a new identity, a discoverable disavowal that nonetheless cannot be undone.[57]

Neither Foucault nor Nietzsche had the pursuit of family history in mind as he philosophized about a genealogical method that refuted the orderly idea of origins and the moral superiority that attached to it (both as pedigree and as the republican God-fearing man) in favor of chaotic emergence. Yet the centrality of descent and morality to the contemporary zeitgeist will become immediately relevant in the first two chapters of this book, even as we study the socially contingent (re)emergence of genealogy. The pedigree of Confucius confers moral inheritance to his ancestors, while the Church of Jesus Christ of Latter-day Saints has emerged from subjugation to bestow a moral afterlife to every common person. And in a strange twist of accidental history, genealogy databases have become rich sources of solving cold cases, moral surveillance repositories that no one envisioned would be an end use for the pursuit of family. Morality has reattached itself to genealogy with a vengeance.

A genealogical method, at once historical and accidental, one that tracks descent and emergence, will help us then understand how the genealogical sublime came to be a technological passion available to everyone, a technology imbued with moral values, a "sacred industry," as Nye calls these kinds of enterprises, borrowing the words from Walt Whitman, that fuses "practical goals with political and spiritual regeneration."[58]

My contribution, then, to the growing family of genealogical studies is to consider the history of some of the major databases themselves and how we have invested meaning in and derived a sense of self from them, keeping in mind the complex family of fields, ideas, and icons that have been brought to the critical conversations about the "innate" need to know from whence we come, in order, in part, to forget or forestall where we are ultimately headed. This historical narrative reveals the extent to which and with what speed technology is changing our ideas of "relatedness," extending family connections beyond anything possible before in history, magnifying their significance and our own. Appealing to the deeply spiritual idea of universal connections, the databases mechanize the idea of relatedness, replacing mystical associations with mathematical computations and infinite cousins, converting the concept of family to a technological and teleological commodity. We pay data to tell us stories of data banks of memory of the past and into the future.

In a fast-moving industry, even a couple of years can change the landscape significantly. So think of this book as a child of its time, a momentary contribution to potentially infinite iterations of how we imagine and write ourselves into genealogical time. Our confrontation with our brief lives as "leaves that die and fall," as one Russian genealogy site put it,[59] gives rise to our infatuation with the genealogical sublime in its technological, mathematical, uncanny, social, and spiritual dimensions.

CHAPTER 1

....

CONFUCIUS
The Oldest Genealogy in the World

To help us understand the mathematical and moral dimensions of the genealogical sublime expressed as descent, pedigree, and inheritance, we will start with a brief chapter on the oldest genealogy in the world. The longest recorded family tree in the world belongs to the Chinese philosopher Confucius (Kong Fuzi, "Master Kong," 551–479 BC), recorded through eighty-three generations, father to son.[1] Confucius helped usher in ancestor veneration toward the end of the Zhou dynasty (1122–256 BC), about the same time as Taoism. A government official who exercised a philosophy of "soft power" during a time of violent cultural upheaval, Confucius dedicated himself to a lifetime of scholarship and teaching, as well as mastery of the warrior arts. Confucius is credited with teaching his disciples the cultivation of personal virtue, parental veneration, erudition, loyalty, kindness, and adherence to custom and ritual. This code of ethical behavior and familial loyalty and responsibility became the moral guidance of Chinese culture for two thousand years, resembling many of the same teachings as Christianity.

The *Analects of Confucius,* "Edited Conversations," is a collection of aphorisms and ideas attributed Confucius and his contemporaries, mostly likely compiled and written by his followers. One of the central principles is *ren,* an outward expression of inward ideals, virtue expressed as altruism, particularly toward one's family—parents, children, and siblings. The Way or the Tao of humanness is through one's interactions with one's closest family and honored ethical figures. Qingjie James Wang argues that the Confucian conception of the self is a "genealogical self," a self established only in relation, that is, relation to one's family and also in relation to figures who "point out to us different ways towards morality and true self."[2] Confucius became over time both an honored ancestor and a family member to a vast and growing number of descendants.

Originally tallied by hand, the first printed version of the *Confucius Genealogy* was produced in AD 1080 in the Northern Song dynasty. By the twentieth century, in twenty-five hundred years, the Confucius pedigree had been revised only four times. After the first modern revision in 1937, the list of Confucius's descendants included six hundred thousand members, strictly organized as a descendant chart, read from top to bottom.[3] No trees here. This vertical, descending structure is the same as the medieval genealogical schemas. "All harbour," as Christiane Klapisch-Zuber writes in the "Genesis of the Family Tree," "the implicit metaphor of a stream of blood, of wealth, of values—flowing from the same source situated on high, down to a group of individuals placed much lower."[4]

In China ancestor worship is a kind of defused religion. In the West we think of genealogy as a mainly secular pursuit (aside from the Mormon doctrinal imperatives). For the Chinese, ancestors are part of a cosmology of both the living and the dead, secular since it is rooted in the family, and supernatural, imbued with metaphysical thinking. While in many genealogical origin myths gods gave birth to humans, for Chinese who still worship ancestors, gods were once humans and humans can still become gods. Deities and the dead live in otherworldly realms and are accessible through spirit mediums and other forms of communication. According to the Chinese Spiritual Life Survey carried out in 2007, almost 70 percent of Chinese practice one form or another of ancestor worship.[5] The three most common forms are visiting the grave sites of ancestors, honoring ancestral tablets kept at home or in an ancestral hall, and updating the family genealogy. Of the three, the continuation of the genealogy is the least practiced, but, in all cases, males with medium to high income status are in the majority of worshippers. Anning Hu summarizes the results of the survey: "Almost all kinds of ancestor worship activities in China are organized by male family members (usually the eldest ones) . . . a finding that is not surprising in light of the patrilineal nature of family life in China."[6]

The early sinologists of the nineteenth century split Chinese religious practices into two dichotomous strands: the practices of the literate elite who followed the three teachings of Confucianism, Buddhism, and Taoism and the folk practices of ancestor worship followed by the majority. All advocate filial piety as a form of reverence that unites kin groups in reciprocal obligations between the living and the dead. Confucianism also formed the basis of Chinese schooling and entry exams for the imperial bureaucracy for two millennia, until the late nineteenth century, when the conservatism of Confucian culture was blamed for Chinese weakness in the face of the innovative developments of the West. The most revered of these lines and kinship groups were the descendants of Confucius himself. From the beginning of the Ming dynasty in the fourteenth century, descendants of Confucius received official titles and honors from the central government. These privileges were revoked only after the overthrow of the Qing dynasty in 1911.

Though it should have been updated every thirty years, Confucius's genealogy was aggressively interrupted when the Communist Party took power in 1949. The party banned ancestor worship and other Confucian rituals as "feudal practices," teaching party loyalty instead. That onslaught was renewed during the 1966–76 Cultural Revolution when Confucius, or Kong Fuzi, was reviled by Chairman Mao as a "stinking corpse." Mao ordered his Red Guards to destroy the rich history of Confucian artifacts as symbols of feudal oppression and to persecute his ancestors as the embodiment of that hierarchy. Confucius was swept aside as part of Mao's order to destroy the "four olds"—old ideas, old customs, old habits, and old culture. But in the 1980s, as China began to pursue a more capitalist model of prosperity, the reintroduction of Confucius proved useful as a buffer against Western values. As historian Francis Fukuyama wrote in the *Financial Times,* "The government has permitted, and even encouraged, this revival of Confucianism in order to provide a justification for a modern, authoritarian China that does not depend on western theories of history."[7] Along with the revival of Confucianism came the resurrection of Confucius himself—and, most important for the purposes of this case history, his genealogy.

In 1998 Kong Deyong, a seventy-seventh-generation descendant living in Hong Kong, established the Confucius Genealogy Compilation Committee to complete a fifth revision of the tree. More than 450 branches were set up around the world to assist in the work. The twenty-first-century family tree update was approved by eighty-seven-year-old Kung Te-cheng, Chairman Deyong's cousin, living in Taiwan, who inherited the millennium-old title of Yan Sheng Gong (Lord of the Saint Blood). Emperor Renzong (1022–63) of the Northern Song dynasty (960–1127) bestowed the title of "Lord of the Saint's Blood" on the head of the philosopher's forty-sixth-generation descendants, and the title passed along with the blood.

Ironically, Confucius himself was probably illegitimate. His father, a warlord named Shu Liang He, and his mother, a member of the Yan clan, "came roughly together," indicating either a rape, concubinage, or some other sort of extramarital encounter.[8] He would not turn out to be a family man, either, leaving his wife, son, and daughter to pursue his politics and writing. Nonetheless a human god of sorts, to the first in Confucius's male line came reverence, property, and prestige. But in 2003, a remarkable departure from tradition indicated that the revision of Confucius's genealogy was tied to larger social contexts: Kong Kaiping became the first woman to have her name included in the *Confucius Genealogy*, breaking almost three millennia of primogenitor genealogy of the revered philosopher.[9] Women in general are rare in Chinese genealogy, a mentality and tradition derived from Confucianism itself. But, says Kong, the eighty-third descendant of Confucius who heads the compilation committee, "The project is about promoting the legacy of the great man rather than the patriarchal clan system of the family."[10] The current revision marked a major break from the past in several respects. For the first time, the genealogy included women, ethnic minorities, converts to Islam, 34,000 descendants from fifty-fourth-generation heirs who arrived on the Korean peninsula at the end of the Yuan dynasty (1279–1368), 900 recovered relatives in Taiwan, and two branches in Shanxi and Henan Provinces that had been "lost" for more than a thousand years.

At eighty volumes, the fifth edition added more than 1.3 million new entries before registrations were suspended, though Kong Dewei, the Confucius descendant who directing the updating work, estimated that there were close to 3 million descendants in total, many of whom had been lost to broken links over time, migrations, and political divisions. Living descendants had to pay five yuan (seventy U.S. cents) to be included. The dead were added for free if their families could prove their pedigree. As the Chinese English-language newspaper *Jinan* reported, with a whiff of irony, "He's been dead for 2,500 years but his family just keeps growing and growing—Confucius, or more properly his descendants, are alive and well and flourishing in China and across the globe, according to the latest version of his family tree which is set to triple the size of his kith and kin."[11]

The rehabilitation of Confucius at home in China was also exported by the Chinese government in an exercise of "soft power," a philosophy descended from Confucius himself. Suffering from an image crisis abroad for the repression of human rights, encouraging industrial globalization with low-wage workers, exporting cheap and cheaply made products, environmental disregard, political and economic corruption, and a general sense of shift in power from the West to the East, China embarked on a cultural offensive, establishing, beginning in 2004, Confucius Institutes worldwide to promote Chinese languages and culture. Similar to his genealogy, the institutes represented both a revival of traditional culture and a branding exercise, as the Chinese government distanced itself from the policies of the Cultural Revolution and Mao.

The registration of new members in the genealogy was finished by the end of 2007. Published in 2009 to mark the 2,560th anniversary of his birth, at forty-five thousand pages, in eighty volumes, Confucius's updated family tree now acknowledged more than 2 million verified members. By 2014 the eighty volumes had been fully digitized—fitting on a thumb drive—to make revision, searching, and verification easier. The digital version was tree shaped and searchable, providing analytical functions for demographic and other statistical information.[12]

In the example of Confucius's family, we see the immediate difference between the idea of genealogy and that of family. They are inextricably linked, to be sure, but genealogy traces strict ideas of useful kinship, while family often doesn't choose its bedmates. The demarcation of genealogical relationships represents a slightly more abstract exercise than sitting down to a family fight or fond photographs hanging on the wall. The narrative need for the resurrection of the Confucian genealogy is part of a rehabilitation more largely of his teachings cultivating fraternity, loyalty, filial piety, integrity, and harmony. However, its other inheritances, a strict adherence to feudal culture primogeniture lines and a patriarchal system that did not tolerate intellectual and cultural differences, have been subdued. In the name of "boosting world harmony," the Confucian line now represents the continuity of his figure and a rewriting of a liberal or neo-Confucianism in the body of his descendants, a sign of the loosening grip of communist repression, and resistance against Western values.

That the women who bore each successive eighty-three generations of baby Kongs have not until now been part of the genealogy points to how absolute the difference between family and genealogy can be. In every major system—Confucian, Jewish, Christian, surname groups, and so on—inheritance is a masculine affair, and women are ancillary, a conception of lineage that the democratization of genealogy has manifestly challenged and changed. So, let us make this observation, which may be obvious, but bears stating: pedigree is a very confined notion of descent, one that locates it absolutely in religion and culture. Genealogy, in this sense, is less about family than it is about an inherited status. Yet blood, the bio, is the matter on which the strict legality of pedigree rests. We are dealing with a concept that is, as with most things human, both physical and cultural, natural and constructed, essential and easily manipulated—in other words, endogenous and entrained. For my purposes, the genealogy of Confucius himself (rather than Confucianism, but still as its manifestation) provides a framing story for some of the issues of the book as a whole: descent, moral and family values, emergent technologies, and the genealogical sublime.

TOO MUCH PROOF

Sometimes proof is the enemy of genealogy. As this brief history of the resurrection of Confucius line reveals, genealogy is manifestly a social practice embedded in political—broadly speaking—demands of the moment. And though practices of tracing pedigrees are grounded in biological inheritance, genealogy and genetics are not necessarily the same thing. As we will see later in the book, the popularity of genetic genealogy is gaining significant momentum in the West, where the popularity of genealogy in general has skyrocketed in the past twenty years; genetic genealogy in China is less compelling yet growing for different reasons. Whereas genetic genealogy in the West focuses in large part on percentages of ethnic inheritance and finding immediate family (often revealing "nonpaternity incidents"), in contrast, in China, where ancestor worship has a twenty-five-hundred-year tradition and 90 percent of the population is Han Chinese, the appeal is linked primarily to discovering links to royalty rather than ethnic roots.[13] But the case of Confucius sheds some light on a resistance to DNA determinism.

Even as the Confucius Genealogy Compilation Committee threw open the doors of the family compound to those who had never been counted before, the process of verification was limited to paper genealogies. The committee was reticent to have the lines confirmed via DNA testing, since the point was not to prove that the sage's blood flowed in his descendants but, rather, to encourage his values. Biological verification would have compromised the cultural project in myriad ways: it might have revealed historically broken bloodlines, it might have disqualified contemporary applicants, and it might have relied on questionable science, given that finding a DNA sample of Confucius was unlikely. Biological verification would have run counter to the idea of the project in the first place, which was to revive the memory of Confucius and to embrace his values as both ancient and modern. The more people who considered themselves related to Confucius, the larger the number of likely adherents. Investing in ancestral identity is to also invest in the attributes of one's ancestors, much as eschewing one's lineage is a way of distancing oneself from the values of preceding generations.[14] In the case of the Confucian line, cultural values and identification were closely aligned. In this case, as Jane Qui observed, "the project hints at the limits of Chinese engagement with the age of genomics, and demonstrates how high cultural stakes can constrain science."[15]

In 2002 Deng Yajun, a professional medical examiner of the public security bureau in Xi'an, Shaanxi Province, became one of the first DNA paternity experts at the Centre of Forensic Sciences and Beijing Genomics Institute. Given her expertise in paternity testing, and backed by the Genomics Institute, Deng proposed that she could use DNA testing to help establish a genetic database of authentic Confucius descendants. "Theoretically, all true Confucian male descendants should have the same genetic information in their Y-chromosomes despite small mutations," Deng said.

Resisting Deng's interest, the compilation committee eschewed DNA testing, since the proposed DNA proof misunderstood the purpose of the reestablishment of the Confucian family pedigree. "We are tracing a cultural linkage instead of a biological one," Kong said. "In addition, the process to re-establish the Confucian family pedigree is to collect lost historical evidence and facts, and the DNA testing has nothing to do with this mission," added Kong, claiming that few people involved in the pedigree revision, including the mostly proven Confucian descendants, had contacted Deng.[16]

Deng claimed DNA fingerprinting might reveal the fallibility of the records, hidden adoptions, and deceit, given the privileges that accrued to those who could claim to be part of the unbroken lineage. "Records and documentations are not foolproof," said Deng. "DNA, however, does not lie."[17] Conservatism shapes the very process of creating a genealogy in the name of tradition. In an interview with Jane Qui, Deng observed that genetic genealogy has attracted far less interest in China than in the West. This might be, Deng reckoned, "because the families interested in genealogy are likely to be the most traditional ones, and therefore unlikely to embrace DNA fingerprinting." Part of it is the cost, too: the project would cost more than one hundred times more per participant if DNA were used.[18]

Debating the wisdom of DNA testing and even the project to revise the pedigree, Qian Xun, a Confucian historian at Tsinghua University, even questioned the necessity of reestablishing a Confucian family pedigree. "What Confucius has left for us are his thoughts. Whether his true descendants could be found is meaningless, let alone through DNA testing," Qian told *China Daily*.[19] Deng didn't want to challenge the work of the compilation committee or the cultural rehabilitation of Confucian values; she only wanted to help by offering "an additional option for some unconfirmed Confucian offspring, who may want to prove their lineage." The only problem was that Deng's plan was impossible without the cooperation of "proven" Confucian offspring.

The idea that DNA will offer incontrovertible proof seems like a dubious claim to make in the effort to verify or disprove a genealogy that stretches over more than two millennia. But in spite of the opposition from the compilation committee, geneticists did not give up on the idea. Since obtaining a DNA sample from Confucius was manifestly not possible, Deng's idea was to use documented descendants of Confucius to form a DNA database against which other claimants could be compared. In 2013 the *South China Morning Post* reported that geneticists at Fudan University in Shanghai found genetic evidence "to prove that most of the people who claim to be descendants of the ancient sage Confucius come from a single bloodline."[20] A significant problem, however, was that a common bloodline didn't prove that it led to Confucius, since none of his actual DNA exists.

Y-chromosome testing was developed in large part by Bryan Sykes, a professor of human genetics at Oxford University, who founded one of the first direct-to-consumer genetic genealogical testing companies, Oxford Ancestors. Sykes tested his own surname first. In an article on Y-chromosome surname studies in the *American Journal of Human Genetics,* Sykes gives the following conditions for the scientific accuracy or inaccuracy of the genetic inheritance linked with specific surnames: "It is a biological necessity that a son inherit the Y chromosome of his father, so it follows that males sharing the same surname might also share the same haplotype in the nonrecombining segment of the Y chromosome. However, this would only hold if (i) there had been no subsequent Y-chromosome divergence, (ii) there were a single common ancestor for each surname and there had been no subsequent surname adoption by unrelated males, and (iii) there had been no nonpaternity events involving unrelated Y chromosomes."[21]

To understand Sykes, we need to understand a bit of specialized language that will be useful in later chapters. A haplotype (haploid genotype) is a group of genes that we inherit together from a single parent. Mitochondria (mtDNA) is inherited from mother to child and so can be used to explore our direct maternal lines in both women and men (and all genders). Mitochondrial testing was the basis for Sykes's 2001 blockbuster book, *The Seven Daughters of Eve,* a compelling combination of science adventure story and origin myth. The Y chromosome is much more specific. This chromosome is inherited virtually unchanged from father to son, so the haplotype allows tracing back through a surname and the extrapolation of ancestors from living descendants. But this is barring the following broad limitations as Sykes's outlines above: recent mutations, multiple sources of the same name (think Smith), no surname adoption (that is, not a Smith by blood), and no "nonpaternity events" (little Smith's father is not who he thinks he is). The magic of the unrecombining Y chromosome is that it passes unchanged through the maternal body, carrying the DNA of the seed but not the womb.

The pursuit of surname genealogies and the Y-chromosomal test echo each other in uncanny ways, but consider this caveat published by two bioethicists in the *British Medical Journal* in 2002:

> Y chromosome tracing will connect a man to his father but not to his mother, and it will connect him to only one of his four grandparents: his paternal grandfather. In the same way, it will connect him to one of his eight great grandparents and one of his 16 great great grandparents.

Continue back in this manner for 14 generations and the man will be still be connected to only one ancestor in that generation. The test will not connect him to any of the other 16,383 ancestors in that generation to whom he is also related in equal measure.[22]

As this exponential multiplication shows, we pick and choose our ancestors and emphasize inheritance against the ever-growing dissipation of contributions. Reflecting the history of pedigree charts themselves, we privilege one kind of DNA inheritance over another. The Y chromosome is the most popular marker in genetic genealogy, because of its haploid character and its close association with surnames and paternal inheritance.[23]

But claims of inheriting undiluted nuclear DNA (from both parents) over generations are statistically naive. To prove this point, Mark Liberman, a linguist and professor of computer science at the University of Pennsylvania, spuriously claimed he may be carrying DNA from Confucius in his debunking blog, *Being Descendant from Confucius,* "Confucius lived about 500 BC. At 25 years per generation, the period between 500 BC and 2000 AD is about 2500/25 = 100 generations. Thus any given person might have as many as 2 to the 100th power ancestors—2 times 2 100 times—at that time depth. $2^{100} = 1.27 * 10^{30}$ or more than 10 to the 30th power. A trillion is 10 to the 12th power. A trillion trillions is 10 to the 24th power. 10 to the 30th power is a million trillion trillions."[24]

We are here again in the territory of the genealogical sublime: incomprehensible numbers into which we vanish or which vanish into us. However, we soon also encounter the historical impossibility of such numbers and a phenomenon known as "pedigree collapse."[25] Exponential ancestor multiplication becomes a mathematical impossibility, given the projected historical population of the world, which was calculated at the time of Confucius to be about one hundred million. The limited number of historical ancestors means that they were the ancestors of all of us, and thus the pedigree collapses. "Obviously there were not remotely enough people for everyone of 2^{100} genealogical slots for your ancestors in 500 BC to be distinct." Interbreeding across genealogies exponentially reduces the number of our ancestors. "Everyone's genealogy must be a tangled web, with lots of people mating with more-or-less distant relatives. That doesn't mean that you or I necessarily (or even probably) have any of Confucius's genes," Liberman continues.

Note that in every generation, half the genes come from the mother and half from the father. So without any reinforcement from interbreeding, after 100 generations you can be expected to have only one in $2^{(100)}$ of the original ancestor's genes, or one in 10^{30} = one gene out of every million trillion trillion. Since the number of human genes is about 20,000, your chance of having one of Confucius's genes is about 20 thousand in a million trillion trillion. This is about one chance in 10 to the 26th poser—roughly one chance in a hundred trillion trillion. This is about the same as the chance of picking one lucky marble out of a pile of marbles the size of the earth.[26]

Even so, Kong Wei, a twenty-one-year-old economics student at the Beijing Normal University, related to almost two million verified Kongs and other Confucius lines, on paper at least, worried that "rejecting genetic-fingerprinting technologies would undermine the authenticity of the revised Confucius family tree." But women, so recently acknowledged in the tree, would be unverifiable, reviving once again the idea that Kong's pedigree can be ensured only by the Y chromosome. In this case, science could undo the work for which Confucius had been enlisted twenty-five hundred years after his death. Given a dubious unbroken chain of eighty-three generations of fathers and sons with 181 lineages with different Y chromosomes, in this case DNA testing would have the unpleasant effect of undermining the authenticity of any number of branches of the lineage. Any past fraud or adoption would introduce a new Y chromosome into the lineage, provoking questions about legitimacy all the way down the line. "You can imagine the kind of havoc this result may cause," observed Sykes. "So people revising the family tree probably don't want to know the answer." Sykes readily admits the limits of DNA testing as a measure of authenticity in this case. "The Confucius family tree has an enormous cultural significance. It's not just a scientific question."[27]

That we struggle to conceive of the numbers (though Liberman's marble metaphor is helpful), we easily develop believable narratives about who we are. We defend ourselves against the statistical improbability of inheriting anything more than a few generations back by telling great stories about being related to great people. We use one cognitive process, imagination, to defend ourselves against another, our confrontation with mathematical dilution.

My explorations of the databases that follow all exhibit the same tendency: each is driven to accumulate greater and greater numbers of ancestors and documents in the name of establishing the intimate relations of family, which become more and more diluted. Each database evinces mathematical and mythic stories of descent.

CHAPTER 2

THE MORMONS

Doctrine and Data

The LDS Church has been the single most important factor in the evolution of genealogy over the past century. There's no question. If you wanted to say "Who created the market out there?" The LDS Church did.

—Dan Taggart, cofounder of Ancestry.com

DOCTRINE

Every genealogist knows that Salt Lake City is the mecca of family history. There, the temple of the Church of Jesus Christ of Latter-day Saints (a.k.a. the LDS, the Mormon Church) looms, pointing eastward and skyward to heaven with Gothic overstatement.[1] Following the direction of Danilo Kiš's "Encyclopedia of the Dead" and its uncanny double, the Mormons' Granite Mountain Records Vault, Utah is clearly the place to start if one wants to understand how genealogy emerged as a potent social and technological force in the twentieth and twenty-first centuries.

The role of the Mormon Church in the development of the popularity of genealogy in North America can't be overstated.[2] I wasn't really aware of the extent of its influence until I interviewed Dan Taggart, the cofounder of the largest commercial genealogical database in the world, Ancestry.com, whose story I will tell in the next chapter. Taggart was a member of the church, and Ancestry's success grew out of the Mormon project itself, so he knew a great deal about the relationship between doctrine and database. His bold statement—that the Mormon Church was *the* key motivator in the exponential growth of family history—is echoed by Donald Akenson, a historian of religion, who offers this proposition at the beginning of his book *Some Family: The Mormons and How Humanity*

Keeps Track of Itself: "By 2025 more human beings will learn their family histories and how world history has evolved through the Mormons' data and theologic-history than from any other source."[3] The scope of the Mormon project is impossible to overstate, given their goal to collect *all* the genealogical records of the world. At the same time, it's all too easy to turn a blind eye to its larger moral and doctrinal purposes that quietly promote our search for infinite family and for life after death, defending ourselves against death itself. These are the pleasures and displeasures of the genealogical sublime.

"Descent" (*Herkunft*), as we have seen, has a history and set of values that are attached to it. The history and involvement of the Mormons are a case study that will lead us to a discussion of "emergence" (*Entstehung*). If we tend to naturalize the idea of descent, that we are part of the human chain of being, how and why we record that chain is deeply social and mythical, reflecting, particularly, our ideas about origin stories. Akenson argues that between any culture's set of genealogical narratives and its basic mythologies is a feedback loop: "Really strong genealogical narratives determine in large part the nature of a culture's gods; and the character of a culture's gods determines in considerable part the sort of genealogical narratives a society will adopt."[4] So what happens when one of those gods happens to be technology itself?

The Mormon story is a combination of doctrinal drive and database technology perceived as a gift of God. A history of subjugation and invented but unshakable doctrine combined with technological savvy led them to the project of collecting all of the genealogical records of the world to redeem the dead and sanctify the living. The records are used to fulfill the doctrine of providing salvation to everyone's ancestors by linking generations together in preparation for the next life and for the ability for men to become gods. How the database came to be reflects all the hallmarks of "emergence": haphazard conflicts, violence, moral superiority, and the eventual domination of the dominated. The strands of messianic purpose, genealogy, whiteness, virtue, technology, and data are tightly woven, but I have had to tease them out to make sense of how genealogy came to play so large a role in Mormon plans to save the world and how, in turn, anyone using the Mormon records or the records of the commercial genealogical companies who have agreements with the LDS Church (almost every company) helps to foster the Mormons' project of uniting heavenly and earthly ancestors, brought together by the enabling gift of technology.

The basic, if fantastic, facts of the "the church" are fairly well known. Mormonism was founded in 1830 in upstate New York by Joseph Smith, a visionary prophet—or a small-time con man (depending on who is writing his history). Akenson provides a discussion of how Smith, "operating on the moral border between being a superstitious savant and a confidence-man,"[5] came to inhabit the position of prophet and how he invented one of the world's most modern religions. As a historian of religion, Akenson gives a detailed account of the development of the Mormon scriptures and their "translations" from both the King James Version of the Hebrew Bible and the New Testament into a rereading of Judaism and Protestantism, creating an entirely new religion—and one that grew rapidly in the twentieth century. Alan Taylor in his work on American religious history narrates another very useful cultural context, arguing that "Mormonism emerged from the lived religion of upstate New York: an open-ended, fluid, porous, multivalent and hypercompetitive discourse involving multiple Protestant denominations and many autonomous clusters of seekers."[6] Significantly, observes Taylor, "the most fundamental issue dividing the evangelical from the orthodox was their clashing attitudes toward latter-day messages from the divine." Wanting direct contact with God, evangelists refuted the idea that the scriptures were historically complete. Smith was only one of many self-appointed preachers who toured rural settlements trying to attract adherents, "independent innovators who created their own local sects by claiming authority directly from God, unmediated and undiluted by any worldly authorities."[7]

Though the Book of Mormon is the best known of Smith's prophetic writings, dictated directly to him by God (though Smith admits authorship in the first edition), for the purposes of our story, the most important revelation came on April 3, 1836. On that day, Smith and one of his adherents, Oliver Cowdry, claimed to have had a vision in their recently built Kirtland, Ohio, temple. Jesus, Moses, Elias, and the prophet Elijah (Smith didn't realize that Elias and Elijah were the same figure in the Old Testament, according to Akenson) appeared in quick succession. Elijah, the prophet of the Second Coming—as prophesied by Malachi at the end of the Old Testament Bible—returned to deliver this message before that "great and dreadful day" when the proud and wicked would be "burned as stubble": the righteous man "shall turn the heart of the fathers to the children and the heart of the children to their fathers, lest I come smite the earth with a curse" (Mal. 4:4–6; Doctrine and Covenants 110:16). This is the scripture from which the church's genealogical drive would come to be derived. To turn the heart of father to the children and the heart of the children to their fathers was destined to mean that the generations of family would become the preoccupation of the faith.

Seeing himself as the "he" of this scripture, Smith was vested with a certain authority and certain responsibilities. "Therefore the keys of this dispensation are committed into your hands; and by this ye may know that the great and dreadful day of the Lord is near, even at the doors" (Doctrine and Covenants 110:16). As Akenson puts it, "LDS scholars take this to mean (and I think correctly) that Joseph Smith was beginning to invent the baptism of the dead."[8] A year later Smith had another vision, in which he saw his much-loved older brother Alvin, who had died in 1825, in heaven with his parents, who were still alive at the time. This vision contributed to the idea that the dead needed a path to salvation and a way to be reunited with family in heaven and thus to the invention of the doctrinal necessity for the baptism of the dead, setting the great Mormon genealogical project in motion.

Not coincidentally, according to LDS lore—and Kory Meyerink, one of the early professional genealogists in Utah—significant things happened right after that revelation in 1836. "For instance, in 1837, England started keeping vital registrations, civil registrations of births, marriages, and deaths, on a nation-wide level. Something no state or country had ever done until that point."[9] The timing was providential if one ignored the reasons for this innovation in record keeping.[10] In 1841 New England initiated the very first nominal census, in which they listed the names and ages of everyone in the country. That year also, New England and Massachusetts started recording vital records on a statewide basis. The United States had been carrying out a census every decade since 1790, but in 1850, for the first time, they named every single individual, including women, children, and slaves, and their ages and their state of birth. Prior to the 1850 U.S. Census, only the names of the heads of households were recorded, while the rest of the household members were tabulated within given age groups.[11] In 1851 the Province of Canada (Upper and Lower Canada) followed suit.[12] Thus were the North American genealogical research tools born with a decade-by-decade snapshot of the entire populations of the United States and Canada. Larger historical or technological trends coincided with the doctrine and practices of the Mormon Church in circular confirmation that the doctrine was divine. Clearly, other entities had heard Elijah's revelation.

Joseph Smith extrapolated much from Malachi's commandment. The "beginning of the massive Mountain of Names that the LDS preserves in Utah is found in scriptures that Joseph Smith articulated in the last four years of his life," writes Akenson,[13] a monumental genealogical project that develops for the purpose of providing saving ordinances for the living and the dead, including baptism and sealing of families for eternity. Church historians concur. Samuel Otterstrom links a 1894 announcement by Wilford Woodruff, president of the church, encouraging "Latter-day Saints from this time to trace their genealogies as far as they can and to be sealed to their fathers and mothers," to the organization of the Genealogical Society of Utah a few months later.[14] A more concise version of the doctrine and why it inspired the world's most comprehensive genealogical collection was given to me by Roger Minert, a professor of genealogy and German history at Brigham Young University. BYU, the largest privately owned, church-sponsored university in the United States, manages a delicate balance between science and belief, offering the only undergraduate degree in genealogy in North America, under the rubric of family studies. Minert explained that "Smith invented posthumous baptism, or relayed the command of the Almighty to invent posthumous baptism, in order to provide an opportunity to the family of the 'Saints,' church members, who might have, but for their death before the revelations of the Church of Jesus Christ, as it was called at the time, embraced its teachings."[15] Smith's doctrine and his subsequent invention of the ritual of proxy baptism were the means by which people who, by the fate of death, had missed hearing Smith's message of the restored Gospel could be provided a release from spirit prison and set back on track in their eternal progression to becoming gods. In his "Epistle of the Prophet to the Twelve," a letter written in October 1840 to the high council and elders proselytizing in Great Britain, Joseph Smith reveals this latest doctrine:

I presume the doctrine of "baptism for the dead" has ere this reached your ears, and may have raised some inquiries in your minds respecting the same. I cannot in this letter give you all the information you may desire on the subject; but aside from knowledge independent of the Bible, I would say that it was certainly practiced by the ancient churches; and St. Paul endeavors to prove the doctrine of the resurrection from the same, and says, "Else what shall they do which are baptized for the dead, if the dead rise not at all? Why are they then baptized for the dead?"

I first mentioned the doctrine in public when preaching the funeral sermon of Brother Seymour Brunson; and have since then given general instructions in the Church on the subject. The Saints have the privilege of being baptized for those of their relatives who are dead, whom they believe would have embraced the Gospel, if they had been privileged with hearing it, and who have received the Gospel in the spirit, through the instrumentality of those who have been commissioned to preach to them while in prison.

Without enlarging on the subject, you will undoubtedly see its consistency and reasonableness; and it presents the Gospel of Christ in probably a more enlarged scale than some have imagined it.[16]

Smith would be pleased to know that his vision succeeded, probably even beyond what he could have possibly imagined. The project was sublime from the beginning. On a more earthly plane, Smith's father, Joseph Smith Sr., had just died. His father's death would have been of some relevance to his doctrine of posthumous baptism, as the loss of a parent is cited as one of the most compelling reasons for starting a genealogy. The very mortal death of his father might have provoked the extension of the church's power to seal families in the celestial realm. Though Smith's father had been baptized in the church well before his death, Joseph Smith's brother Alvin hadn't been, and Smith desired to reunite the family in heaven. He had also lost four children in infancy, and, perhaps not coincidentally, infants were exempt from needing posthumous ordinances.

Early proxy baptisms were carried out starting in 1840 in the Missouri River near Nauvoo, Illinois.[17] But the prophet Elijah, via Smith, insisted that these baptisms deserved a consecrated pool. The first baptismal font was dedicated in 1841 within the unfinished walls of the Nauvoo temple. And the great Mormon project began in earnest. With the doctrine of baptism and a pool in place, in the early 1840s Smith revealed the "New and Everlasting Covenant," a theology of family that superseded all earthly bonds.

Enthusiasm for the practice grew quickly alongside the parameters of its meaning. Not only were the dead to be baptized in a mission to save them, but they would all be reunited with their earthly flesh and blood. Further, living families were themselves to be "sealed" together for eternity, wives to their husbands, children to their parents. Until sealed, mortal relationships would die at death; those that had been blessed would continue in celestial marriage. Similarly to posthumous baptism, couples and families could also be sealed retroactively. So sealed, the faithful Saints were promised godliness after death. Section 132 of the Doctrine and Covenants is the primary scriptural reference for sealings—and for plural marriages—as the doctrines of plural marriage on earth and in heaven are very tightly connected to the practice of sealing. Less faithful Saints also found redemption in baptism, sometimes for the second time. "Rebaptism" for "Remission of Sins" was a common practice for men who had "exploited numerous women under the guise of 'spiritual wifery.'"[18]

Though the Mormons were imagining a loving reception in heaven, they were not popular on earth. Joseph Smith had invited persecution since he was a teenager and his band of Mormons no less. They were driven out of Kirkland in 1838 for debt and regrouped in Missouri, where they were not welcome, but swore to defend themselves this time. The governor of Missouri, Wilburn Boggs, issued an "extermination order," directing the militia to drive the Mormons out of the state. A few days later, eighteen Mormons were killed. A truce was called and the Mormons agreed to leave, though Smith was arrested for treason on the grounds of mobilizing resistance. He bore his sentence with saintly patience. While he was in jail, his disciples moved on to Illinois, where they founded a new town, Navuoo, putting themselves in charge of the local government. Released from prison, Smith joined them. But then Governor Boggs was shot and injured. Smith's bodyguard was the main suspect, and Smith went into hiding.[19]

While he was in hiding on a small island in the Mississippi River, Joseph Smith wrote the 127th section of the epistles. And here we see a central idea in "emergence," that haphazard conflict is sometimes a factor in the sudden manifestation of an idea or practice. With a lot of time to think, Smith wrote an epistle, a letter to the church synthesizing a variety of teachings that he had received as a prophet, something he did only a few times in his career. In that epistle, Smith repeated the scripture in Malachi and tells us with "great precision" what that means. "And what that means," said Shipley Munson, the vice president of marketing for FamilySearch, the LDS family history database, "is tracing the lineage of mankind and to do the work that we are now engaged in. Still."[20]

Here then are the paragraphs from the epistle in the Doctrine and Covenants that reinforced the great record-keeping project and the doctrine of "sealing" families. The Doctrine and Covenants is a series of revelations given to the prophet Joseph Smith, which read the way you might read Paul's epistles. The letters are answers to questions. "We get the answers, but not the questions, so we have to infer what the questions might be," explained Munson. Presumably, the questions, given the answers, were about how to keep track of the practice. "And again, I give unto you a word in relation to the baptism for your dead";

6 Verily, thus saith the Lord unto you concerning your dead: When any of you are baptized for your dead, let there be a recorder, and let him be eye-witness of your baptisms; let him hear with his ears, that he may testify of a truth, saith the Lord;

7 That in all your recordings it may be recorded in heaven; whatsoever you bind on earth, may be bound in heaven; whatsoever you loose on earth, may be loosed in heaven.[21]

In the uncanny foretelling of the archives to come, Smith is very specific about the sanctity of the records themselves:

9 And again, let all the records be had in order, that they may be put in the archives of my holy temple, to be held in remembrance from generation to generation, saith the Lord of Hosts.[22]

Smith presciently outlines the process from start to finish, with the records coming to an orderly end in an archive, the archive that would become the Granite Mountain Records Vault, an archive built as the repository of immortality.

Over the next two years, Joseph Smith was instructed, and instructed in turn, how these proxy baptisms should be conducted. The baptisms should be gender specific: a man is baptized in the name of a man, a woman for a woman. And each baptism would be witnessed by two people, one who would attest that the baptism by immersion had been done correctly and one a scribe who would record every one of these events: the name of the person baptized, the date of birth, and the place of birth of that person, enough genealogical data to identify that person. The next step would be to keep a record of all these in a coherent manner so that the ordinances would not be duplicated. Two sets of records were needed for the practice: the genealogical records that confirmed, or "concluded," an ancestor's existence and the set of records for those for whom the ordinances had been performed, a database for the unbaptized and unsealed and one for the baptized and sealed. Key here is that the Mormons had to collect the records before they could perform the rituals of baptism. Every record in the vast Mormon project has been collected with saving ordinances and the sealing of families as the goal.

Smith would come to a violent end in 1844, two years after he received the doctrine of baptism for the dead. Arrested again, this time with the entire Nauvoo city council, he was charged with treason. The jail that held him was stormed, and he and his brother Hyrum were shot, Smith multiple times. He left an indeterminate number of "wives" widowed. Estimates vary from sixteen (the official number in FamilySearch) to more than forty, since many of the marriages, other than his marriage to Emma Hale, his first wife, with whom he eloped, were not recorded in any civil or church documents. Many of the marriages, including those to other men's wives, were secret or celestial, complicating the genealogical record considerably.[23]

The prophet was dead, but his church only gained traction. The pioneers fled once again, this time over the mountains to the vast flats of Salt Lake City to commit themselves to family, alive and dead. The records they began to archive and organize in aid of the sealings and posthumous baptisms would become a vast act of familial generosity, embracing everyone who has ever lived.

François Weil tells the story of the growth of the Mormon genealogical activities in *Family Trees: A History of Genealogy in America*. From the 1880s on, "a growing number of Mormons served as genealogical missionaries, mostly traveling east to meet with distant relatives, copy family records, search old registers and cemeteries and contact genealogical societies."[24] The existing missionary corps was soon adapted to service the genealogical cause. Armed with missionary zeal, missionary cards, letters of appointment, and a special blessing from a church authority, the genealogical missionaries visited relatives, copied family Bibles and other records, and asked an unending stream of questions regarding their ancestors. They visited parish churches, where they spent long hours searching through old registers, and trekked to cemeteries, seeking the gravestones. Many missionaries reported spiritual experiences that gave them firm assurance that the Lord was with them and had miraculously directed them to their needed sources.[25] The need to collect and keep good records for posthumous baptism then led to the establishment of the Genealogical Society of Utah in 1894, sponsored, supported, and mostly funded by the Church of Jesus Christ of Latter-day Saints. The Utah organization wasn't out in front of the turn-of-the-century enthusiasm, but its motivations were very different.

In "John Farmer and the Making of American Genealogy," Weil discusses the interesting problem for early American colonial genealogists. They were seeking to elevate themselves, or "secure social standing within the British Empire," at the same time that the revolutionary republicans sought to overthrow the hierarchies that pedigree inferred. "Many in the first generation of Americans questioned the compatibility of genealogy and republicanism," fearing that it would endanger the nation's collective identity. The "Adams" of the new nation, as Thomas Jefferson declaimed, should look to the future rather than the past. Nonetheless, the aspiration to be part of history regrew as an interest in local history (or "antiquarianism") was established, most tenaciously in the New England states by the early 1800s. Weil points to Daniel Webster's speech at the bicentennial celebration of the Pilgrims' landing as a turning point. "There may be, and there often is, indeed, a regard for ancestry which nourishes only weak pride," said Webster. "But there is also a moral and philosophical respect for our ancestors, which elevates the character and improves the heart."[26] Here Webster played what we see are familiar themes of marrying moral goodness with genealogical pursuits.

I hear echoes of Malachi's instructions to turn the hearts of fathers to sons and sons to fathers, without, of course, the threat to smite the earth. The Mormon enthusiasm for family history lagged somewhat behind that which began to beat in the hearts of the New England patriots in the 1820s. What both movements shared, however, was the emphasis on evidence rather than narrative or family lore for establishing family trees. For the early American antiquarians, scholarship was the mark of a well-respected tree; for the Mormons, a "conclusion," evidence that an ancestor had indeed existed, was necessary for a successful baptism.

The growing enthusiasm for family history in the early nineteenth century was not without its prescient skeptics. Joseph Willard, the printer of John Farmer's 1829 *Register,* predicted future fantasies of genealogical interest. "You will incontinently set the universal Yankee nation to hunting out their pedigree, and we shall find one man who considered himself the artisan of his own fortune priding himself on being descended from Tom of whom he never before heard or imagined in all his fancies—another as coming from the loins of Dick & a third from Harry."[27]

Nonetheless, the first genealogical society in the Western world, the New England Historical Genealogical Society (NEHGS), was established in 1845. It still exists in a patrician building on Newbury Street in downtown Boston and maintains its dignified status among the wild west of genealogical databases, though its collections too are now fronted by a branded database, "AmericanAncestors." It holds a fascinating collection of American family history artifacts, diaries, letters, photographs, needlepoint, family Bibles, and registers and prides itself on the quality of its research. In spite of the society's very different aims, the interest in genealogy fostered by the NEHGS became part of the Mormon project. Between 1845 and 1885, New England, New York, Pennsylvania, New Jersey, Maine, and Wyoming all established genealogical societies, but these were few compared to the hundreds, if not thousands, of existing historical societies across North America, many of which had a strong interest in genealogy.[28] Mormons interpreted the growing interest "over genealogical matters" in the United States as "the hand of the Lord." And, indeed, the end of the nineteenth century through the beginning of the twentieth was another boom time for genealogical interest, driven, in part, by non–western European immigration and fears of race suicide.[29] The church-controlled *Deseret News* explained in 1885 that "thousands of men [were] laboring assiduously to prepare the way, though unconsciously, for the salvation of the dead."[30]

Between 1885 and 1900, at least 178 Saints became genealogical missionaries, a mix of elders and younger folk. They collected records close to home, but the majority went to the British Isles, the beginning of the church's mission to collect records worldwide. The establishment of the Genealogical Society of Utah was an effort to systematize record gathering rather than rely on the haphazard and expensive work of the missionaries.[31] Its membership grew from forty-eight in 1895 to twenty-five hundred by 1915.[32] The society began to recruit field agents in New England, Germany, Switzerland, and Scotland. Then the society made a crucial decision that would forecast its future. They decided to be open to anyone of "good moral character," not just church members, setting a precedent for engagement with genealogists everywhere. The society's vision was prescient. Founder Nephi Anderson wrote in 1912:

> I see the records of the dead and their histories gathered from every nation under heaven to one great central library in Zion—the largest and best equipped for its particular work in the world. Branch libraries may be established in the nations but in Zion will be the records of last resort and final authority. Trained genealogists will find constant work in all nations having unpublished records searching among the archives for families and family connections. Then as temples multiply and the work enlarges to its ultimate proportions this society or some organization growing out of this society will have in its care some elaborate but perfect system of exact registration and checking so that the work in the temples may be conducted without confusion or duplication. And so throughout the years reaching into the millennium of peace this work of salvation will go on until every worthy soul that can be found from earthly records will have been searched out and officiated for and then the unseen world will come to our aid. The broken links will be joined the tangled threads will be placed in order and the purposes of god in placing salvation within the reach of all will have been consummated.[33]

Women played a large role in the early society, particularly Susa Young Gates, one of Brigham Young's fifty-nine children, who bore thirteen of her own (only four of whom survived). Family lines grew exponentially, helped along by polygamy and the genealogy-minded Daughters of Utah Pioneers, founded in Salt Lake City in 1901 in the model of other national lineage societies such as the Daughters of the American Revolution. Susa compiled a thirteen-volume genealogy of the Young family that contained twenty thousand names. Her later *Surname Book and Racial History* (1918) was sent to every known genealogical and historical library in America and Europe. Based on the fifth chapter of Genesis, the names begin with Adam, Seth, and Noah, and the races—the Black or the Ethiopian Race, the Yellow or the Mongolian Race, and the White or the Caucasian Race—which were aligned with the descendants of Noah, Ham, Shem, and Japheth. Interestingly, Gates acknowledged that the three racial lines shaded into one another, given the "original unity of the human race," but church doctrine was quite clear that dark skin was a curse for sins, as opposed to the "white and delightsome" appearance of the righteous.[34] Deeply racist doctrine would permeate the church until a 1978 revelation changed the policy of not allowing individuals of African descent to become Saints.[35]

Gate's nearly six-hundred-page book is surprisingly erudite and comprehensive, a combination of the Bible, the Book of Mormon, the *Encyclopedia Britannica,* a mishmash of religious genealogies, and quite meticulous onomastics, detailing the history and origins of proper names. In the introduction, Gates says that the data of the genealogical record might be called "the tabernacle of the departed spirit, even as the word is the tabernacle of the thought which it embodies."[36] Here we have another element of the sublime, that the data/document embodies an element of the divine, that the document houses the dead soul.

At the first International Congress of Genealogy in 1915 in San Francisco, 48 out of the 106 official delegates were from the church, equally split between men and women. The congress was part of the Panama-Pacific International Exposition and was coordinated not to conflict with the American Historical Association, which met the week before, and the American Genetic Association and the Second International Conference on Race Betterment, which would meet the week after.[37] The Mormons made an impression on the congress and staked their place as the world's record gatherers. Books constituted a large part of their collection; by the late '30s, they had the fourth-largest genealogical library in the United States. Only the Library of Congress, the New English Historic Genealogical Society, and the Newberry Library in Chicago had more. The church threw its resources behind the genealogical project in every part of its institutional reach. Even children were enlisted to perform vicarious temple work, saving nearly fifty thousand souls in 1923.

And here's where the story merges into the present. Temple work had become so popular that data management emerged as a significant problem. Ordinances were duplicated, costing the church and the members who performed the ordinances by proxy time and money, because there was no effective system of cross-referencing from temple to temple or family to family. The new Temple Index Bureau was established in 1932. Its first director, Harry H. Russell, conducted elaborate durability tests on index-card stock. Five typists completed 126,000 index cards in five months, and by the late '30s more than six million names had been checked with more than five hundred thousand duplications avoided.[38] Significantly, the Temple Index Bureau and its recording technologies took a turn with the introduction of microfilm in 1935.

One of the extraordinary aspects of the Mormon genealogical mission is the technology that they have recruited to accomplish their mission of amassing all of the genealogical records of the world. Or, to follow the logic of doctrine and divine Providence, new technologies have been synergistically provided for them in order that they might fulfill their role as the world record keepers and saviors. The success of their mission has necessitated staying at the forefront of storage technology. Miraculously, similar to the worldwide interest in genealogy that the Mormons took as a sign that Elijah's message was divine, the technology developed on pace with the church's acquisitions of records. The sublime technology was all part of God's plan.

THE PROPHECIES OF TECHNOLOGY

We believe that the technology is placed here by our Father in Heaven for a purpose. And one of the most important purposes for all these technological tools is to give humans the ability to re-create the family tree of the human race.

—Shipley Munson, vice president of marketing, FamilySearch

Under the Gothic gaze of the Salt Lake City Temple, across West Temple Street from the silver-domed Tabernacle, sits, in rather stolid fashion, the modern bunker building of the Family History Library. It's an ordinary-looking library that would not look out of place on any university campus, except for the wall-long mural of Christ with his hands held wide, welcoming the peoples of the world and those who cross the threshold of this temple of the dead. Opened in 1985, this sixth iteration of the main library has already outgrown itself.[39] In January 2018, the new FamilySearch Centre opened in Lehi, just south of Salt Lake City, about five minutes away from the new headquarters of Ancestry.com. These modern structures invite all who search to enter their doors to use and to contribute to the records of the church. The genealogical records are open to everyone, the temple records to church members only. Collecting genealogical records is a more straightforward exercise than keeping track of the temple records (the records of who has been posthumously baptized or sealed), the two branches of the Mormon genealogical project that demand different technologies.

The data-management problem that surfaced with the popularity of ordinances of sealing and baptism and the duplication of records made the society keenly interesting in record-keeping technologies. Much of how that technology developed has been outlined in James B. Allen, Jessie L. Embry, and Kahlile B. Mehr's exceptionally useful account, *Hearts Turned to the Fathers: A History of the Genealogical Society of Utah, 1894–1995*. Its primary author, James B. Allen, was a church historian whose detailed histories of the church—and its controversies—in its historical context made many members unhappy. He was shuffled out of the position of assistant church historian to the History Department at Brigham Young University after writing *The Story of the Latter-day Saints* in 1976, falling under suspicion repeatedly for writing church history that was too secular. But Allen was a scrupulous historian, and he had access to all of the minutes and official church documents. His historical work is balanced and meticulous and, fittingly, for my purposes, full of statistics. The church's own investment in numbers—presaging the mathematical element of the genealogical sublime—becomes abundantly clear in Allen's culling of these revealing quantifiers. The growth of the church and its genealogical collections, the numbers of records, microfilms, users, genealogical missionaries, family history libraries, and so on, announces the unstoppable genealogical drive of the church, bound up in the technology they found and developed to contain it all.

The Genealogical Library of the 1930s had only printed and handwritten materials and could satisfy only a small portion of the genealogical needs of the church. Moreover, war was on the horizon, and European church members felt a sense of urgency about saving public records from possible destruction. The society's attention was drawn to new microfilm technology, and as the church began to investigate, it discovered that many genealogical materials had already been microfilmed by government agencies and could be bought in that format. The LDS were part of the wave of academic institutions to embrace the technology after Eastman Kodak perfected a 35mm microfilm camera that reduced the size of a record to a twenty-fifth of the original. The *New York Times* began filming and publishing the paper on microfilm in 1935, and that same year Harvard started using microfilm technology for its Foreign Newspapers Project. Under the right conditions (and with newer film materials), microfilm is one of the most stable information-storage technologies, theoretically lasting three to five hundred years, enduringly readable with a strong light source and a form of magnification.[40] Only paper and parchment last longer. The society bought its first camera in 1938.[41]

The society raised money to buy as many European records as it could and pleaded the emergency of the situation to church members. Archibald F. Bennett, a dedicated employee of the society, a.k.a. "Mr. Genealogy," wrote genealogical representatives in each stake,[42] praising the new technology and urging each stake to act swiftly: "With a world trembling on the brink of wholesale war and devastation there is every possibility that unless we act swiftly and decisively the records of millions upon millions of our ancestors will be destroyed beyond all recovery. Apparently the lord has granted us a lull to seize this opportunity to rescue the records before it is too late." The invention of microfilm was not only fortuitous but ordained. "At the same time he has inspired the development of microphotography by which records can be copied quickly accurately and so cheaply that it is almost unbelievable. It is up to us to act NOW!"[43]

European churches welcomed the society's help, and it received permission to photograph nearly two and a half million pages of Danish parish records, with promises of similar arrangements in Germany and England. Other countries balked, but Germany was particularly receptive. The German Bureau for Racial Research had already amassed one of the largest microfilm collections of genealogical information in aid of Hitler's racial purity laws. The bureau had filmed seven thousand of the oldest books of parish records and the society was keen to buy copies of the microfilm, but the war broke out before the deal could go through. Nazi and Mormon enthusiasm for genealogy, albeit for different reasons, made them natural collaborators.

In *Moroni and the Swastika,* David Conley Nelson has provided the first detailed study of the relationship between the Mormon Church and Nazi Germany. Nelson shows that the two ideologies shared many of the same values of purity in behavior and blood.[44] The *Deseret News* published laudatory editorials about the German genealogical project, spurring Fawn McKay Brodie to write to her uncle a scathing indictment of the church and its lack of concern for Jewish refugees.

> Of course, there is latent anti-Semitism that exists in every area as provincial as Utah and which is not dispelled by the church doctrine that we are all "of the blood of Israel." Add to this the fact that the persecution of the Jews had made 8-million people "genealogy minded"—so much so that according to a recent campus acquaintance, a former Berlin lawyer, genealogy is the first subject of conversation in German. I can just hear the good brethren of the Genealogical Society at home saying "Of course, the persecution of the Jews is terrible, but God moves in mysterious way, his wonders to perform."[45]

Her sentiments would later earn her excommunication for her biography of Joseph Smith.

At the war's end, German Mormon missionaries were granted permission by the Russians to look for the records. A store too big to move was found in Stassfurt, a quarter mile deep in a salt mine. Another large store was retrieved from Rothenburg Castle, high on a mountaintop in Thuringia, that Allen recounts with the urgency of a thriller. With some divine help from the weather, they were able to bring the records down to the railroad. "A huge store of Jewish records" was removed from Castle Rathsfeld. The records were returned to Berlin and the Germans, where they were photographed by missionary Paul Langheinrich, who had been instrumental in saving them. He estimated that he had filmed more than one hundred million names.[46] Allen reports on these postwar genealogical adventures admiringly, ignoring the irony of saving the records over the people. Even though the Jews are venerated as God's chosen people, controversy over these Jewish records and others would erupt in 1992 when Jewish genealogist Gary Mokotoff discovered that Jewish Holocaust victims had been posthumously baptized by the church. Embarrassed, the church agreed to desist, signing an agreement with Jewish groups committed to removing the approximately 360,000 entries of "posthumously baptized Jewish Holocaust victims who were not direct ancestors of living members of the Church from the IGI."[47] In reality, the church did not remove the names, hiding the ordinances from public view instead.[48] Controversies with other faith groups would surface again later, but none were very successful in protecting their records or their ancestors.

Filming in the United States, the society began brokering deals that would become the model for their later efforts. In exchange for access to the records, the filming would be carried out cost-free to the institution, and film copy of the records would be returned to the archives. This arrangement, along with the benefits—and drawbacks—to public archives, would be repeated as the technology shifted from film to digitization.

In 1944 the Mormon Church made an important corporate decision that would affect the control of the genealogical records for the future. The Genealogical Society of Utah had, for its first fifty years, been an entity independent of the church, incorporated as a public institution, supported by paying members, though mostly by the church. In the interests of restricting access to sensitive records, the church leadership suggested that it would be better to repay those who had taken out lifetime memberships so that the church alone supported the society as an institution wholly under control of the church. Thus, the world's fastest-growing genealogical database became a private entity, a move that would presage the biggest databases to follow. "In November the Society became a church corporation with a new name, the Genealogical Society of the Church of Jesus Christ of Latter-day Saints. The requirement for membership fees was rescinded."[49]

As Allen tells us, "As soon as the war was over the [microfilming] program grew dramatically, particularly in Europe and Mexico. This growth is illustrated by the rapid rise in the amount of exposed film received. In 1944 and 1945, the Society received 24 and 69 rolls respectively. In 1946 the number went to 462, in 1947 it jumped to 4,501 and in 1948 it made another jump to 10,012." Scandinavia and England were next, but the real prize was the existing German microfilm that had been cached as the war neared its end. By 1949 there were microfilm projects in most of Western Europe and the Nordic countries to the tune of $750,000. The costs of filming were mounting, so the society negotiated a film dealership with Dupont Film, and costs dropped dramatically. As Allen observes, "Genealogical work not only used high technology, but had also become a significant business." By the early 1950s, the society had 150 million pages of records on nearly 200,000 rolls of film. In the parallel data-collection effort, the temple records were still being created using index cards. Twenty-two million cards had been created, twenty-nine million names checked, and six million duplications avoided, all typed manually, almost exclusively by the society women, under the supervision of men, President Joseph Fielding Smith in particular.[50]

The church had three arms of record keeping: the genealogical records themselves; the index, which was used to verify family lines and ancestors for baptism; and the temple records, which recorded the baptisms and other ordinances that had already taken place. The databases overlap and are constantly being reorganized, renamed, and updated with newer technologies, so the genealogy of the databases themselves is very difficult to track. Let's just say that there is a before and an after database that will one day merge entirely.

In 1944 almost fourteen thousand patrons used the library. The holdings included forty-two thousand volumes. In that year, three thousand books, 10,637 rolls of microfilm, and 125 manuscripts were added. Postwar, the number of people using the library grew dramatically. In 1960 more than eighty-five thousand people accessed the holdings, over a thousand a day—99 percent of them church members. The success of its own mission had the society scrambling to keep up. Several times, the society shuttered its doors in order that the legion of typists could deal with the backlog of records and the demands that they be cross-referenced before ordinances were performed. The demand for temple-ready names outstripped supply. "In 1957, for example, the Society forwarded 780,464 names to the temples, but during the year 950,379 endowments had been performed. Another problem arose because women consistently attended the temple in greater numbers than men and the supply of female names diminished much faster than male names."[51]

The church was footing the bill, and when the expenses topped $2 million in 1961 it started to balk. The mission was slowed at various points, but never stopped, and the society gained recognition for its efforts internationally and at home, not only for the record collections but also as technological leaders. In 1968 the Eastman Kodak Company gave the society an award for its "significant contribution to the advancement of the science of information technology." The society was the second-largest user of Kodak products and had pioneered storage, indexing, and classification systems. With recording technologies in full swing, storage now became the issue.

Overflowing with records, the society began to discuss how to store them and announced the plans for a buried vault in 1954. In 1959 they chose a site just outside Salt Lake City to construct an underground storage facility, the "Granite Mountain Records Vault," the material equivalent of Danilo Kiš's imaginary vault in "The Encyclopedia of the Dead," the story that catapulted me into this research. Between 1960 and 1965, the church blasted the stone vault out of the mountain in Little Cottonwood Canyon, four tunnels each 190 feet long, 25 feet wide, and 15 feet high, 65,000 square feet under 700 feet of mountain stone. "The vault" was designed to protect the records from decay, natural disasters, and "man-made calamities." Carved from granite and lined with steel, entrances to the secure archive areas were guarded by specially constructed Mosler safe doors weighing fourteen tons at the main entrance and nine tons at the two smaller entrances, all designed to withstand a nuclear blast. The pure mountain spring under the vault proved a problem, but also supplied water for the workers and for processing of the film and helped to keep the temperature in the vault at fifty-five degrees; humidity is a controlled 35 percent. Dust-free fresh air circulated throughout the vault (blue-jeans dust is deadly), creating ideal conditions for the preservation of the now 2.5 million rolls of film containing 3.5 billion images. It's hard now to argue with Joseph Smith's archival prophecy.

Not surprisingly, conspiracy theories about the vault abounded. Some speculated that the Mormon presidency also had quarters in the bunker to which they would retreat in the case of a nuclear attack, leaving ordinary Mormons to fend for themselves. Other rumors swirled around the seventh vault where the church keeps its most valuable historical documents and, perhaps, hides the evidence of fabricated histories. The intense security surrounding the site makes it a perennial favorite for conspiracy lists dedicated to the most secure archives in the world, many owned by private interests that severely restrict access. Indeed, the Mormons closed Granite Mountain to visitors in the late 1970s, citing contamination. The secrecy and security of the archive only helped to generate intense interest. To ward off the inquisitive, the church released a seven-minute "whirlwind" video tour, in which viewers are allowed "a glimpse of a place few people will ever get to see."[52] The church counts the archive as one of the seven wonders of the Mormon faith, after the tomb of Joseph Smith and before the BYU University Centre on Mount Scopus in Jerusalem.

Around the same time that the vault was being constructed to house the microfilm collection, the church realized that newer technologies could help solve their name-flow problem. The bottleneck in the process was the necessity of verifying the family charts so that the appropriate family "sealings" could be performed before the baptisms. By 1960 the supply of names was critical, with less than six weeks' supply on hand. In Salt Lake City, society workers ran back and forth to the temple every day in an effort to keep it open. The church realized it would be "shortsighted" to keep building temples with an inadequate supply of names. The solution was twofold. Given that everyone was related in the end, there was no need really for families to be the exclusive owners of their ancestors. The Lord had supplied these names by inspiring genealogists to compile and publish them. Surely, the books had been compiled in order to serve the larger purpose of making the names available for temple work, regardless of any family ties. Just as important, the new technology of electronic recording was at hand. "The genealogical society and, consequently, the temples moved with solemn deliberation into the computer age."[53] The doctrine proved to be malleable in the face of new technologies.

THE COMPUTER AGE DAWNS

Although the church did not yet own a computer, it started the Advanced Planning Department in 1962. The society had started to use "Flexowriters" the year before. Working from the records, typists punched out streams of paper tape in a room that clattered with the sound of automation. Every record was typed by two different typists for accuracy. The data from the paper tapes was then transferred to a magnetic tape, ready to be fed into a computer for comparison. It wasn't long before the data could be entered directly on magnetic tapes. In 1964 the president of the Genealogical Society, Elder Howard W. Hunter, went to San Jose, California, to attend a weeklong seminar hosted by IBM in the developing technology of data-processing equipment. Five years later, "the Department unveiled a comprehensive computer system designed to automate the submission of names for temple ordinance work. Introduced to the public as the Names Tabulation Program, it was known within the department as GIANT." The program "combined the names extracted from genealogical sources under the records tabulation program (R-TAB) with the names from the manual method of patron name submission. All names went into one computer system programmed to detect duplicates and confirm unique entries. It served as the primary names processing system for the next twenty years."[54] The computer was a room full of mainframes run by magnetic tape.

By the 1970s, the department (now the Family History Department) began the massive project of automating the data it already had and setting up systems for the submission of new data, both genealogical records and temple ordinances. At the same time, the family group sheets were eliminated, the rules for ordinances were changed, and the "extraction" program began. No longer did children need to be sealed to individual parents; the presumptive *parents* would be good enough for admission, and it didn't matter if the parents had already been baptized. Ditto for spouses. The promise and the limits of the technology dictated changes in doctrine that fundamentally undermined previous practices. The technology won out over the objections of more conservative members.

Roger Minert explained the process to me: "We were given, for example, the records of a Protestant parish in a certain part of Germany, and instructed to write down the name of every child Christened from, for example, 1650 to 1885. The birth date, the Christening or baptism date, the names of the parents. Those are all recorded. They were not grouped in families, but simply taken literally one by one chronologically from the record. Those then formed the gigantic database that people could use as finders, so to speak." No longer burdened by the necessity of grouping names with families, the cost of clearing names for the temple dropped from a high of $1.37 in 1967–68 to $0.64 in 1973.[55] Families were still encouraged to "turn their heart to their fathers," but ordinances could continue unabated.

The availability of microfilm duplication and the computer records generated by the extraction program allowed the library to branch out. The Logan library, the first branch, was opened in 1964. By 1968 there were seventy-five branches worldwide. The branches were established with a basic set of microfilms, and additional ones could be borrowed from the main library in Salt Late City. Technology, hand in hand with doctrinal adaptation, provided the conditions for the rapid expansion of the church's genealogical research. In 1963 the Correlation Committee made genealogy one of the four major responsibilities of the priesthood, along with missionary work, welfare, and home teaching. Genealogy was no longer an auxiliary function of the church but a basic priesthood assignment.

Over the years, the society pushed the limits of microfilm, commissioning lenses and cameras that could produce 42x reduction on 16mm film, which meant new reading technologies as well. Every technological innovation meant vast changes across a network of libraries, film laboratories, and storage facilities. The society made excursions into oral genealogies, sending interviewers to collect information from indigenous cultures across the South Pacific, Taiwan, Indonesia, and Africa. But they soon gave up, as the process was much more expensive per name. It was cheaper to return to their obsession with microfilming records around the world. Three-quarters of the records held by the church come from countries outside of the United States.

At first, the society focused only on countries in which Mormon Church members and ancestors had lived, but beginning in the early 1970s, the society expanded into Asia, Southeast Asia, Africa, and the Middle East. In the 1980s, China granted the society access to the State Archive Bureau. Microfilming around the world was interrupted only by armed conflict, localized opposition, and some government, religious, and institutional resistance. In 1992 the United Church of Canada voted against the wishes of its chief archivist that the Mormon Archive be allowed to microfilm certain archival holdings of its Central Archives. The decision was reaffirmed by the General Council Executive in the late 1990s. At issue was the ethical question of trust. The United Church has held firm in its policy that the information in the church registers was given by individuals for a specific purpose and considered to be held in sacred trust. Accordingly, the United Church resisted further overtures by the LDS and by Ancestry, committing itself to never transfer its records to other institutions, though the sharing of information by individual genealogists has probably rendered the United Church's resistance somewhat futile.[56]

Allen provides an extensive discussion of when the society started filming records in most of the hundred countries in which it has filmed and under what circumstances. It's an intriguing read in persistence and pluck.

In 1975 the Genealogical Society was wholly subsumed into the church, acknowledging that its functions were quite different from every other genealogical organization in the world. It became the Genealogical Department of the church, while the corporate body of the society was retained for the business end of negotiating microfilm contracts.[57] The main responsibilities of the department were aligned with the two databases and the mission: gathering records that could be used for genealogical research, providing names for the temples and keeping an official record of the temple ordinances performed, and encouraging family history research for church members, and, as we will see, ultimately, everyone else as well.

By the late 1980s, advancements in microcomputing allowed the department to decentralize the process of clearing names for ordinances. This was a major step forward, and the "TempleReady" database was born. The International Genealogy Index (you remember all those typists typing on sturdy filing cards) was transferred to CD-ROM and distributed to the network of Family History Centers. Family historians could then check the names they had extracted (for that work too had now been completely decentralized) against the IGI in TempleReady and then go off to the temple with the name of the newly-to-be-blessed. The number of ordinances performed soared, creating another "inventory" crisis. Again, and all through the early 2000s, the church was faced with a supply of names that ranged from about a year to less than two months, particularly for young women who were the most enthusiastic about performing temple ordinances. At approximately fifteen to thirty seconds a baptism, the number of temple-ready names on hand couldn't keep up with the demand. In order to curtail demand, the church reduced the number of baptisms that could be performed by youth baptism groups from five per saint to two and reduced the number of times they could visit the temple in a year.[58] In part, the shortages were a result of the increased cost and difficulty of extracting names from non-English-speaking countries. The pragmatics of data acquisition stifled the sublime desires of the church and its members. But not for long.

Of course, the other end of the data stream, the recording of the ordinances, also had to be automated. Another new system called the "Ordinance Recording System" was designed to handle the flow at the temples and to return the information to Salt Lake City. Disks with names gathered from members or the department were processed by each temple. Printed slips were given to the proxies, who then, duly dunked, handed them back to be recorded in the temple database. Disks with the newly saved names were then sent back to the Family History Department to be entered into the Completed Ordinance File. Between 1991, when the ordinance file was instituted, and 1994, it grew to 21 million names. Add this to the 187 million in the IGI in the 1992 edition multiplied by the intervening thirty years of ordinance work, and my best guess is that they are nearing or over the 1 billion mark now. The slips are printed at home by church members, complete with bar codes in order for scanners at the temples to send the data directly to the latest iteration of the central database.

"The vault" also serves now as the growing repository of the digital future. The library is shifting its collection, storage, and dissemination technologies online, digitizing its millions of microfilms in the process. The preservation of digital data is much more difficult than microfilm, as storage and reading formats change rapidly and digital information corrupts quickly. But the Mormons have weighed the pros and cons of

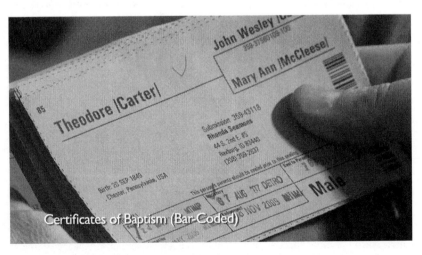

FIGURE 2. Certificates of baptism (bar-coded). Courtesy of the author.

developing data storage. Unlike the image reproduction of microfilm, which deteriorates with each copy, digital copies are perfect, even though digital media must be copied to new media every few decades. Every digital image is copied to two separate vaults. The Mormons now own and protect thirty-three times the number of records as the U.S. Library of Congress, according to the *New Republic*.[59]

"FamilySearch" is now the nonprofit organization that, in addition to its website and the thousands of pages of wikis, holds all the contracts, all the entities, all the record contracts, the records themselves, and the rights to the records. FamilySearch is a relatively new entity, a digital project launched in 1999. It was immediately a victim of its own success. Much like the crash of the UK 1901 census website just days after its launch in 2002 by the UK Public Record Office, FamilySearch was overloaded by visitors within days of its launch as well. After a few more iterations and a good deal of beta testing with church members, the latest version of FamilySearch was fully launched in December 2013.

After the church launched FamilySearch as a public database, it rolled out a second database to its members and then to the general public, FamilyTree (at one point called New FamilySearch), a database for LDS Church members that combined four large data sets, family trees, and ordinances mostly still on CD-ROM: the IGI (the temple ordinances); the Ancestral File (the family pedigrees of LDS members who had completed their assigned Three and Four Generations Projects from the 1960s to the 1980s); the Pedigree Resource File (a project that had encouraged the general public to submit family trees to the LDS databases); and the church membership database.[60] According to Don Casias, the senior vice president of patron and partner services who oversaw the Family History Library and all the genealogical support services worldwide from 2002 to 2015, the launch of FamilyTree revealed the extent of the duplication problem that had been a problem since the beginnings of the ordinance record keeping. The duplication problem had long been known, but the implementation of FamilyTree revealed that approximately 30 percent of the names submitted for temple ordinances by members were duplicates, though the records provided by the extraction program had nearly no duplication. FamilyTree allowed members who hadn't completed the research to see all the information that FamilySearch had about their family.[61]

One of the hallmarks of the FamilyTree is that it details almost the entire documented population of the United Kingdom. When the extraction program began, the church largely used British parish records for the temple inventory. Many church members had British ancestors, and the church had access to a large set of records from which it could draw for temple ordinances when the supply had diminished from members submitting names. The end result is that nearly every documented person who lived in the United Kingdom has been baptized posthumously by the church.[62]

The completeness of the UK ordinances reveals how futile resistance to the church's project has been. In 2008 the Catholic Church also expressed its displeasure with the Mormons. The Vatican had never recognized the Mormons and so had ignored the issue of proxy baptisms.[63] But according to Tom Heneghan, a religion reporter for Reuters, the widespread availability of records on the Internet and questions of privacy made it harder for the Vatican to disregard the proxy baptisms of large numbers of names of saints and popes and historical pontiffs, some of whom had been "sealed" in Mormon marriage to imaginary wives, despite having lived in celibacy. The Vatican wrote to Catholic dioceses worldwide, urging them not to "cooperate with the erroneous practices of the Church of Jesus Christ of Latter-day Saints" by providing them with parish records.[64] Mormons were dismayed, finding it difficult to understand why anyone would object to their saving ordinances and arguing that the parish records were public information. Once again, doctrine trumped worldly annoyance.

In 2012 the controversy erupted again, as Helen Radkey, an excommunicated Mormon devoted to being a thorn in the side of the church, scoured the IGI for inappropriate baptisms.[65] She discovered proxy ordinances had been conducted for the slain journalist Daniel Pearl and the parents of Holocaust scholar Simon Wiesenthal. Radkey had been trying for years to draw attention to the church's baptismal chicaneries. She had tried to involve the Vatican years before they recognized it might be a problem and then turned to the Jewish community, where she found a receptive but relatively isolated audience. This time, the baptisms were so high profile and outrageous that the story attained traction and widespread media coverage, amplified because of Mormon Mitt Romney's run for president in the 2012 election.[66] Joan of Arc, Charlie Chaplin, Hitler,

Anne Frank, and Marilyn Monroe all made the celebrity ranks of posthumous baptisms. Who would get to have the conversation with Hitler at the pearly gates? Satirists had a field day, converting all dead Mormons to Judaism and homosexuality and debaptizing Romney's father-in-law. The church responded by cutting off public access to the IGI, in no small part in order to keep Helen Radkey out.[67]

Given this remarkable confluence of record acquisitions and storage technology put to the service of religion, I was curious about how the Mormons understood this relationship. Jay Verkler was the CEO of FamilySearch in 2010 when I interviewed him at the Family History Library. As Verkler somewhat gleefully confessed, "There's some great technological challenges when you're dealing with billions of records and complex questions being asked of those records, and how you do that for tens and hundreds of million people. There's some really interesting technology challenges there." Even given the comparison with the Library of Congress holdings, trying to figure out the size of the Mormon record holdings is not at all straightforward. The first challenge is what constitutes a record. Verkler broke it down for me in a really useful way. The church has more than a billion "conclusions" in its database. A "conclusion"—and this is essential for the process of baptism—is the verified record of someone who once lived. In Verkler's words, "conclusions are things that 'I've done the research, and hey—that's a person.' We've got a billion of that, actually a little more than a billion of those." Then there are the records that the church has been acquiring for more than eighty years. Those 3.5 billion genealogical images on microfilm might contain multiple names; for example, an image might contain four different birth certificates or the ledger of a census with a page of names. And even one record might contain multiple names. A birth certificate might have the birth of the principal, as well as the mother and father. "So when you add that all up and you think about 3.5 billion images, you have a whole lot more names than just that," said Verkler, somewhat bemused himself by the complexity of how one would count the number of names secured in the vault.

The Mormons' ambitions are not daunted by scale. They estimate that there are 50 to 60 billion genealogical records in the world. The 3.5 billion images they have now contain somewhere in the neighborhood of 12–15 billion records. "So we think maybe we're a quarter of the way done. There's a lot left to find, acquire, and to help people find their ancestors," said Verkler.[68] The church has already acquired records from about 110–20 countries, and their ambition is to finish the job of acquiring the remaining three-quarters of the world's records within a generation.

Here we are in the territory of the mathematical version of the genealogical sublime, where the numbers far outstrip our ability to imagine our place in pedobytes (2^{50} bytes, 1,024 terabytes, or 1 million gigabytes) of information. Verkler admits that the Mormon project is grander than the technological solutions at hand. "And, by the way, when you have pedobytes of information and you're an archive, you start thinking pretty deeply about how am I going to make sure that that information exists for tens, hundreds, even thousands of years." The industry does not have a solution to that problem. "Certainly not an economical solution, and arguably not a solution at all."

But Shipley Munson has faith that the technology will manifest. "We also believe that these technologies have been placed on the planet for a purpose at this time so that this work can actually be accomplished. Can you image trying to do this with the means of communication and transportation that they had available in 1843?" Munson projects the impossibility of the project historically even further. "Or, when Malachi was preaching to the restored Jews in the temple district in Jerusalem in the 4th century before the Common Era? Can you imagine trying to do that? Impossible to imagine." But in the present, the technology has caught up with the task. "But when you think of the power of computing today, the amount of data that can be stored in ways that can actually be fit into spaces and accessed, all of a sudden, you'd say, 'Hey. Maybe this can really be done.'"

The prophets prophesied not only the necessity of the vicarious work for the dead of the world, but also that technologies would be developed to make the work possible. "And then you say, 'How did Joseph Smith know that? How did Malachi know that?' And so the answer we always come back to is, if you compare us to Ancestry.com, we have a different boss." Shipley smiled broadly.

Shipley offered God to me as a self-fulfilling philosophy in answer to my questions about the relationship between technology and genealogy, allowing that humans haven't always had the wisdom to benignly deploy the technology that has been given to them, invoking the myth of Prometheus stealing the fire from Zeus in heaven, a kind of overreaching of human invention into dangerous areas of knowledge. His example was the atomic bomb: "Were we given the atomic bomb before we had the wisdom to not use it? It's that kind of question." He wasn't suggesting, however, that the church had been given technology beyond its capacity to use it wisely—though I might have made that inference from his invocation of Prometheus and our commonplace notion of playing with fire. The case is quite the opposite: "So in a much more prosaic, in some ways, but we would consider a more profound and divine application, is that we believe that the technology is placed here by our Father in Heaven for a purpose. And one of the most important purposes for all these technological tools is to give humans the ability to re-create the family tree of the human race." Munson made a surprising assertion. "We're primarily at this point a technology company, so we have to figure out how you can capture that and record that, and make that available for those who are searching for answers." At that, he teared up with emotion, the sentiment of people searching for answers outweighing the absolutely pragmatic observation that the database arm of the Mormon Church is a "technology company."

The miracles of technological advances are understood as confirmation that the goal is good, though Sisyphean. The Mormons have a "leaky-bucket" problem. "On the planet today, we're creating more records than we have the capacity to preserve, and catalog, and make accessible. So we're always losing ground in one respect," said Munson. And were technology to freeze in its current state, it would not be enough. But what we have today, particularly the capacity to access records online from anywhere, is a sign, as long as we demonstrate the wisdom to use it well. "And that's just a taste of the technologies that our Father in Heaven will make available to us in the years to come. That's what we believe. But in order to get that technology, you have to demonstrate that you know how to use it, you know how to absorb it, you know how to apply it in a manner that is aligned with the reason that it was brought to you in the first place."[69] The reasoning is circular—the technology will allow the task of preserving the world's records to be accomplished, and each technological advancement affirms the goal—though the church is far from passive when it comes to encouraging the development of genealogical tools and their dissemination to users.

RootsTech, a genealogy conference sponsored and organized by FamilySearch that started in 2010, is now billed by FamilySearch as "the world's largest celebration of families across generations." According to FamilySearch, "RootsTech is all about preserving and sharing family stories through technology and innovation." RootsTech is a technology incubator for the user side of the business, where the Innovator Summit and Showdown events are designed to facilitate connections between investors and entrepreneurs seeking to build the next big thing in the genealogy industry. Technology has two faces in the Mormon project: the massive data-storage needs of the vault records and the technological toys that encourage individual genealogists to be as productive as possible.

In 2017 twenty-five thousand participants gathered for the third annual RootsTech conference, a seamless merging of family, faith, and technology. The stage for the opening ceremonies was designed as a family home, complete with kitchen and family room. President Russell M. Nelson and his wife, Sister Wendy Nelson, gave an hourlong homily on the importance of family, using Russell's family of fifty or so and growing (multiplied from ten children) as the basis of all church life. Enter Elijah and his prophecy as a segue into family history and temple work. Wendy Nelson reinforced the message: "The spirit of Elijah, the holy ghost, is prompting family to do those things that will allow families to be sealed eternally." President Nelson told the story of another spirit, that of his great-grandfather, who made a ghostly visit to his son, Russell's grandfather, in 1891 to tell him, in part, that he too was involved in missionary work among the spirits waiting to be saved and to not worry too much about the accuracy of earthly records, since absolutely correct records are kept on the other side (though we know now that the Mormons are sticklers for accuracy). The Nelsons urged the gathered to make sacrifices of their time to carry out the work of family history and temple ordinances, as the most precious thing one can confirm is an ancestor's ordinance-qualifying information that would release them from being confined to their spirit prison. Their talk hit every now familiar adage I have learned about the Mormon mission—without a word about the technology. But the technology was integrated everywhere, from the hundreds of exhibitor booths with all the major players to sessions devoted to instructing genealogists in the use of the latest software and hardware. Accompanying these earthly pursuits were LDS sessions, given by many of the senior leaders of the church, that kept the family, the mission, and the doctrine at the fore.

In 1937 President Joseph Fielding Smith instructed the society to keep abreast of all the latest technical developments in record work, not only to be informed of new accomplishments in the field but also to be leaders. In 1957 L. Garrett Myers declared that the prophecy of the Lord had been fulfilled. He had indeed provided the technology for the ever-increasing tempo of the salvation of the dead, and the custodians of the great record repositories had indeed been moved to open their records for filming. In 2017 FamilySearch announced that it would stop microfilming records as of September 1. Ninety years of microfilming had come to an end.[70] Few microfilm suppliers still existed, and the prospect of long-term storage and duplication costs of microfilm had almost doubled the cost of microfilm.[71] The born-digital age for the Mormon records had begun.

Shipley Munson was quite forthright about this goal:

> If we want to stay true to our mission, which we think is actually a larger mission than for most companies, we need to get many, many, many more people involved in researching their families, and their family histories, than are involved today. We need to engage beginners at the point of entry and attract more people who are interested but haven't started yet, and tip them into the first steps. And we are just now beginning to figure out what it takes to do that, and that's what you should see coming from us in the next two or three years.[72]

In 2016 Jay Verkler, the former CEO of FamilySearch, became the CEO of the for-profit company FindMyPast, bringing with him his expertise developed with the FamilySearch database. As we will see in the next chapter, for-profit databases have been integral to the LDS project of baptizing the family of man, since almost every company shares its family trees with the church, in exchange for access to the church records.[73] The LDS project has been central to the incubation and profitability of the industry as a whole.

Multiple accidents emerged and merged to produce the world's largest genealogical database: the invention of the world's most modern religion—Mormonism, born out of persecution; Joseph Smith's doctrinal directive to baptize the dead as moral imperative to save the world; the invention of microfilm as a recording technology; and the development of the Internet as the ideal platform for genealogical research, allowing the records to be undisturbed in their entombed archive, while the church's genealogical sublime spreads across the world. "Emergence" is a useful concept here.

CHAPTER 3

ANCESTRY.INC

It is hard to imagine, having started all of this without having some relationship with the LDS Church.

—Dan Taggart, cofounder of Ancestry.com

DAN AND PAUL: IN THE BEGINNING

If the Mormons created the contemporary genealogical market by proselytizing the importance of family and family records worldwide, just down the road from Salt Lake City in Provo, Utah, best friends Dan Taggart and Paul B. Allen were the first to capitalize on it. Provo is a scrubby place of low buildings on arid land that looks up to white-capped mountains and the campus of Brigham Young University. The monetization of the industry of family history runs parallel to the Mormon venture, born of it, but advancing more nimbly, as entrepreneurial enterprises often do. Institutions run by rules and doctrine and bureaucracy are slow to change; companies that make up—and change—their own rules, that embrace disruption, are beholden to none except mammon. As the founders of Ancestry.com—now the biggest for-profit genealogy company in the world—Taggart and Allen were the first to recognize that the digitization of records and their online availability would revolutionize the practice and profits of genealogy. Dan Taggart welcomed me and my crew into in his very comfortable Provo colonial house with its circular driveway, Doric columns, and room for eight children. He was eager to talk about the company he had founded and its phenomenal success.

Born in Utah, and practicing Mormons, Taggart and Allen were graduate students at BYU casting around for ways to fund their studies when

they hit on an idea to digitize some of the key LDS family history resources for the LDS market. They, like all other LDS Church members,
were constantly encouraged, mandated even, by the church to create
family records. It was a time-consuming business that relied on library
visits, archives, microfilm, and other family members. In 1990, sensing
an opportunity, Taggart and Allen founded Infobases, Inc., and began
publishing LDS genealogy resources on floppy disks, selling them out
of the back of their car.[1] They had hit on a rich vein, tapping into such a
demand for easily accessible genealogical information that they dropped
out of their graduate programs to do the business full-time. They began
by looking for family history books that they could publish electronically,
discovering a small company in Salt Lake City called "Ancestry," which,
according to Taggart, "had the best ancestry, or genealogy, reference
books on the planet." And so they began licensing those books from that
company, publishing them on CD-ROM.

In 1995 they created a boxed set of CD-ROMs called *The LDS Family
History Suite,* selling it in the want ads in local newspapers. The suite was
several different products—software, databases, reference material—
bundled together, all helpful to Mormons doing family history research.
The church itself was not yet publishing any of its records on CD-ROM,
except for the purposes of temple work. *The LDS Family History Suite* was
an immediate success. It became the top seller at Deseret Book and other
stores throughout Utah and was picked up by Walmart regionally, becoming a regional top-selling product. As Allen recalled with sheer glee,
"It was so wildly successful that we realized that there was a huge possible
industry, or market, for genealogy products." Their first genealogy product in 1995 was targeted only at the LDS market. "And it made a million
dollars in five months. And that was for us—in a very small start-up—that
was a lot of money, a lot of interest from our small customer base."[2]

By 1996 Infobases was named one of the nation's fastest-growing private companies by *Inc. Magazine.* Between 1991 and 1995, Infobases's rev-
enues had grown by 630 percent, which was enough for it to crack the
top 500 companies at 454. "We started this company with the vision of
empowering people with the information they need to engage in noble
learning activities—whether they be religious, educational or historical in nature," Allen told *Newswire.* "We are pleased to report, and have
verified by *Inc. magazine,* fact that there truly is a world-wide need for the

FIGURE 3. Dan Taggart: "Just an interesting piece of history." Courtesy of the author.

kinds of products we are providing on CD ROM and the Internet." Allen and Taggart hadn't just tapped into an existing worldwide need; they were reaping the rewards of a century of Mormon genealogical fervor.

"It is hard to imagine," Taggart said reflectively, "having started all of this without having some relationship with the LDS Church. The LDS Church has been the single most important factor in the evolution of genealogy for the past century. There's no question. And it's because they don't have a need to make money on genealogy. For them, it's a matter of faith." Faith backed up with considerable resources. "The church spends an awful lot of money making it possible to do that work for the members of the church, and for anyone else that wants to. So over the past century, they have been aggregating and digitizing records from all around the world, where nobody else would have been able to afford to do that, where there was no commercial opportunity at the time."

It was at this point in our conversation that Taggart made the claim that made me think about the surge of interest in genealogy in less than natural terms. "If you wanted to ask who created the market out there?" Taggart asked rhetorically. "The LDS Church did." Taggart reiterated the importance of the LDS project, the centralization of information via the Genealogical Society of Utah's microfilm projects, and the creation of the

Family History Library and the vault. "You cannot overstate the importance of what they did in making all of this possible."

But the church was like a glacier. Taggart changed metaphors, trying to make the point absolutely clear. "The wheels at the church grind exceedingly slow, but exceedingly fine. They could do huge projects because they had thousands of people involved, or tens of thousands of people involved, in amassing the information, but in terms of actually getting something to market quickly, or developing software quickly in a way that a commercial enterprise would do, that wasn't something that they were very good at."[3] They were amassing the world's information, but it was small companies designing software programs that eventually made a commercial market for genealogy.

Taggart and Allen anticipated the next big step. Paul Allen was at an online developers' conference in San Francisco when he realized that the Internet, the World Wide Web, would overtake CD-ROM, that CD-ROM would go away. And, he thought, "What better content to put on the Internet than all of the genealogical records of the world?"[4] This was a eureka moment for Dan Taggart and Paul Allen, and another moment of technological convergence from which the industry of family history emerged.

In September 1995, Taggart and Allen invented the commercial industry of online genealogy. They launched Ancestry.com's first site in June 1996, and, as far as Taggart knows, Ancestry.com was the very first to publish commercial genealogy databases on the Internet. "We started with the Social Security Death Index [which had more than fifty million records], and a couple of other small databases that were of great value, and made those available free of charge, just to attract a lot of traffic. And it went crazy."

"How did you get access to those databases?" I asked. "Well," Taggart explained, "the Social Security Death Index is a publicly available database from the government, and they publish it, and they provide it on CD-ROM. We just purchased the CD-ROMs from the government and reformatted them to make them more accessible and searchable online."

"Did you have to sign any agreement with the government to do that? Did you tell them that you were doing that?" I asked. Taggart replied, "There were actually several companies that were licensing or purchasing the data from the government to publish on CD-ROM or in other ways. And there wasn't any very involved or complicated process for licensing, because this was public domain material. You just had to purchase the data, and that was a fairly simple process, and then they sent you the discs."

"So if you don't mind me asking, how much did you pay for those discs, and how much money did you make from them?"

"We probably paid . . . several hundred dollars for the initial data is all. And then there was a renewal fee each year, because they would update it. I think the initial purchase might have been $1,000 or $1,500 for the full set, and then several hundred dollars for the updated material, so it wasn't very expensive."

"And how much income did that generate?"

"Zero. Because we made that available free of charge. We thought, you know, we don't need to make money on the Social Security Death Index. We'll use that to generate traffic on our website, and then we'll start finding other records that are inaccessible to people. Publish those. Really add value. Make those available."[5]

The second data set was also publicly available information, though this one generated by users. User-generated information is now a staple of the genealogy industry, and Ancestry was the first to capture it online. An Ancestry.com engineer figured out how to crawl[6] and index the RootsWeb Surname List (RSL) message board, pulling data from the millions of messages people had posted saying, "I'm looking for the Israelson surname, or the Matheson surname." Those were Ancestry's first two data sets: the Social Security Death Index and the ROOTS-L surname message board. But the real ploy and play was to disrupt the industry, which they did, in part, by hoovering up information genealogists had shared for free with other people also looking for roots.

By the time Ancestry was crawling the Web, the idea that the Web was an ideal place to exchange genealogical information was already a decade old. Genealogists themselves were way out ahead of the industry and some of the earliest adopters of online networking. The newsgroup net.roots, named after Alex Haley's enormously popular television series *Roots,* was launched in 1983. In 1987 Alf Christopherson from Norway and Marty Hoag of North Dakota State University started the ROOTS-L mailing list. In the late '80s, the Web was still mostly the domain of university researchers, but that was about to rapidly change. Karen Isaacson and her husband, Brian Leverich, were the next online genealogy innovators. In 1989 Isaacson took over the maintenance of the newly established RootsWeb Surname List.

Isaacson and Leverich were both working at RAND Corporation—home of the 1960s network designers, a military think tank devoted to U.S. national security issues, for the most part—and had access to the company server. They convinced RAND to host the RAND Genealogy Club, creating one of earliest genealogy websites, which soon became so popular that it attracted more traffic than the official corporate site, eventually making the corporation suspicious. As Leverich tells it, "Sensing a problem in the making, K & B [Karen and Brian] registered the name of RootsWeb.com and started serving the RSL and other genealogical material out of their mountainside cabin in February of 1996."[7] Soon, they were getting fifty thousand hits a day. By late 1995, just as Ancestry.com was coming online, Isaacson and Leverich were already concerned about the future of genealogy on the Internet, that the data would soon be under lock and key, held behind paywalls and pay-per-view. They too were prescient. Much of the user-generated genealogical information on the Web would end up being monetized in one way or another.[8]

Allen continued to explain Ancestry's strategy to me: "I think instinctively we believed in disruption. Meaning that if you have a competitor that is selling product, but you can find a way to give that product away for free, that you end up obviously, potentially, getting more customers and certainly a lot of awareness. And so we were very excited about the possibility of putting a lot of genealogical records on the Web for free, and then finding other ways to generate revenue from customers."[9]

Taggart and Allen's only real competition was Brøderbund (literally, "band of brothers—and one sister). Brøderbund had grown from a company established for marketing Galactic Empire, one of the first gaming softwares, into a software publishing house that included CD-ROMs of the family trees that the company had amassed, along with their genealogy software Family Tree Maker.[10] The software was originally developed by Kenneth Hess of Banner Blue Software in 1989, which Brøderbund bought in 1995, publishing Family Tree Maker in a set of five three-and-a-half-inch diskettes. In 2000 Brøderbund teamed up with the Arts and Entertainment Network and Mattel to create Genealogy.com.[11] Brøderbund's genealogy business model was lucrative but questionably ethical. It built family trees by asking people to submit or donate their family trees that they would then publish and sell on CD-ROM. "Some family historians weren't very happy that they would donate their family tree, and Brøderbund, in turn, would sell those family trees for a profit," Taggart told me. This practice set the monetizing pattern for what was to come.

Brøderbund had amassed quite a large number of records for the time. Taggart thought they might have had "fifty million or a hundred million names in those family trees. Family historians would have to buy fifty or sixty discs to get them all, and each of the discs were approximately thirty-nine or forty dollars. I remember it seemed quite expensive, and most people couldn't afford buying very many of them."[12] Taggart and Allen believed that you could take all of that information and make it available in one database online. And since it was being donated, they decided they would also make that database available for free. They started a project called the Ancestry World Tree. Every user could submit their tree at no cost, and Ancestry.com would index all the records in their records, and all the records in everybody else's trees, and then users could download any records or any branches from anybody else's trees. "You could imagine what that did to the revenue model for this other company. It was devastating to them." Taggart reveled in the success of the strategy. "In fact, where they had been the giant—they were the 600 pound gorilla to begin with—a few years later we acquired them. We actually bought that company."[13]

Taggart and Allen's plan was to attract as many users as possible to their site and worry later about how to generate revenue. It was a huge success. Allen: "I'd say within a year or two, we were the most popular genealogy site on the Web. Our philosophy was all user-generated content should always be free." Taggart and Allen gambled that by offering for free everything that Ancestry.com's competitor was selling, they would end up being the largest player in the genealogy database industry. The gamble worked beautifully. Part of their for-profit strategy was to offer a subscription service for new databases. They made a difficult promise to add one new database every day. "And at the time," Taggart said, "that was a tall order to fill." Inadvertently or advertently, they had tapped into the data-consumption desire that still drives the industry.[14]

Anne-Marie Kramer, a British sociologist who has studied the industry extensively, has considered the addictive quality of genealogical information. "I think that the heritage industry very much plays on the fact that knowledge is compulsive."[15] They market every new data set, "selling genealogy to people as yet uninitiated, and reselling genealogy to those who might have been pursuing it, but have dropped it." People go in and out of dormant phases with genealogy. The industry attracts and reattracts people by adding new material all the time, using genealogy blogs as one way of advertising those new additions. "So we scoured the Family History Libraries," Taggart continued.

> We found all kinds of published books that were all so old that they were in the public domain, and we began scanning that information or having it typed in, and before we even announced that service, we had a pipeline of forty-some available, ready to go, so that we could continue just adding a new database every day. And then we just started accumulating more and more. Well, you know, that sounds like it was a lot. Now they are probably adding more like a million records a day. Probably a thousand times that every day is going into Ancestry.com.[16]

Ancestry.com was rapidly growing. They were now the publishers of *Ancestry Magazine,* the "Official Magazine" of the 1997 PBS *Ancestors* series, which boosted the subscription rate of *Ancestry Magazine* from eleven thousand in November 1996 to sixteen thousand in January 1997. Those numbers now seem laughably small, but they indicate the extent to which genealogy had a relatively limited appeal before online databases attracted users. The February 1997 "Editor's Note" encouraged people who had access to the Internet to "put *Ancestry Home Town* (www.ancestry.com) on your list of favorite websites." This was an early example of a "virtuous circle," where the TV series fed the magazine, and the magazine led people to the Ancestry website, which linked with existing online newsletters, and around again. The increase in genealogy interest was exponential. Loretto Szucs, the longtime editor of *Ancestry Magazine,* exclaimed, "Talk about changes! With a new database posed each weekday, no wonder 20,000 visitors are stopping at the site daily."[17]

Ancestry had managed to attract a number of small angel investors from Utah, the company was cash-flow positive, and Taggart and Allen thought that their potential to digitize all of the world's genealogy records was within their grasp. Genealogy by its very nature—again, a sign of the genealogical sublime in an era of technological extension—is an exercise in hypermemory. Some of the world's records are not enough; in parallel fashion, some family history doesn't satisfy many genealogists. It's an addictive and obsessive search that multiplies in the same fashion as family lines themselves.[18] Most genealogists have a sense of humor about the addictive qualities of their searches, including the frequent observation that their immediate families think they have gone mad.[19] The goal is to get it all.

With huge ambitions, Taggart and Allen approached all the major venture firms, targeting, in particular, CMGI, the biggest Internet venture fund at the time, because they felt that Ancestry.com was pure Internet play. Peter Mills, the West Coast representative for CMGI, was so excited about Ancestry's prospects that within a week they had put together a $12 million deal, the largest first-round funding event in Utah history. CMGI and Intel were the largest investors, along with several other smaller investors.

And they were off and running. Allen and Taggart took positions in management, hiring Paul Allen's brother Curt Allen as CEO, and Ancestry started growing very rapidly. "And you know, the rest is kind of history," said Taggart, without observing the pun. Along with the subscription service, the moneymaking arm of the company, Ancestry still operated a sizable "freemium" component that held dear the higher purpose of bringing living families together. Their flagship program was the MyFamily.com site, a precursor to Geocities and Facebook, which provided a sharing platform specifically for families.

MyFamily.com was free for the first three years. In that time, it became the top photo-sharing site on the Web. Some 2.8 million families shared their content and their photos and built trees together. The strategy was that from those families and the free sites they built (all of which Ancestry took as propriety information) was a strong likelihood that one person would appoint themselves the family historian. The company used that truism as its tagline, "Every family has a genealogist." It could be a distant cousin, an aunt or uncle or grandparents, but, typically, somebody would get hooked on genealogy and subscribe to the paid site to access records. Taggart and Allen believed deeply in the bedrock of family and that making genealogy into a moneymaking venture would serve to support the work of bringing families together. Doctrine and dollars have never been antithetical to the Mormons, making them one of the most entrepreneurial and wealthiest groups in North America.

THE MISSION AND THE MONEY

We thought that Ancestry's mission was to digitize the genealogical records in every nation and make them available online affordably.

—Paul Allen, cofounder of Ancestry.com

Taggart and Allen's "freemium" philosophy proved to be one of the most effective in the industry. Writing in the online business magazine *Fast Company* about the remarkable rise of the genealogy industry, Neal Ungerleider observed that MyHeritage, an Israeli company founded in 2005, had become "one of the big players on the genealogy block," and one of Ancestry's biggest competitors, by using the freemium model. As Allen knew, and as Ungerleider discovered by interviewing executives from all the major companies, "sign-ups tend to have a network effect. If one or two relatives with an interest in genealogy sign up for a service, their cousins, aunts, and uncles come along as well. If a service is able to secure hard-to-find resources like old family pictures, church records, or scans of antique documents, that gives them an edge versus their competitors." MyHeritage cleverly leveraged that philosophy in 2015 by asking its eighty million users for photographs of members who strongly resembled their ancestors. According to Ungerleider, "Responses poured in from around the globe." Those photographs graced the front page of the site. Split in two halves, the MyHeritage records side featured black-and-white photographs of dead relatives and the MyHeritageDNA side that ancestor's uncanny double in living color.[20] Once again, Taggart and Allen were clearly precocious in their understanding of how to motivate families to click for ancestors.

For a couple of years, the company and its mission of gathering families dead and alive were fine. Ancestry's valuation went from $20 million, when they raised their first venture money in December 1998, to $100 million and then to $300 million in about a two-year period.[21] Because the value of the company was so inflated, Taggart and Allen only had to give away about 10 percent of the company to raise that capital. By 1999 it had attracted $45.5 million in investments.[22] CMGI was the largest investor. The Internet bubble had created a lot of companies with unwarranted value. As long as the company's valuation was growing, the investors left the management team in place, and Dan Taggart, Paul Allen, and Curt Allen were able to run the company according to the principles of their mission to bring families together in the process of finding ancestral records.[23]

By the end of 1999, CMGI had a market value of $41 billion. It was the best-performing U.S. stock of the preceding five years, returning 4,921 percent. By July 2000, CMGI lost $1.4 billion on revenue of $898 million, and by November of that year when almost all of the investment community admitted that the bubble had burst, investors demanded that companies had to be profitable immediately, including Ancestry.[24] Another round and another $15 million of fund-raising saved Ancestry in the short term, but the heady days of fast money were over. Ancestry downsized quickly, a painful process in which they closed their San Francisco offices and retreated to Utah. The last round of funding came from Utah investors, and even though the company was once again cash-flow positive, the new management team enforced a new philosophy.[25]

The MyFamily group of sites combined were in the top fifteenth to twentieth worldwide in overall page views (depending on who is reporting), keeping company with the big Internet plays such as eBay, Amazon, Yahoo, and Google.[26] Ancestry had recognized the value of user-generated information, and its online success was in no small part a result of acquiring RootsWeb, which Isaacson and Leverich could no longer afford to host. RootsWeb itself was one of the largest user groups online. In May 2000 alone, it had more than "149 million page views (according to Nielsen NetRatings combined home and work statistics), sent over 155 million e-mails, and handled over two million downloads of files from the various archives hosted at RootsWeb."[27] Ancestry pledged to keep the site free and open to all users who registered on Ancestry.

But along with all the dot-com plays, Ancestry's value plummeted, and along with that tumble, the percentage of the company that Taggart and Allen actually owned. The venture capital investors, now in control of the majority shares in the company, removed Curt Allen from his role as CEO and other Mormon executives, replacing them with Silicon Valley executives to take the company public. Ironically, the decision to raise a lot of capital to accomplish the mission had already undermined the mission itself. Family historians and genealogists, particularly those who had been involved in the hobby or professionally long before the boom, could see the changes, and they weren't happy.

In order to make the company more profitable, the new management cut things Taggart felt were very important and would affect a lot of people. MyFamily was going to be shut down because it was costing a few million dollars a year to host. "We were growing by twenty to thirty thousand new users a day before the site turned into a paid site. I just kind of do the math in my head, and I think, well, that's six to nine hundred thousand new users a month. And that's millions . . . almost ten million new users a year. And if we can keep this site free for a long period of time, we can have tens of millions, maybe hundreds of millions, of families someday that are using our free services." Taggart was excited about the numbers. "But . . . there was so much pressure on all of our investors to clean up all of their portfolio companies and make sure every company was profitable that they just felt that they had to turn the MyFamily site into a paid site. That was devastating to me, because I felt that the MyFamily.com idea was ten times bigger than the Ancestry.com idea."[28]

In a lot of ways, MyFamily.com was a social networking site before social networking. The site already offered voice chats in 1999, years before Skype was invented. In 2000 MyFamily.com teamed up with ThirdAge Media, an online media, marketing, and consumer-insight company directed specifically at baby boomers (adults born between 1946 and 1964), and Onebox.com, a "free" communications company that provided a unified phone and online messaging service. Uniting the family unit online made it into a marketer's dream.[29]

Allen said sadly, "The investors and management team didn't see it that way." The new management started unwinding the founders' family values. "They thought that the fastest way for us to stay profitable would be to focus 100 percent on genealogy," by creating databases for end users. "They first unwound the free family sites. And then a lot of the free databases started disappearing from the site," said Allen. Ancestry turned MyFamily.com into a subscription site, and users had to pay to keep their family trees in place.

Though Taggart was exuberant remembering the whirlwind success of their venture, Allen was sadder about the cost of that ride. "We didn't understand the small print. We were anxious to take the capital, but probably not as anxious as we should have been to understand all the terms and conditions that are associated with venture capital. So, who's now in charge of running the business? We lost control very quickly of Ancestry.com."

"And what were the ramifications of that?" I asked

"How long do you have?"

"You can talk. We've got lots of tape."

"Okay, well. What happens when—and this is very typical, and I don't see anything wrong or evil with the venture capital industry, per se—but it turns out that in venture-backed companies, the VCs change the CEO within a year. Of course, they don't tell you up front that when you raise all that capital that they're now in charge of who the CEO is going to be, and therefore what the philosophy and strategy for the company is going to be."[30] Allen left the company in February 2002, but he kept an eye on its business practices. When I interviewed him, he was literally keeping an eye on Ancestry from his mostly empty offices kitty-corner to the corporate headquarters of Ancestry in Provo, Utah, which he could see directly out his window.

In 2003 MyFamily.com (Ancestry.com under a new name) released a new version of Family Tree Maker, which had passed through the hands of the Learning Company, Mattel, Gores Technology Group, and Riverdeep as Brøderbund was sold on. The company had built itself into one of the largest online subscription businesses, with more than 1 million paid subscribers and over 10 million Web users every month.[31] By 2004 MyFamily.com, growing by about a 100 percent a year, had 1.5 million subscribers and had outgrown its old headquarters in Orem, Utah. It leased a mothballed Sears, Roebuck call center in Provo, anticipating that it would almost double its workforce. Spokeswoman Mary Dondiego predicted that the industry was just getting started: "More than 60 percent of the U.S. adult population is interested in family history," Dondiego said. "That's 120 million people in the U.S."[32]

The company that we now know as Ancestry.com had grown branches faster than any family tree. The pedigree of Ancestry.com would run something like this: the marriage of Ancestry Publishing (1983) and Infobases (1990) begat Ancestry.com (1996) and its younger sibling MyFamily.com (1998); Ancestry then acquired RootsWeb.com (2000), soon reaching the

1-billion-name milestone (2001); it went international launching Ancestry.co.uk (2002) and made its first DNA play (which quickly failed); then, changing its name to MyFamily.com, it acquired genealogy.com (2003) and FamilyTreeMaker (2003) and Heritage Makers (2005), then begat a series of offspring, Ancestry.ca (Canada, 2006), Ancestry.au (Australia, 2006), Ancestry.de (Germany, 2006); and then, changing its name again, this time to the Generations Network (2006), begat another set of offspring: Ancestry.fr (France, 2007), Ancestry.it (Italy, 2007), and jiapu.com (China, 2008).

In 2007 Spectrum Equity Investors purchased the majority interest in the Generations Network for $300 million.[33] The DNA partnership with Sorenson Genetics was fired up again (I'll discuss this partnership in detail in chapter 5 on genetic genealogy). In 2008 Ancestry made $1.24 million in the first 6 months and $8.8 million in the first six months of 2009.[34] Ancestry filed its initial public offering (IPO) prospectus with the NASDAQ in 2009. It makes for interesting reading. The prospectus notes that its biggest competitor was FamilySearch, the free database of the Mormon Church, and that government privacy protections of vital statistics posed a significant risk to the company's business model.[35] Nonetheless, Ancestry's 2009 IPO was a huge success. CEO Tim Sullivan rang the NASDAQ stock exchange opening bell to start trading on November 6, 2009, launching the IPO and the company over the billion-dollar capitalization mark, making it one of the most powerful in the industry.[36] Ancestry had created a network effect. It had amassed the most trees and the most user-generated content acquiring RootsWeb, and it had built the largest number of genealogy databases, created or purchased from other companies, governments, or partnerships. The company fostered a wide-reaching company of online affiliates, paying commissions to every genealogy website that sent visitors to them.[37]

One of the most effective branches of the company was its marketing organization and the television presence that the company built with the existential television reality show *Who Do You Think You Are?* The program concept was borrowed from the United Kingdom, where sleuthing the ancestors of celebrity figures had been a staple of British television since 2004 (rolled out in Ireland, Canada, Israel, Sweden, Norway, Denmark, the Netherlands, Russia, and South Africa between 2007 and 2009). The U.S. series was launched by Ancestry.com in partnership with NBC in

2010. It was an immediate hit, reaching approximately 6 million viewers an episode, and ranked as the top-watched show of its time slot for popular celebrities like Susan Sarandon and Brooke Shields. Not everyone was enamored. Neil Genzlinger, a television critic for the *New York Times,* quipped that the show should come with a warning screen that "you may find that everyone you're related to was nothing but a drone in the vast hive of humanity, living unremarkably and dying unexceptionally, just as you probably will."[38] Ancestry.com's prominent presence on *Who Do You Think You Are?* "contributed to a 42.6 percent spike in its online subscriptions, to 1.87M," for the first two years of the show.[39] Observing the success of the program in Australia and the growth of the industry, the historian Graeme Davison coined the term *speed-relating,* which he likened to "driving a high-powered car down a freeway compared with walking or cycling," annihilating space along the way.[40]

It was all part of what Allen called a "virtuous circle." "Every time someone's exposed to that social proof, either from a friend or a television commercial, or an episode on a reality show, I think that unlocks that innate desire. I don't think it creates the innate desire. I think it unlocks it. It lets you know—that's possible. And therefore you realize you want that, too." The more records and technology exist, the more social proof is broadcast, either through word of mouth or online or television. That social context then "touches that latent desire for each person to know how do they fit into this scheme of things. Where did their ancestors come from? Why did they inherit the appearance or the tendencies or, you know, whatever they inherited from their ancestors?"[41] That's the virtuous circle. Ancestry.com warned its investors that the show's cancellation by NBC in 2013 might affect share price, but TLC stepped into the breach, and the infotainment meets genealogy infomercial show was saved.[42]

Allen's assessment of Ancestry, in spite of his reservations, was unbridled admiration. "Ancestry's got a great brand and has very effective ways of reaching millions of people online, on television, and getting them interested in trying things out. And once someone tries it out, they have a very effective hint engine that kind of spoon-feeds genealogy to the newbie. And helps them find actual records about themselves or grandparents that they didn't know existed. So really, the whole company is working very well. The content side, the marketing side, the brand side. Ancestry's definitely a huge success today." He really couldn't argue against that since he was part of the 2013 buyout that saw Permira buy the company for a whopping $1.6 billion, making Allen and Taggart multimillionaires.[43]

To continue the pedigree: Reverting to its maiden name, Ancestry.com, Inc. (2010), became a publicly traded company, sponsoring and promoting *Who Do You Think You Are?* It then acquired genline.se (Sweden, 2010), ProGenealogists.com (2010), iArchives, Inc., and footnote.com (2010), as well as, moving into the business of biodata, GeneTree (the not-for-profit database of Sorenson Genetics), launching Ancestry.DNA (2012). Eschewing public life, Ancestry returned to the family compound and was bought for $1.6 billion by intimates Permira Advisors, Spectrum Equity, and the management team, including Tim Sullivan and chief financial officer Howard Hochhauser. It continued its acquisitive ways, buying photo site 1000Memories (2012), FindAGrave (2013), and the records of the defunct South Africa company Ancestry24 (2013). And in 2013, in a marriage made in heaven, Ancestry reached an agreement with FamilySearch to digitize one billion records from the Granite Mountain Records Vault. Ancestry.com reached its "Next Generation" milestones: one million subscribers, one million people's DNA tested—all waved along by Ancestry's trademark little leaf.

I'll return to the genealogy of Ancestry shortly—and I'll devote the next chapter to a discussion of the dawn and accession of DNA testing. In the interlude, let's have a look at the courtship, separation, and eventual nuptials between Ancestry.com and FamilySearch, the database of the Mormon Church.

ALL IN THE FAMILY

While Ancestry listed the LDS Church as its biggest competitor in its 2009 IPO, that was during a trial separation. The longer history is more familial. Taggart's claim that the Mormons created genealogical demand moves us toward the idea that the industry emerged from Utah because the largest concentration of materials and genealogists were already there, along with the fact that few other entrepreneurs would have recognized the opportunity had they not been party to the Mormon project. Very early on, Taggart and Allen approached the church about licensing its information. The leadership wasn't against the idea, but they were slow to move. Initially, Ancestry didn't get very much information from the church. But once Ancestry proved that it was a serious company and could be trusted—and had developed the technology to digitize records—then the church was keen on the collaboration.

"At a certain point in time," said Taggart, "we approached the church, or we came together to discuss how we could cooperate in getting some of their material digitized. They had thirteen billion records on microfilm and microfiche, and we had become the world's leading digitization company for digitizing genealogical records. We actually did most of that work in China, to tell you the truth."

Ancestry would batch material and send it to China, where it would get double keyed—two different people would key in the same information. The people who keyed in the information probably didn't read English, Taggart surmised, and they just keyed in what they saw. Those two records would be compared, and the errors that surfaced between the two copies would show what mistakes had been made. A third person would go through and fix those. The process yielded very accurate digitized material. "So the church respected that competency that we had, and we began digitizing their records and scanning the images of those records with the understanding that we would make them available to the church to offer through the Family History Departments and Family History Centers throughout the world, and especially throughout the United States, for free to their members."[44] In return, Ancestry could offer the same digitized records online as part of their subscription service.

The Genealogical Society of Utah began digitizing in 1998, and the church's website FamilySearch.org went live in 1999, joining, as Erik Davis, writing for *Wired Magazine,* put it, "open-source time in the great beyond." The digitization arrangements between Ancestry and the church in the early years are not publicly available, though the deal went on for several years, since it was good for both Ancestry and the church. But in 2007, the relationship soured. "I don't know exactly how that broke down later," said Taggart, professing to know very little about the family feud.[45] No one I talked to in Utah affiliated with Ancestry or the church seemed to know anything about the disagreement over license fees that Ancestry wanted to charge the church, given the valuable data sets that Ancestry had digitized. Genealogists working at the Family History Library and at the Family History Centers knew that bad blood had come between the Generations Network (a.k.a. Ancestry) and the church, but few commented on it publicly. The *Voice of Utah*, an anonymous blog writing "sarcastic observations of Utah politics," reported on the story. "Uncharitable doings at the LDS Family History Library" begins: "In this corner: The Church of Jesus Christ of Latter-day Saints, operator of the largest genealogy library in the world. And in this corner: The Generations Network, Inc., operator of the largest genealogy website in the world, Ancestry.com. Caught in the middle: 800,000 genealogists in Utah and elsewhere who are getting the shaft." The story was also picked up by "Ancestry Insider," a blogger, also anonymous, who had been an insider at both industry heavyweights, who argued that privacy issues were the reason for cutting off church users. The necessity of anonymity for industry critics located in Utah hints at a sense of vulnerability. "Voice of Utah" provided this gloss, which seemed pretty accurate. "Over the past year, Ancestry.com's parent company has shifted focus. It changed its name from MyFamily.com to The Generations Network. It launched a national ad campaign. It sent a cease-and-desist to FreeOnAncestry. com, which had originally operated with its predecessor's blessing. It began foisting unwanted ads on paying customers. It changed RootsWeb (which it bought in 2000) to make formerly free features available only to Ancestry subscribers. And—the biggie—it decided to hit the Church up for licensing fees." Discussion boards on RootsWeb (archived on Ancestry and now no longer publicly available) were full of comments on all these issues, particularly how the Ancestry ads made patently false promises.[46]

The marriage made in heaven was strained by the partnership deals that the church was signing with a number of other companies and institutions, including MyHeritage.com, FindMyPast.com, and the National Archives and Records Administration (NARA) in Washington, through its new Records Access Program, leaving Ancestry out in the cold, as far as even the insiders could tell.[47] "Ancestry Insider" thought the deals would be structured so that the church would provide the images to the commercial and institutional sites, which would index the images, alone or with the church volunteers, and provide the indexes to the church and its members. The church was less than transparent about how it was acquiring the records.

After talking to Don Casias, the former vice president of partner services, who knew these deals intimately, the conflict became much clearer.

Indeed, the church had vast repositories of record images that needed indexing, and indexing is a time-consuming and costly operation. The church had the right to sell 60 percent of its records; 40 percent of the records could not be sold under the agreements made with the original records' custodians. The church would swap images for indexes (often two for one) with the understanding that all of the information entered into the family trees of the for-profit companies would be made available to LDS members for their genealogical work. The church realized that the more players there were in the industry—particularly ones that appealed to specific identity or heritage groups—the more the church and its members could pursue their mission by integrating the family trees built by consumers on the commercial sites into the LDS FamilyTree database. The church's support of Ancestry's competitors—in the name of gathering every ancestor everywhere—was undermining the profitability of Ancestry's proprietary data sets, and the company started looking for ways to recuperate some of those costs from the church.

But that didn't seem to upset Ancestry publicly, as Tim Sullivan, CEO of Generation's Network, applauded the new deals, in part because the church's volunteer indexers (you remember the "extraction" program) couldn't compete with Chinese labor. "We absolutely do not view the church as a competitor," Sullivan said. "There are gazillions of records that all of us need to get online. We are thrilled that others can get into it. It's only going to help us as a company. The church's model to have volunteers, nonpaid indexers, is intriguing but unproven and has a ways to go before it could scale to the way we digitize records."[48] In other words, the church needed Ancestry more than Ancestry needed the church.

And Ancestry had bigger fish to fry, as it was headed for a buyout under the chair of the board, David C. Moon, born and bred in Utah. Ancestry, though not owned by the church, was, nonetheless, a Mormon company through and through. Shipley Munson answered the question about the relationship between the church and Ancestry in several ways. "The fact is, Ancestry.com is based in Utah County. We're in Salt Lake County. Salt Lake County has a population that is 60 percent LDS. Utah County has a population that is 90 percent LDS. And so, if you look at the entire workforce of Ancestry.com, it reflects the demographics of its geographic location." As Munson put it, the workforce of Ancestry probably understood the church better than the management.

By 2008 the marriage was being consummated once again. Ancestry and FamilySearch sealed a deal that would see the two significantly enhance online offerings of the U.S. Census material, originally NARA records. The child looked something like this: FamilySearch would digitize its master microfilm copies of the original U.S. Censuses from 1790 through 1930 and give these images to Ancestry.com to sell to subscribers. The images would be available for free in NARA reading rooms and FamilySearch's forty-five hundred Family History Centers. In exchange, Ancestry.com, which held indexes and images of the entire publicly available U.S. Census collection, would give FamilySearch copies of its existing Census indexes. In effect, the two Census databases would merge.[49]

Munson's assessment of the business relationship verged on saccharin but made it clear that the church had come to see Ancestry in a new golden light. The different business models were not incompatible, and, ultimately, the prosperity of each institution helped the other. Only their bosses were different. "The church has a very different goal from Ancestry.com. Our goal is mission driven, and now they are answerable every quarter to their shareholders. So that will, by necessity, create a certain divergence. But I will tell you," said Munson, "that our view is that we are as committed to Ancestry's success as we are to our own, because we are trying to build a community, and we understand that they need to make money on certain collections." The community is both competitive and cooperative, all in the name of attracting the largest number of users. "So, in many cases, we have chosen not to publish collections that are only available on Ancestry, because they need oxygen to breathe. And at some point, those collections will be made public, and at some point, those records will be commoditized so that they can be available to all the world."[50]

In 2013 Ancestry and the church renewed their vows, making them virtually indistinguishable (except for their very different missions), sealing them forever in the afterlife. FamilySearch, realizing the pace of the industry and the limitations of its volunteer indexers, who, even in the millions, couldn't keep pace with commercial sites farming out the records to China, the third world, and prisons,[51] announced partnerships with Ancestry.com (and its subsidiaries), the British Company FindMyPast, and the Israeli company MyHeritage. The CEOs of all of these companies knew that the church would use their clients' trees for ordinances and accepted the church's deals as both beneficent and Machiavellian.[52] The Ancestry.com deal was the most contentious for church members.

The *r/exmormon* Reddit blog reported on the 2013 deal. "LDS church signs over a billion records indexed by volunteers (roughly everything to date) over to ancestry.com in exchange for $60 million and 5 years of free access to the site for LDS members. That was roughly 25 percent of ancestry.com's total subscription sales for that year." Brother Dennis Brimhall, then CEO of FamilySearch, offered this anodyne response to people who felt their volunteer efforts were being sold: "FamilySearch honors the sacrifice of its volunteers by freely sharing what it freely receives." The deals would have FamilySearch provide the records' images, which their commercial partners would then index with time-limited embargo for public access. Ancestry users responded with both glee and skepticism. "Carol" astutely observed, "Ancestry is a business for profit up front, and FamilySearch is under the partial tax-exempt cover of the LDS Church. This could become a monopoly."[53]

Indeed, if the church wanted a monopoly, it could have it. The church considered buying Ancestry several times. Even without the acquisition, the church would have been the biggest player in the market had it chosen to commercialize its records. But each time the question of monetizing the church's records was discussed—an obvious way to finance the church's long-range goals—the decision against it held firm. To run a commercial operation would dilute the spiritual dimensions of the enterprise. And, in reality, the commercial companies and all of their clients are doing the church's bidding without the church needing to enter the commercial space.[54]

WHO OWNS THE INFORMATION?

This consolidation of world records in Utah raises a question: Who owns the information? Taggart's answer to that question is telling: "Um, ownership of genealogy data is at best a gray area. And it depends really what you are talking about. The data itself . . . the birth dates and names and places . . . that is public information for the most part in the United States." Outside of the United States, that's not necessarily true. In many European or Asian countries, vital information is not public. It belongs to the government. But in the United States, it's public information—paid for by taxpayers. Information in the public domain is not protected, and anyone can access it. But the information alone isn't the issue, as Taggart explained. "When a company goes in and adds value by aggregating a lot of data, and then combines it with a retrieval system, that aggregated information, just like a phone book, becomes copyrightable." Taggart joked that they called the databases themselves "phone books for the dead." "And so," he continued, "that is where you have the added value that allows you to protect what you've put your work into. Otherwise, companies couldn't do this, right? And you wouldn't have any ability to commercialize those kinds of things, and companies like Ancestry wouldn't exist."[55] The commercialization of public information would more likely to lead to privatization than free public access, Taggart predicted.

Susan D. Young, a professional genealogist with more than forty years and forty thousand hours of experience, had this to say about the tactics of the industry:

> Copyright begets a marketable product. Therefore, it is in the best interests of the profitability of any mass data marketer (e.g. Ancestry, FindmyPast, etc.) to claw back from their subscribers the right to repackage anything that a subscriber posts to their website through online family trees, message boards and even the aggregation of a subscriber's on-site search results. I don't believe the average user realizes just how much money is being generated by their information and use of these websites for these companies. In essence, the user has become an unwitting partner and slave in the profit-making of the site(s) they use.[56]

In the extra-fine print of the terms and conditions at the bottom of Ancestry.com's homepage, one reads the all-too-familiar clause:

> By submitting User Provided Content through any of the Services, you grant Ancestry a sublicensable, worldwide, royalty-free license to host, store, copy, publish, distribute, provide access to, create derivative works of, and otherwise use such User Provided Content to the extent and in the form or context we deem appropriate on or through any media or medium and with any technology or devices now known or hereafter developed or discovered. . . . We will also have the right to continue to use your User Provided Content, even if you stop using the Services, but only as necessary for us to provide and improve the Services.[57]

Ancestry's rights to use your information continues even if you stop using their websites or services. Now add the consumer/contributor to our ever-growing virtuous circle of technology, family values, trees, religion, and commerce.

Paul Allen and I continued to explore this question of user-generated content. "So, they're doing some maybe not-so-savory things?" These were the kind of questions that Allen had been nervous about. "The biggest one for me," he admitted, "is kind of the lock-in for online family trees and all of the records that someone might discover." He explained how it works: "Let's say that ten years ago, you became an Ancestry subscriber, and you've spent now three or four thousand dollars over a ten-year period, and of course thousands of hours of your time to go in and find all the records pertaining to your family . . . and so you're successfully finding all kinds of records and you link them to your tree. But there's a lock-in, there, where you really can't export your tree with all the associated links and records. . . . There's a real lock-in." "Locking in" users helps Ancestry retain subscribers. If you want to keep seeing the records that you've identified, you need to keep subscribing to Ancestry. "My biggest concern is if a person spends ten years of their life preserving their heritage for themselves and all their relatives and posterity . . . what if they pass away? What happens to their tree? What happens to their links? What happens to the records?"[58]

Allen's question about what happens to your account was a good one, and nowhere did I find an answer to it. For a company so heavily invested in the dead, Ancestry doesn't seem to acknowledge that its users die. You can't delete an account on Ancestry; the best you can do is cancel a subscription.[59] You are given guest privileges for eternity.

Allen's reservations continued. "I think even though some people in the genealogy community have a concern about the church and its motives, and its mission and theology, there's also the concern about the corporatism of Ancestry.com, maybe locking up the records."[60] It was at this point in the interview that I began to understand why Allen had almost balked. We had met briefly before the interview, and he was visibly anxious, worried that he what he was going to tell me would harm his relationship with Ancestry, with whom he still did business. In 2015 Ancestry.com shut down MyFamily.com altogether, giving users little notice and deleting user content. Similarly, Family Tree Maker, which had been, according to Ancestry.com, "the world's No.-1 selling family history software," was discontinued by Ancestry.com in 2015 and sold in 2017, much to the dismay of its users.[61] In 2017, citing a privacy breach, RootsWeb, now fully hosted on and merged with Ancestry.com since 2008 (again, much to some users' dismay), was shut down.[62] While Ancestry restored access to some of its functions, access to decades of discussion groups have not as yet been restored, hiding, in effect, the history of genealogists' discussions of the development of the industry and the technology itself.[63]

"You know," said Taggart to me, in 2010, "we haven't even talked about DNA genealogy work. We haven't talked about where that's going. If you want to talk about the future of genealogy, that's where it is. It's in very, very sophisticated algorithms, computer-based algorithms that will actually analyze DNA and tell you a lot about your family history and tie you into all kinds of family history information. Even if you don't know the names of your ancestors, you can find out who they were."[64] Indeed. The rest of this book is really about that. Records are almost old hat. The real money and future for genealogy is in the lab and under our skin, in places entirely hidden to us without the interventions of new genealogical technologies. The true genealogical sublime is observed under a microscope in mathematical abstractions that have become the irrefutable science of where we come from and who we are.

....

CHAPTER 4

ICELAND
End Games

ÍSLENDINGABÓK

In 2013 three software engineering students came to international attention with the announcement that they had won a million-krona contest for the best cell phone app to celebrate the ten anniversary of Íslendingabók, "The Book of Icelanders," Iceland's genealogical database. The winning entry was a Facebook phone app whose function was, primarily, to keep cousins from sleeping with each other. The app allowed users to bump their phones together to see instantly how closely related they were. The tagline made the point clear: "Bump in the app before you bump in bed," and the app sounded an "Incest Prevention Alarm" if the mating was a little too proximate.

Media outlets outside of Iceland had a field day with the winning app, making Icelanders both cool (they must be having a lot of sex if they need an app like that) and silly at the same time ("I almost put myself into sex with my aunt," says the mortified pretend Icelander in a Jimmy Fallon skit, mangling English syntax in a way that few young Icelanders would). One wag commented, "I bumped my iPhone with sister, and it says we're not related. . . . I guess that's a green light . . . ?" The story of the app drew a lot of attention to Iceland and to the database, and it served, I must admit, as an intriguing introduction to the wonders of Iceland genealogy.[1] I began to research Iceland to follow up on the story of the app, which I thought was the most amusing application of genealogical data I had heard about. But I soon found the backstory much more interesting and one that proved to be the proverbial canary in the coal mine for the end uses of genealogical information and the sublime ambitions for complete databases.

If North America has the biggest genealogy databases, one of the genealogical wonders of the world belongs to Iceland. Iceland is home to the most complete national digital tree in the world, *Íslendingabók,* named after one of the earliest historical accounts of the island's settlement—and paid for by the Iceland biotech giant deCODE Genetics. The population of Iceland is a genealogist's—and a geneticist's—dream. A little Icelandic history will help us to understand the phenomenon.

Iceland, a volcanic outcrop in the North Atlantic, was first settled by Gaelic monks sometime before the 800s, who perhaps used it only as their summer retreat or for hermetic isolation. The monks were displaced, not wanting to live among heathens, or perhaps dispatched by the Vikings who drifted onto the island by mistake, off course on their way from Norway to the Faeroe Islands.[2] A few intrepid Vikings returned on purpose and, surviving a difficult winter, were astounded when the island turned a verdant green in the spring. The first permanent settler, Ingólfur Arnarson, arrived in 874, looking for a place beyond the grasp of the tax-happy King Harald Fairhair of Norway. Arnarson and his family, his men and their enslaved Irish women, established a population whose patrilineal lines were Norse and matrilineal ones were strongly inflected with Gaelic. More settlers arrived. By 930, with the settlement firmly established, Iceland convened the first parliament in the world, the commonwealth of Alþingi.

The story of Iceland's early settlement and its geographic isolation is only half of what makes it exceptional in the history of genealogy. Icelanders were—and are—one of the most literate societies in the world, frequently referring to themselves as the "Book Nation."[3] That literary inheritance—crucial to the databases to follow—begins with the medieval sagas, around 1200, a "literary tradition which far exceeded in scope and volume anything produced by their continental kinsmen."[4] These secular stories, "Family Sagas," recorded in the eleventh and twelfth centuries, amalgamated oral traditions, histories, and genealogies of the previous centuries with new literary innovations, creating a set of origin stories for the island that rival the other mythic and religious chronicles of late antiquity and early Christianity. The sagas are dramatic, full of conflict and intrigue and fantastic stories and creatures. They belong to three main types: poetic and narrative biographies of kings and bishops and of prominent families and popular outlaws; sagas or chronicles of regions

and geographies; and family sagas, records of the feuds and violent conflicts that lay at the heart of great family histories. Each type mingled elements of the others. Oral and written genealogies were used for political
unity and sometimes skewed to bolster land claims—all of that violent
death left the ownership of much land in question. Both historical and
fantastic, the sagas ascribed to some of the early kings genealogies leading
back to the Norse gods Thor and Odin, detailing godly battles with mon-
sters at sea. Theodore Murdock Andersson, a scholar of the sagas, writes
of the transition from the oral stories to the written sagas that "there must
have been genealogical traditions of a copiousness and complexity that is
hard for modern people to imagine."[5]

These sagas included the original *Íslendingabók,* written on durable
hide. "The Book of Icelanders" recorded the oral histories of the major
events of Icelandic history, avoiding all supernatural material and
Christian theology alike, unlike the much more popular sagas. The pro-
logue of *Íslendingabók* invites correction and the addition of "what proves
to be more accurate," making it the most reliable extant source on early
Icelandic history.[6] Roughly contemporaneous is the *Landnámabók,* "The
Book of Settlements," which tells the story of who settled the island by
geographic areas, tracing the most important events and family histories
from the tenth to the twelfth centuries. The *Landnámabók* names more
than 3,000 people and describes more than 1,400 settlements, providing brief genealogies of 435 early settlers, men like Thorolf Twist-Foot,
Bolverk Blind Snout, Herils Knob-Buttocks, and Eyestein Fould-Fart.[7]

One obvious consequence of a small, isolated population is the necessity of avoiding marriages between close relatives. After the tenth century,
marriages, and thus bloodlines, were regulated by the Catholic Church
in Iceland. Catholicism (another source of Icelandic literacy) dominated
religious life from the tenth until the sixteenth centuries, converting the
Norse from paganism until Danish rule abolished Catholicism in favor
of Protestantism. The church restricted marriages, making those who
wanted to marry their second or even third cousins pay a fee to the parish
or get a special exemption from the pope, for an even bigger fee.[8] Keeping
the family genealogy was fiscally prudent.

The fledging country grew through the Middle Ages, only to be
decimated by several disasters. The bubonic plague in the early 1400s
killed 40 to 50 percent of the island, only to return in the last years of the

century and wipe out another 30 to 50 percent of the remaining Icelanders. Approximately 40,000 people perished between the two bouts. The population had just begun to recover when it was ravaged by smallpox in the early 1700s, killing a quarter of the inhabitants, mostly young adults. Then the eruption of the Lakagigar volcano in southern Iceland in 1783 flooded 220 square miles with fire and rock and spewed a poisonous ash across the country (reaching mainland Europe as well).[9] The ash killed crops and half the livestock, and about 20 percent of the population died of starvation in the "Mist Famine."[10] By the middle of the eighteenth century, Iceland's population was fewer than 50,000 people, with a limited genetic diversity, all descendants from lines that had managed to survive a thousand years of devastating events. The culmination of these disasters was "as if a giant tree had been pruned again and again until only its trunk and a few of the sturdiest branches remained."[11]

Not surprisingly, not many people wanted to move to this harsh place of wonder and terror. Iceland's population was still only 300,000 people by the 2000s (smaller than most North American cities). Many people emigrated from Iceland, particularly to Canada in the late nineteenth century, but few immigrated to this volcanic outcrop.[12] Geographic isolation and a population winnowed over a millennia by disease and natural disaster combined with a highly literate population entranced by history and family lore laid the foundation for the world's most homogenous and traceable nation.[13]

FIGURE 4. Vikings. Courtesy of the author.

Gunnar "Viking" Olafsson looks every bit the part. He's a tall, barrel-chested man, with a broad face, long red-blond hair, and a scraggly beard. *Gunnar* means "warrior." He is every inch "Warrior Viking Son of Olaf." I met Olafsson in his clubhouse, a barracks on the now abandoned U.S. Army base just outside Reykjavik, empty for twenty-five years. Olafsson is the leader of a band of Viking revivalists, "Einherjar: Víkingfélag Reykjavíkur," the "Army of One: The Vikings of Reykjavik," or, in another loose translation, "Odin's Army," an army of equals for "The One," a god with two hundred names who will admit to Valhalla the warriors who die in his name. Olafsson's car license plate is "Viking" and his motorcycle "Odin." He sounds American, having grown up in California, but the lure of heritage brought him back to Iceland at the age of eighteen. Olafsson claims he can trace his roots back to the year 632 to King Harald of Denmark. His thirty-fourth grandfather was King Harald Fairhair (ca. 850–932), who united Norway but drove Norse "malcontents" to find other lands, the impetus for the settlement of Iceland. Although the amount of genetic material Olafsson would have inherited from Harald Fairhair is less than 1/1000th (mathematically, 34 generations of ancestors would include a potential 34 squared or 1,156 contributors to his genetic material—though probably considerably less because of marriages between close relatives and the concentration of genetic lines in Iceland), Olafsson doesn't care. The science doesn't matter to him; it's the stories that are important, the words, the documents, knowing to which family tree he belongs—or to all of them, cementing his identity as a Viking. His sense of being part of a continuity makes him feel a bit sorry for those who can't know that heritage.

"For some abroad, they can only talk about two grandmothers, two grandfathers. Possibly great-grandfathers or great-grandmothers, if you can remember, but we have a whole family tree and we like talking about way back in the past."[14] Icelanders like to talk. "And before the TV, everybody talked about who your family was. Everybody knew something about who you are. It was enough for you to travel to another town in Iceland that somebody would say, 'Ah, I can just see from your reflection that you come from this family tree.'" Iceland family names, one of the last Scandinavian countries to hold on to a patronymic naming system, do not follow the conventions of the West, but, rather, are context dependent, where the son or daughter takes the first name of the father (or sometimes the mother). Thus, Olafsson's sister's last name, if he had a sister, would have been Olafdottir, "Daughter of Olaf," where Olaf was the first name of the father. People are known by their first names, which are much more distinctive, and it is those names that they pass on to their children. Without family names, there's a greater sense of equality, of good families rather than pedigrees. Reputation is important.

According to Olafsson, one-fourth of the Icelandic character is dedicated to talking about from whom they come. In the countryside the elders always ask, "Who was your grandfather?" "Ah, yes," they say, "Let me tell you a story." You don't hear the bad stories, only the good ones, though Olafsson readily admitted that the stories were also a form of gossip, that neighbors watched each other and recorded the outcomes of furtive visits—or kept that information quiet. That history extends not just to people but to places as well. "You don't have to go far to go out into the country. You know, every hill has a name. Everything, every town, there's a name from way back into the Viking ages." After the financial crash of 2008, when many Icelanders lost their livelihoods, their cars, their apartments, Olafsson felt it was more important than ever for people to retain their sense of identity. "We still own our land," said Olafsson. "I want to bring the proudness back into the Icelanders."

His band of Vikings stood on the edge of a dune, backlit against the low afternoon sun, banging their axes and swords and lances against round shields bearing the rods and waves insignia of Reykjavik, ready to fight, looking every bit a thousand years old. They play "slay each other" for my benefit. One of his band explains, with that wry Icelandic humor, that they are all descendants of that first settler, Ingólfur Arnarson, but that most of them can also trace their heritage to King Harald Fairhair—Ingólfur's enemy.

It's a serious game, for that pride cuts other ways as well. On his Facebook page (a very popular page that was mysteriously hacked in 2017), Olafsson offered his support to Soldiers of Odin everywhere, anti-immigrant street patrols that started in Finland. Pride of bloodlines, and the nationalism that runs through it, makes outsiders easy to identify.

REWRITING *ÍSLENDINGABÓK*

"Some people call genealogy," Friðrik Skúlason said dryly, "the national hobby of Iceland. Others call it a general genetic disease that affects a substantial part of the Iceland population, but typically only manifests after the age of fifty, with the symptoms generally getting worse after retirement."[15] He's a funny, lovely man, as close to a living hobbit as one might imagine. Skúlason is a computer programmer and founder of FRISK Software, a company that programs antivirus software. He is also an avid genealogist, like many Icelanders. Skúlason was one of the early adopters of database technology for genealogy, developing genealogical software called Espólín in 1987. Because of Iceland's naming system, diacritical complexity, and unusual kinship categories, genealogical software had to be designed specifically for the culture. "There used to be a category for the official mistress of a priest," explained Skúlason. "Which brings up the rather interesting subject that just about everybody in Iceland is a descendant of the last Catholic bishop in Iceland, Jón Arason. Which is kind of funny, since they are not supposed to have any children, but he had a mistress and five or six children with her, and we are all his descendants. Then he got beheaded, but that's besides the point." Like everything new with a historical antecedent in Iceland, the pedigree software was named after Jón Espólín (1769–1836) and his 1821 *Íslands árbækur,* the "Annals of Iceland," a history of Iceland from 1262.

From the software, Skúlason began to build a database. "In my spare time, I started adding data. In 1996, on January 17, I had added 299,999 people, and the number 300,000 happened to be my daughter, born on that date." Shortly after Skúlason added his daughter's name to his database, deCODE Genetics, an Iceland biotech start-up, contacted Skúlason. "Now, I had planned to continue just adding data by myself in my spare time. I estimated it would take me forty years or so," he said with a dry lilt, "and I would complete it at the retirement home or whatever. But the people at deCODE said, 'We need this database. We cannot wait twenty or thirty or forty years. We need it in two or three or four years. So, how much money do you need?'"

DeCODE was interested in the genetic causes of diseases. One of its cofounders and the most public face of the company is the hero-villain visionary Kári Stefánsson. Stefánsson was a Harvard neuroscientist who returned to Iceland in 2006, drawn by the possibilities of mining the genetic homogeneity of the population—and by his own Icelandic genealogy, which he proudly traced back to the murderous tenth-century poet Egil Skallagrímsson. Restricted by the sample size at Harvard, Stefánsson

escaped the confines of academic research for free-market research frontiers. He raised $12 million to start deCODE, a company that drew the
world's attention to Iceland and its exceptional genealogical and genetic
resources. Most Icelanders were closely related to the "founders," and the
bloodlines were very clear. He would also draw the world's attention to
the country's failure to protect that exceptional resource.

Friðrik Skúlason and deCODE called the database Íslendingabók, a
new "Book of Icelanders." This was a name that was dear to the heart of
the country, in the tradition of naming databases after people or books,
making the technology part and parcel of the mythology of the nation
and lending to the database the sublime quality of human transmission.
Landnámabók and *Íslendingabók* and the dramatic sagas were crucial to the
assembly of the modern-day genealogy, which technologically reinvented
a copious and complex medieval art. More than money, what Skúlason
needed to complete the database was manpower to scour the sagas and
the genealogies, the census and the parish records, many of which, fortunately, had been microfilmed by the Mormons in the 1960s. DeCODE
agreed to provide the researchers and programmers, and for the next
four years, from 1999 to 2003, roughly the same time frame in which the
growth of genealogical databases worldwide began to accelerate, twenty
deCODE employees worked full-time adding genealogical data. Skúlason
provided his extensive library and project management.

"Instead of looking for individual people and tracing their ancestry"
Skúlason explained, "we approached this as a data-mining operation."
They logged the parish records, including birth, death, and marriage
registrations, which started as early as 1668 in some places, and the old
genealogies. They then computerized national censuses—about twelve
between 1703 and 1930 and the partial Farmer censuses of 1735, 1753, and
1760—programming comparisons between data sets to find out what
matched and didn't, manually adding and analyzing mismatches. "We
were not tracing the ancestry of individual people," explained Skúlason.
"That appeared as a side effect of going through the entire mountain
of data."

The Íslendingabók project was not without controversy (though more
was to follow), as the publishing company Genealogia Islandorum took
deCODE and FRISK (Skúlason's company) to court for using Genealogia
Islandorum's previously published genealogies compiled from much

the same sources.[16] DeCODE rejected the claim, on the grounds that genealogical facts on their own do not constitute private property and that they had added significantly more information as well as storage and a retrieval system.[17] The case was appealed to the Supreme Court of Iceland, where deCODE and FRISK won because, as the evaluators argued, the researchers who had assembled Íslendingabók had cited their sources and used the same methods that genealogists always had: "This approach testifies to scholarly methods which resonate with the finest procedures applied by genealogists in recent times when composing their writings. . . . All published genealogies naturally add to previously available information . . . making it easier at the same time to connect persons or acerbating the process."[18]

As a gesture to the public ownership of the records, deCODE made a limited version of Íslendingabók available to every Icelander who had a social insurance number, upon request. When the database was completed in 2003, approximately half of the population requested access to it, making it one of the most popular databases in the world per capita. "Overnight," writes Gísli Pálsson, a professor of anthropology at the University of Iceland, "*The Book of Icelanders* became a popular pastime."[19] The database became a party game of sorts, gossiping families and church surveillance supplanted by a database. Similar to the origins of Facebook and presaging the "bump before you bump" phone app, the younger generation used it as a dating site, exploring connections and good matches. People used it at work, hoping to establish rapport and collaboration with colleagues. As usual, people searched for connections to fame. Björk's family grew substantially.

No less important were the extended family gatherings, a popular phenomenon in Iceland, where dating couples could be unwittingly confronted with awkward family ties. One young couple who used the app told me this story exactly. They had dated only a few weeks when she invited him to a children's birthday party. "We walked into a birthday party, and half the people there, her relatives, were mine." He shook his head at the discomfort of the memory, "'Oh, oh,' he thought. 'I'm sleeping with my cousin.' Fortunately, they checked the app, and these two families were related by marriage, not blood." "What would you have done if they had been blood relatives?" I asked. "We would have canceled," his wife answered. He didn't look so sure. There were unpleasant surprises, as people tried to correct records that revealed secret biological fathers and half siblings or a family relationship to a convicted criminal. It turned out that just about everyone in Iceland, like Kári Stefánsson, had the famous tenth-century poet and homicidal maniac Egil Skallagrímsson as an ancestor. Egil, the subject of one of the most popular biographical sagas, wrote his first poem at three and killed his first person at seven over an argument in a game.[20] "Then he went on to probably write a poem about it," said Skúlason. "You have to understand the Viking philosophy to really appreciate that."

In the end, Íslendingabók traced 70 percent of all Icelanders who have ever lived since the founding of Iceland in AD 874, including 285,000 contemporary Icelanders and 400,000 of their ancestors.[21] This is as close as any database has come to the sublime ideal of capturing everyone.

BIOPIRACY

Iceland is a captive biomedical community.

—Richard Lewontin

The bigger backstory of deCODE and Íslendingabók is its own Icelandic saga, complete with larger-than-life characters, cutting-edge science, exuberant capitalism, hubris and greed, unwitting dupes, and political intrigue. And, indeed, the technological vision and its opponents drew on Iceland's cultural traditions with powerful narrative and persuasive effect.[22] The value of the limited genetic pool, a source of the genetic risks of inbreeding, combined with the genealogical database was a gold mine for deCODE. For example, virtually every case of breast cancer in Iceland caused by the BRCA2 mutation could be traced through the combined genealogical and genetic records to a sixteenth-century cleric named Einar, whose descendants survived the plagues and fires, contributing in magnified fashion to the much-winnowed genetic diversity of the island.[23] In 1998, after deCODE accelerated the compilation of Íslendingabók, the first of its "three-legged database stool," the company began to push the development of the other two: the country's medical records and genetic samples from as many Icelanders as they could get.

Kári Stefánsson and Jeffrey Gulcher explained that their "genealogical approach," linking patients to generate large, extended pedigrees, boosted "the size and power of the patient cohorts." The size of the population, the genealogical records, and the genetic structure of Iceland meant that the researchers needed "twenty times fewer people to do the same research in the U.S." and could do it "twenty times quicker and twenty times cheaper," as Nick Short put it. Short was the editor of *Nature* who had jumped on board the Iceland genetic express. Michael Specter explained it this way in the *New Yorker*: "The raw genetic facts (called genotypes) are . . . compared to the physical condition of each patient (the phenotype). At the same time, deCODE turns to its genealogical database to search for familial patterns of illness." Specter continues, "That way, specialists are able to make highly sophisticated statistical interpretations of genetic relationships among people, and to find the best places in the incomprehensibly large universe of human DNA to look for genes that may cause illness."[24] The popular science of the "genealogical approach" found willing buyers.

In 1998 deCODE signed an agreement with Hoffman–La Roche (the Swiss pharmaceutical company that owns Genentech, now partnered with 23andMe). The agreement promised $200 million over five years if deCODE could identify genes of some of the most genetically complicated diseases in the world: schizophrenia, Alzheimer's, stroke, heart disease, and emphysema. Roche would then develop diagnostics and drugs, which, in turn, would be available free of charge to Icelanders. The funding was tied to the development of the three-legged database—braided genealogical records, genetic samples, and medical records—unique in the world.[25] DeCODE and the Iceland government, led by Kári Stefánsson's university friend Prime Minister David Oddsson, took Iceland and the medical community by surprise when they introduced a bill in the Icelandic parliament authorizing the creation of the Icelandic Health Sector Database.[26] The HSD would allow Hoffman–La Roche, via deCODE, access to the medical records of the entire population of the country. Iceland has a national medical insurance system and had kept immaculate records on diseases since 1915, along with a tissue bank. In return for developing the database, which would be a boon to the health of Icelanders—and the world—but would be very expensive, the government would give deCODE an exclusive twelve-year license to the medical records and tissue samples, hoping to attract further billions in pharmaceutical investment to Iceland.

The 1998 bill provided no direct consent from the people whose medical records and genetic samples would be studied, but instead assumed "presumed consent," requiring Icelanders to opt out if they didn't want to be included in the database.[27] The dead, whose tissue samples remained in the medical records, and children were presumed to have given consent. Kári Stefánsson argued, pragmatically, that informed consent would be too difficult to obtain from every Icelander and would have to be obtained not just once but in every instance of a new research study.[28] The promise of the database, its financial and its health rewards, generated strong support among the general public, but fierce debates followed about privacy rights, medical ethics, and the ownership of pubic information, including the genealogy records.

There was also the question of who should profit from such a database. Should it not be the nation and not a private company? The situation in 1998 was, as Skúli Sigurdsson describes it, "a mixture of a shouting match, an elaborate advertising campaign by deCODE, overwhelming media attention and marathon sessions in the Icelandic parliament."[29] A sector of the population found the idea and ownership of the database to be Orwellian, which was diplomatically dismissed as "unduly paranoid." Opponents accused the company of having an "incestuous relationship" with the government. The implications of that accusation would have resonated in Iceland. Critics also saw a path toward Nazi-era eugenics.[30]

The database bill was debated more extensively than any other bill in the history of modern Iceland. Seven hundred newspaper articles, 150 television programs, and the endless debates produced approval for the bill in the end, forestalling some of the foreign criticism. Articles surfaced in the *New York Times,* the *New Yorker, Science,* and a host of international academic journals in the fields of biotechnology, genetics, law and ethics, and population studies. One of the most scathing critics was Richard Lewontin, whose op-ed in the *New York Times* on January 23, 1999, "People Are Not Commodities," became one of the most cited in the English media. Lewontin, a Harvard population geneticist and ethicist who knew Kári Stefánsson well, argued that the bill had made Icelanders into "a captive biomedical community."[31] That phrase stuck. Other people called it "biopiracy," the robbing of a nation's unique biological assets.[32] Countering the perception that the company was a homegrown Icelandic enterprise, Lewontin pointed out that it was a Delaware corporation (the state of

Delaware has the most favorable corporate laws anywhere in the United States) and that "its financial backers include American companies whose representatives hold seats on Decode's board." Lewontin went so far as to call for a scientific boycott of deCODE's results. Besides Kári Stefánsson, the only Icelander on the board was a former president of Iceland, Vigdís Finnbogadóttir.

But the bill was passed, with major revisions between second and third readings that pointed to end moves around critics. Stefánsson, famously intolerant, tolerated some of the criticisms and the bill was amended, but by 1999 he was fed up. Michael Specter quotes him in the *New Yorker*: "Those who are opposed to what we are trying to do are a small group. They are not important. And they will lose." Providing support, Prime Minister Oddsson went on record saying, "It certainly would be nice if the gene responsible for all the wrangling and quarrelling which had often obstructed progress in this country could eventually be identified and isolated."[33]

In June 1999, Icelandic state banks bought out the original investors and began selling the shares back to the Icelandic public, making deCODE Iceland's most valuable company. Its value soared from $12 million to $500 million in two years, and shares rose from $5 to $60 in 1999.[34] There was unbridled optimism about the company and rumors of a NASDAQ offering. A lot of people invested and borrowed money to invest. "It was like the gold rush in America in the nineteenth century," recalled Dr. Steindór Erlingsson, an Icelandic historian of science in Hördur Arnarson's documentary *Decoding Iceland: The DNA of Greed*.[35] The public invested heavily, as did the government and the national banks. People took out loans, mortgaged houses, used life savings to buy shares. They were on board for selling their genetic purity as long as they saw some of the rewards. Much like Ancestry, deCODE was another company swept up in the dot-com rush.[36]

In January 2000, the license legislation passed, and deCODE received its license to the country's medical records to build the Health Sector Database. In March 2000, deCODE filed papers for an initial public offering on the NASDAQ; Hoffman–La Roche is listed as owning 13 percent of the company. *Forbes* called it "a risky business." It raised $178 million on 9.6 million shares. The shares shot up and then fell, even though the company had a market capitalization of nearly $2 billion. *Forbes* noted that even given its valuable data sets, "DeCODE isn't even as unique as it's cracked up to be. Salt Lake City–based Myriad Genetics has been finding genes in a Mormon population in its hometown since its inception in 1991"[37]—and wasn't making that much money from it. Genetics and genealogy became bedfellows quite quickly, but no one was quite sure what those matings would produce. Morgan Stanley Dean Witter was the main underwriter, and Lehman Brothers acted as comanager.[38] If you remember the catastrophic financial events of 2000 in the Ancestry.com story, you see where this is going.

The filing papers are a fascinating read, full of caveats about why deCODE might not be able to fulfill its promise, including the difficulties maintaining the goodwill and cooperation of the Icelandic population; that government supervision of the database, including the Iceland Data Protection Agency, might prove to be an obstacle; that they might not derive any profits from their research; that their assumptions about disease might be wrong; that ethical and privacy concerns may lead to litigation against the company and the Icelandic government;[39] that data confidentiality could fail, resulting in a loss of the license; that they might not be competitive with other biotech companies; and, significantly, along with volatility and no guarantees about stock prices and so on, that others might claim intellectual property rights to "our genealogy database."[40]

"Recently, two holders of copyrights in approximately 100 Icelandic genealogy books have filed a copyright infringement suit against us in Iceland claiming that we have used data from these books in the creation of our genealogy database, in violation of their rights. The claimants seek a declaratory judgment to prevent our use of the database and monetary damages. . . . We believe that this suit is without merit and intend to defend it vigorously." Indeed, deCODE would win this case, but its offering makes it clear that the intellectual property rights over the genealogy database were crucial. DeCODE had successfully privatized and monetized the public's interest in genealogy and their families' histories. "In establishing links between the transmission of language and the transmission of genetic material," observe Arnar Árnason and Bob Simpson, "deCode succeeded in making genetic traditions an entirely logical extension of Icelanders' preoccupations with their cultural traditions."[41]

DeCODE was now an Icelandic success story, employing hundreds, reversing the brain drain, and fostering a sense of optimism and pride in what Iceland could accomplish by punching far above its weight. Bio-information might just do for Iceland what offshore oil had done for Norway. More than 75 percent of Icelanders showed enthusiasm for the potential of the company to exploit one of the great natural resources of the island, a just reward, "poetic justice," said Kári Stefánsson, for all the misery Iceland had suffered.[42] It was about to suffer again.

In May 2000, the Biobank Act set the rules for deCODE's collection of DNA samples.[43] Consent applied to those people who were donating new samples, but no consent was required for samples collected in the past for clinical purposes. "Presumed consent" was at the center of the contro-versy.[44] Icelanders were granted a six-month opt-out window after the bill was passed. By 2001 almost twenty thousand Icelanders had applied to have their records removed from the database, which had yet to be established. One-third of Icelandic doctors refused to hand over patient files, citing confidentiality requirements. One psychiatrist explained his concerns: "Patients come and talk to me, and at night I'm supposed to send the information to a third party that can sell it on the world mar-ket. . . . That is extremely troublesome."[45] Privacy concerns were still central, but so was the question of which companies might buy access to the database in the future, health insurance companies in particular. Those who opted out became their own database. They became "entities in a second-order HSD, registering those socially deviant where the first-order HSD is still empty."[46]

Like all start-up biotech companies, deCODE was very expensive to run, with a "burn rate" of about $12 million a month. To raise operating capi-tal, deCODE turned to the "gray market," Iceland's own lightly regulated trading system. Professional investors could sell shares directly to investors without the oversight of an official initial public offering as long as they did not actively promote the company. Customers had to ask to buy. But with the company profile everywhere in the press, everyone was aware of its potential. Icelandic financial institutions borrowed money from foreign banks in order to loan money to Icelanders to buy shares in the company. And here's where the trouble really began. Michael Fortun documents a complicated shell game in which Biotech Invest, a company set up in Luxembourg, was used to sell deCODE shares, for a commission. Biotech sold the shares to Icelandic financial institutions, which then sold the shares on to Iceland investors.[47] DeCODE made almost $70 million via this route.

DeCODE shares hit a peak of $56 on the gray market in Iceland, but shares in the IPO in the United States never rose much above $30.[48] Part of the dot-com bust, shares on both markets declined rapidly. By 2002 shares of deCODE tanked, trading on the gray market for $6 and hitting a low of $0.23 on the NASDAQ. The trading frenzy was over. The same dot-com bubble that cost Dan Taggart and Paul Allen control of Ancestry wiped out the share price of deCODE. Virtually every Icelander had a financial stake in the company through pension plans, individual investments, or local government investment. The market value of deCODE accounted for 7 percent of the gross domestic product of Iceland.[49] James Meek reported on some of the more egregious cases in the *Guardian* in 2002. Even though Icelanders had lost their shirts, they still did not want to blame deCODE or the government and believed that deCODE would rise from the ashes and make them all rich. As Meek wrote, Stefánsson dismissed Icelanders who lost money after buying deCODE shares on the gray market as "the victims of their own recklessness; of banks and brokers he didn't control; of local politicians who had demanded he let Icelanders share the profits from a gene bonanza; of global financial markets which didn't put a high enough value on science; of anyone, in short, save deCODE. Stefánsson suggests that only a politically motivated left-wing journalist would think of asking him questions about the grey market."[50] In spite of exploiting everything Icelandic, deCODE bore no responsibility.

RAGNHILDUR AND GOLIATH: PRIVACY AND GENETIC INHERITANCE

In 2003 deCODE faced a new setback, a Ragnhildur and Goliath story. On November 7, the Iceland Supreme Court ruled in favor of eighteen-year-old Ragnhildur Gudmundsdottir, who did not want her dead father's records transferred to the database. She challenged the company's encryption system, arguing that it would be easy enough to identify her through her father's records, given that she shared half of his DNA. The data was not anonymous, given that the family links were absolutely necessary but, as was the case in all three of the databases, would be encrypted when braided with any other.[51] She was right, of course, that deCODE would always have the ability to identify people.

Roberto Andorno, a bioethicist, explains the case: "The court said that the one-way encryption system was, in general, a sufficiently sage mechanism for data protection, but in this case, the possibility of an indirect identification is increased by the fact that the Health Sector Database would allow information to be linked with data from genetic and genealogical databases. Consequently, including the records in the database might allow the plaintiffs to be identified as an individual at risk of any heritable disease her father might be found to have had." The Court was far from sure that her privacy could be protected, which had the wider implication of making the 1998 law unconstitutional because it failed to protect personal privacy.[52]

Ironically, Kári Stefánsson has similar qualms and isn't one of his own research subjects. The question of privacy cuts two ways. Research subjects might not want their results revealed to others, but they may also not want to know themselves. Unlike Craig Venter, the pioneering geneticist who published a draft of his own DNA in a race with the Human Genome Project, Stefánsson has no wish to know his own. "My mother died at the age of 62. My father died at the age of 67. And therefore I have been very diligent about avoiding to learn anything about my own disease predisposition. I want to die ignorant of my weaknesses."[53] The ironies of a man who would expose the weaknesses of a country not wanting to know his own are deep.

Stefánsson offers an example of how the database allowed deCODE to identify the mutation of BRCA2, the inherited breast cancer gene, in Iceland. Only 0.8 percent of the Icelandic population carries it, but of those women, there is an 86 percent probability of developing potentially lethal cancer. "We can, at the push of a button, find encrypted ID of all these carriers," Stefánsson said, belying the notion of the privacy of deidentified data but raising the question of the ethics of disclosing that information.[54] "If society would want to use this, they could find these women, they could approach them, and they could mitigate most of this risk." But, "for the moment, society is struggling with whether or how to use this. One of the concerns . . . is that by approaching these women, you would be violating their right now to know."[55]

It's worth reading Masha Gessen's *Blood Matters: From BRCA1 to Designer Babies, How the World and I Found Ourselves in the Future of the Gene.*[56] Gessen is one of those women who inherited the breast cancer gene from her mother, who had died of the disease. *Blood Matters* is a long meditation on inherited genes and the process of trying to decide whether to have prophylactic surgery, a double mastectomy and her ovaries removed, in order to forestall the possibility of developing breast or ovarian cancer. Her risks at thirty-seven were low, 14 percent, but would increase to 50 percent by her fifties. In order to understand the pros and cons of her decision, and the science that was both a blessing and a curse, she interviewed medical experts, religious thinkers, scientists, historians, and many people who faced decisions similar to hers, trying to ascertain how genetic information had irrevocably altered who we think we are, how we feel about those from whom we inherited bad code—and who we think we will become. Genetic information has provided a new way of knowing the self, and its lurking dangers, but it is by no means a panacea or an unadulterated good. Disease prevention through testing of potential parents raises all kinds of questions about what counts as an unacceptable disease versus the potential for an acceptable one—should we eliminate the possibility of all children with Down's syndrome, for example? Icelanders are in the middle of this question.[57] Some people find out they have the gene for diseases for which there is no cure—Huntington's—and become hyperobservant about behavior that might indicate its onset. We know much more about genetic risks than genetic cures.

The legal challenge brought against deCODE might well have factored into the decision not to finish the Health Sector Database. DeCODE gave up on the idea of the database, firing approximately two hundred employees who had been inputting the data. But even without the database, deCODE had amassed about 110,000 blood samples with their medical records from Icelanders who had voluntarily submitted samples through their doctors, more than half the adult population of Iceland. DeCODE created industrial-scale genetics, one of the first companies to do so.

Even without the Health Sector Database, deCODE was still able to make significant discoveries using the samples combined with the genealogical information in Íslendingabók. For example, as *Time* reported in 2006, Icelanders with a particular variant of the LTA4H gene turn out to be 40 percent more likely than average to have heart attacks. Scanning the DNA of other populations, deCODE scientists found that for African Americans, the variant indicated an increased risk of 250 percent. DeCODE had bought the license from Bayer for a prospective drug that could have a lifesaving effect if the drug ever reached the market. Critics worried that it would lead to further discrimination, thinking in future terms when insurers and employers might have broader access to the genetic histories of clients and employees. Quoted in *Time,* Stefánsson scoffed at that notion: "'You guys never needed genetics to discriminate against African Americans,' he says. 'You've done that completely unassisted by genetic discoveries.'"[58]

Kári Stefánsson's visionary determination, the company's driving force—Stefánsson was selected by *Time* the following year as one of the one hundred men and women "whose power, talent or moral example is transforming the world"—was also one of its biggest impediments. His dismissal of critics' concerns was cited as one of the major factors in the resistance that deCODE encountered in Iceland and from geneticists and ethicists internationally who raised red flags. Stefánsson, nothing if not blunt, hypothesizing that we might also inherit brain function from our parents, said of himself that he fears how much he takes after his father, a "nasty bastard."[59]

The ambitions of deCODE are not to be underestimated. The company's groundbreaking work on the genetic markers for Alzheimer's disease is designed to provide a "proof of concept" for the efficacy of beta secretase inhibitors as treatment for dementia. "The implication there," said Stefánsson, "is that if big pharma finally develops an effective inhibitor of beta secretase, it should not only be given to those at high risk of Alzheimer's disease, it should probably be put into the drinking water!"[60]

"I'm not joking, not at all," he continues. "I think it makes infinite sense to use for people who become sufficiently old who suffer age-related cognitive decline." Stefánsson uses statins as his precedent: "The pharma industry developed statins to treat very high blood lipids. Now we have started to give statins to people who were previously considered to have normal blood lipid levels, because it has been demonstrated that you can prevent a normal decline in vascular health by giving statins to a very large percentage of the population."[61] While these kinds of claims seem to support the idea that Icelanders have given up their genome for the greater good of the world, the analogy with statins is troubling. Allow me a brief sidebar into statins—one of the most popular, and possibly ineffective—drugs of the twentieth and twenty-first centuries.

In 2014 major controversy erupted about the efficacy and side effects of statins in controlling cholesterol. Researchers reviewed Angel Key's foundational research of the 1960s, particularly the "Seven Countries Study" in which he established the link between saturated fats and heart disease, which was to become unimpeachable science.[62] Even by the 1970s, his study was shown to have been deeply flawed.[63] He had ignored the effects of tobacco, sugar, and lack of exercise on the radical increase in heart attacks in the United States, using only the data that supported his hypothesis—that the consumption of cholesterol, an American diet high in saturated fats, was to blame for the spike in heart disease.[64] Much like Stefánsson, Keys was intellectually gifted and charismatic, and was so convinced of the rightness of his theory that he would tolerate no opposition.

Agrobusiness jumped on board, launching low-fat foods (spiked with sugar), and became a major sponsor of the American Heart Association. Scientific naysayers were blacklisted. The sugar industry joined the party, promoting the connections between cholesterol and heart disease in order to divert attention away from the links between sugar and heart disease. The Sugar Research Foundation commissioned Harvard scientists to review and critique research that pointed to any link; the resulting article published in the *New England Journal of Medicine* in 1967 did not mention any support from the industry.[65]

French cardiologist Michel de Lorgeril's research in the late 1990s confirmed Key's observation that diet and particularly the Mediterranean diet, full of saturated fats, olive oil in particular, produced one of the lowest levels of heart attacks. But his conclusions about the causal relationship were entirely different. The clinical trials for statins had indeed been impressive, and he, at one time, had also been a true believer. But the trials were 90 percent commercially funded, and the sponsoring companies had a vested interest in the outcomes and owned the data. The data, unlike experiments that are conducted in independent laboratories, belonged to the companies who paid for the research. It was proprietary information and was never released to independent researchers. Lorgeril's 2014 *Cholesterol and Statins: Sham Science and Bad Medicine* revealed the toxicity of statins, leading in particular to memory loss, and said that they worked because they reduced inflammation; lowering cholesterol was a red herring. De Longeril concluded, "Physicians should be aware that the present claims about the efficacy and safety of statins are not evidence based."[66]

De Lorgeril's research did little to slow the prescription of statins, and they became a multibillion-dollar business, the most prescribed drug of the twenty-first century. Statins have been prescribed to people who had

had heart attacks already, those at high risk, and, more recently, echoing Kári Stefánsson's hopes for Alzheimer drugs, those who were simply at a higher risk because of age. Patients began asking for statins because they had been frightened by sixty years of fat and cholesterol demonization. Some compared the discourse about cholesterol and complicity between doctors and industry to claims in the 1930s that smoking was good for your health. Nonetheless, in 2013, new standards for cholesterol levels were lowered to the point where one in six Americans could potentially be advised to take statins at a cost "of approximately 30 billion dollars a year." Once particular disease models take hold, they can be very difficult to dislodge, even if disproven.

SHIPPED OFFSHORE

In 2008 the demise of Lehman Brothers in the U.S. subprime mortgage crisis—the company that had underwritten deCODE on the NASDAQ—pushed deCODE over the edge. In spite of an impressive number of research publications, deCODE had yet to turn a profit and had lost $700 million. It filed for Chapter 11 bankruptcy protection. DeCODE's shares plummeted to forty cents, and assets that it had given to Lehman to manage were frozen. DeCODE fought to retain its listing, but failed. To stay afloat, it declared bankruptcy in 2009.[67] DeCODE sold off its subsidiary Islensk Erfdagreining, which conducted deCODE's human genetics research, managed its population genetics resources, and provided its personal genome scans and DNA-based risk assessment. DeCODE sold the core assets of the company—the country's genome—to a U.S. investment company, Saga Investments. Reviewing the sale in the *Genomics Law Report,* Dan Vorhaus observes that the deal was conducted at "fire sale" prices. The bankruptcy court refused an objection that a consumer privacy ombudsman be allowed to review the deal.[68]

Saga, including the original investors, rescued the company. "Even though we are [venture capitalists], it's not just about financial returns," said Terry McGuire, a cofounder of Polaris Venture Partners in Waltham, Massachusetts. "We decided it really was a world treasure."[69] The fate of its database was unclear, though Stefánsson maintained that it and the biological samples themselves could not be sold because of the legal restrictions on their use. "The database will never be managed by a foreign organization," he said. "The data are sensitive," said Stefánsson. "We are a proud nation, and the data are not for others to manage."[70] But there were few international laws, if any, that applied to the Icelandic database.[71]

DeCODE, like Iceland, had pluck and fortitude. The country recovered, thumbing its nose at foreign banks that had borne the burden of insuring the savings of their own nationals who had invested in Iceland's banks.[72] And in 2012, with many more research papers, and a growing wealth of data and analysis, but no developed drugs or genetic therapies, the company was sold again, this time to U.S. biotech giant Amgen for $413 million. Observers noted that the genetic data was easy to come by; the real value of deCODE was the additional access to medical and genealogical records.[73]

The investors who saved the company in 2009 made a significant profit, multiplying their investment eightyfold in three years. At the heart of this deal was what Icelanders had given to deCODE in the first thirteen years: 140,000 blood samples and full medical records to go with them, mostly provided to deCODE through discrete collaborations with doctors interested in specific diseases. But those donors and the people who had invested in the company prior to 2009 saw none of the profits of the sale.[74]

In the early days of deCODE and Roche, there had been a robust discussion of public compensation for the Iceland resources of health information, genetic material, and genealogies.[75] In the end, neither Roche nor deCODE ever paid Icelanders any compensation, and the free drugs promised to the country never materialized—which might have been a good thing, since Icelanders would have then become a testing ground for newly developed drugs, their efficacy, and their side effects. Stefánsson argued that the value to Iceland was in the form of homegrown employment for the country's best and brightest and the development of a high-tech industry, moving the country away from its dependence on fishing. Indeed, the scientific studies and references generated by the database have been extensive.[76] The trade-off has been the development of a resource by auctioning off a nation's genome.

DeCODE had struggled to discover drugs or diagnostics in spite of its treasure trove of information, in part because, ironically, the Icelandic database was too narrow. Homogeneity and a small population sample turned out to be not so good for identifying the genetic causes of common diseases because the pool of Icelanders with particular diseases was even smaller. Amgen had other ideas about how to use the data, to predict the usefulness of drugs that were already in development. Stefánsson stayed on as the president of deCODE and became a vice president at Amgen. He emphasized, again, that the new ownership would not affect the management of the Icelanders' data. The DNA samples would remain in Iceland, and deCODE would continue to control access, subject to the privacy protections and ethics policies already in place.

In 2014 Stefánsson was third on the list of highest taxpayers in Iceland. DeCODE and the Icelandic records had made him a very wealthy man, and the Icelandic databases, a model of completeness, were the envy of the biotech world and the fantasy of every genealogist. "We have sequenced the whole genomes of 2,500 people. We have genotyped about 120,000 Icelanders with an Illumina chip. We can impute whole genome sequence down to variants with less than 0.1 percent frequency into about 370,000 Icelanders—there are only 320,000 living today! . . . We basically have the whole genome sequence of an entire nation."[77] As Stefánsson explains, "Human genetics is the study of human diversity." But the genome on its own is not enough. "What you are trying to do is to figure out how information lies in the genome that has an impact on human diversity. And having, for example, the genealogy gives you the avenue by which this information is passed from one generation to the next."[78] Indeed, it was the pedigree of the nation, the historical sagas of *Íslendingabók,* that allowed deCODE to impute the whole genome sequence in spite of having consent of only half of the population.[79]

The value of that database has become ever more apparent. Finding it had little use for the diagnostic arm of deCODE, Amgen created NextCODE in 2013. Originally developed from deCODE's population data, NextCODE allowed physicians to establish genetic matches for rare and common diseases. Amgen's announcement was enthusiastic about the potential of the database. "Leveraging the power of the database architecture developed at deCODE and licensed by NextCODE, this information can also be used by hospitals and research institutions for future diagnostics work to potentially find new insights to help other patients with rare diseases. This is both medically and commercially valuable to patients, to NextCODE, to its partners, and to Amgen. Simply put, everyone wins."[80] It took less than two years for Amgen to become the biggest winner. In 2015 it sold NextCODE to Chinese WuXi Pharmatech for $65 million, which then merged NextCODE and its own genome database into a new company called WuXi.[81] China has set its sights on becoming the world leader in genomics testing.[82] Ironically, in light of the world-wide circulation of genetic information, China tightened the rules on foreigners using Chinese genetic data; for Iceland, that ship sailed long ago.[83]

Myth, history, pedigree, science, and capital collided in one of the least populated nations on earth to create the world's most complete genealogical and genetic databases. In Iceland the idea that "we are all related" is a statistical probability; in the rest of the world, it will appear as a sublime nightmarish dream of complete connectivity.

CHAPTER 5

....

GENETIC GENEALOGY
The Double Helix of Inheritance

Family trees with their roots somehow mirror and are intertangled with
the double helix of genetics.

—Catherine Nash, human geographer

THE NEW "MUSEUM OF ME"

Dan Taggart, the cofounder of Ancestry.com, told me in 2010 that DNA
testing was the future of genealogy. He couldn't have been more right. By
2017 Ancestry.com had become the world's largest consumer genomics
provider.[1] The double helix of genetics and genealogy is now intimately
entwined as the bioinformatics industry made these two taxonomies of
inheritance into one lucrative root system. The history of these databases
and their role in the industry of genealogy more broadly is a story with
more branches than I can possibly chop, but the broad sweep is worth
synthesizing. In order to understand the drive to know our past at further
and further remove, we need to turn, once again, to a genealogy of the
commercialization of genealogy.

Like many scientific advances, genetic genealogy emerged on several
fronts at the same time, motivated by personal and scientific voyages of
discovery—and the necessity of involving others in those voyages. Four
projects in particular drove the industry forward, all with very different
starting points, resources, and narratives.

In 1997–98, the magazine *Nature* published several articles on new
Y-chromosome studies of inheritance. The Y chromosome is found in-
side cells like any other regular chromosome, but not in a matched pair.
Its partner is the X chromosome. With two X chromosomes, one is

biologically female (or somewhere on the spectrum); the Y transforms the fetus toward masculinity. While every other chromosome recombines in every generation, mixing the genetics of our parents and grandparents unpredictably, the Y chromosome doesn't recombine and is passed virtually unaltered from father to son (through a necessary but unremarked mother)—which is what makes it so valuable for the study of (male) genetic inheritance. The Y chromosome attracted attention in two studies: one tracing the priestly Jewish Cohen line and the other President Thomas Jefferson's possible patrimony of his slave Sally Hemings's male children.[2]

In the Cohanim (the plural of Cohen) study, the authors, scientists from the Universities of London, Haifa, and Oxford, were trying to prove that the Cohen tribe, biblically descendants of Moses's brother, Aaron, should be identifiable through the DNA of contemporary Cohens and distinct from the Levites, the descendants of Moses. The study did indeed prove a genetic relationship between modern Cohens and ancient ones, though the authors' confidence about the timing of the origin of the line had a wide statistical variance. Assuming a generation time of twenty-five years, they had a 95 percent confidence interval "of 84–130 generations for the combined Ashkenazic and Sephardic samples, 2,100–3,250 years before present," placing the origin of priestly Y chromosomes sometime during or shortly before the Temple period in Jewish history. They were less certain about the mutation rate, given the rapidly expanding and dispersing population. "Uncertainty in the mutation rate significantly broadens these intervals (conservatively taking 95% confidence intervals on both the distance and the mutation rate leads to an interval of 34–455 generations) as would a different assumption about the shape of the Cohen Y-chromosome genealogy."[3] The possible spread of 34–455 generations (850–11,375 years) makes the biblical correlation of the story Exodus and the origins of the priestly Cohen line a little more questionable. Moreover, the Levites, the lesser of the two priestly castes, showed significant genetic diversity, making the line from Moses impossible to trace.

While the study suggested that Jewishness was a biological inheritance, as the molecular scientist Ian Vincent McGonigle, an anthropologist of science in Middle East studies (with a PhD in molecular neuroscience), explains, given that the "Y chromosome mostly contains non-coding DNA, sequences that aren't thought to translate into a physically expressed trait, it is unclear whether identification of the Cohanim signature holds any

valid indexicality as to the nature of the bearers' body in terms of a physio-
logical or biometric characteristic, even though it might be read as a valid
inscription of ethnic history." The bigger issue is that the study raised
the fundamental paradox of what constitutes "Jewishness," even biologically. While genetic analysis can trace Jewishness genealogically by reading DNA up the paternal line, Jewishness, as it is rabbinically defined,
"can only be reproduced in the present, that is 'passed on' through the
maternal line through the process of gestation in a Jewish womb."[4] The
original Cohanim studies did not ask any questions about the cultural
significance or implications of these findings, even though they raised
the historically sensitive question of whether Jewishness was a racial or
religious category—or, in this case, a conflation of the two.

In the second study, of President Thomas Jefferson and Sally Hemings,
the question of race and historical harm was central. The Jeffersonian Y
chromosome was used "to throw some scientific light on the dispute" about
whether Jefferson was the biological father of one or more of Hemings's
sons. Since Jefferson fathered no known sons, the authors "compared
Y-chromosomal DNA haplotypes from male-line descendants of Field
Jefferson, a paternal uncle of Thomas Jefferson, with those of male-line
descendants of Thomas Woodson, Sally Hemings' putative first son, and
of Eston Hemings Jefferson, her last son."[5] The authors concluded that
the molecular findings failed to support "the belief that Thomas Jefferson
was Thomas Woodson's father," but provided evidence that Jefferson
"was the biological father of Eston Hemings Jefferson." The study was
quickly challenged for not considering a wider range of Jefferson males
who might have been genetic contributors to the "inbred" community
of the plantation. The scientists were forced to qualify their findings, but
maintained that their "modest, probabilistic interpretations" were ten-
able.[6] Rumors and debates more than two hundred years old were swayed
by the DNA evidence, provoking extended debates about the nature of
the relationship and its implications for American history and cultural
questions.[7] But in 1998, the novelty of the study and its seemingly conclusive evidence of a sexual relationship between a sainted president and an
enslaved woman, a probably coerced sexual partner, changed the face of
American genealogy.

Inspired by these two stories, Bennett Greenspan, a dedicated genealogist frustrated by the "dead ends" in his paper-trail research, had the idea

FIGURE 5. American DNA. Image courtesy of the author/Library of Congress.

that he could use molecular biology to break through genealogical blocks.[8] Greenspan convinced a "VERY reluctant male NITZ cousin in California and one of the several very willing NITZ males in Argentina" to take DNA tests to bust through his genealogical dead end.[9] The only problem was no commercial Y-DNA lab existed. Greenspan struck a deal with Michael Hammer, the coauthor of an earlier 1997 University of Arizona Cohanim study on which the 1998 study had built.[10] Hammer would test two dozen men of Greenspan's choice, as "a proof of concept." ("Proof of concept" goes against standard scientific methodology, which tries to prove or disprove a hypothesis. In this case, you test to prove true.) In exchange, if the proofs worked, Greenspan would be committed to starting a commercial enterprise. The University of Arizona would provide the science, and Greenspan would build the company. Greenspan obtained the DNA from his Nitzes; Hammer proved the concept. The haplotypes—a set of DNA variations that tend to be inherited together—of the Argentine Nitzes' Y chromosomes and those of Greenspan's Nitz cousins matched perfectly. The haplotype did not match any of two dozen control samples. The first genetic genealogy lab testing Y-DNA was launched in May 2000.[11]

The field of Jewish genealogy exploded in the decades after the Cohanim study, particularly as the study of genetically inherited diseases common to Jewish lines had already been the subject of medical research since the 1950s in Israel, based on data that had been amassed from immigrants who poured in after 1948.[12] It became clear, ironically enough, that there were no mtDNA markers that could definitively distinguish Jewish female lines beyond Europe, which led researchers to hypothesize that the history of dispersion was also a history of conversion, with many Jewish men taking non-Jewish wives as they migrated.[13] From where they migrated was particularly contentious, since the return to Israel was predicated on the tribal roots in the region. Debates continue, with definitive positions constantly under challenge and new as well as old theories gaining ground (for example, the Ashkenazi are really Khazar converts).

The science, the results, and the cultural meaning of the results are nowhere near settled and grow more contentious all the time. I have reduced this origin story of Jewish genetics to little more than a nub; a host of recent books provide very different summaries of the science and its meanings, including David Goldstein's *Jacob's Legacy: A Genetic View of Jewish History* (2008), Harry Ostrer's *Legacy: A Genetic History of the Jewish People* (2012), and Steve Weitzman's *The Origin of the Jews: The Quest for Roots in a Rootless Age* (2017). Given the status of Israel as a nation devoted to providing a homeland for Jews, the question of Jewish genetics and genealogy inevitably became a question of national belonging. Ian McGonigle put the problem starkly: the "epistemic value of 'ethnic genetics' and the political milieu appear to be 'coproduced,'[14] which is to say they beget and stabilize each other. . . . Crucially then, ethnic genes may serve to make states into more stable political realities, whilst states simultaneously create the conditions for the meaningful misrecognition of genetic material as bearing an essential identity."[15] And, indeed, in 2013, "the Israeli state announced that it may begin to use genetic tests to determine whether some prospective immigrants are Jewish or not. If implemented, the state would be enshrining Jewishness at the level of DNA, rendering 'Jewish genes' legally legible, and making DNA signatures a basis for decisions on basic rights and citizenship for the first time in its history," writes McGonigle.[16]

Raphael Falk, a geneticist at the Hebrew University of Jerusalem and persistent thorn in the side of those who would prove a genetic "race" of Jews, sums up the circularity of the research this way: "Obviously, what kept Jews' identity were their language, culture, tradition and religion. Thus, whatever their biological hereditary kinships, both the transgenerational vertical, and intra-generation horizontal relationships are secondary consequences. However, the increasing reliance on scientific reductionism in biological thinking of the last two centuries eventually culminated in turning the evidence of DNA sequences into the essence of the characterization of Jewishness rather than its consequence." But all the major direct-to-consumer testing companies offer to tell their questing buyers what percentage Jewish they might be. Suspicious of this science, in 2016 Eran Elhaik, a bad boy of computational genetics, invited/ challenged academic researchers, the public, and 23andMe to use his benchmark to test claims that Jews are genetically distinct from non-Jews. He didn't get many takers, and those who did failed the test.[17]

What Y-chromosome studies did for the popularity of Jewish genes and male lineage, Bryan Sykes, a geneticist at the University of Oxford, did for mitochondrial DNA. Mitochondrial DNA, derived not from chromosomes in the cell nucleus, but the cytoplasm, is also valuable, but of a different order.

THE SCIENCE OF TRIBAL ORIGINS

MtDNA is used to track maternal inheritance. While the Y chromosome is much more distinct, allowing geneticists to pinpoint patrilineal lines, mitochondrial DNA is much more plentiful, allowing for the grouping of peoples around the world. Unlike the DNA in the chromosomes, which we inherit from both our parents—boys the Y chromosome from their father only—all children inherit mtDNA from their mothers, but only females pass it on to their daughters.

We have in our cells, according to Sykes, "upwards of a hundred times more of it than any other type of gene."[18] Mitochondrial DNA "turns out to have special properties which make it absolutely ideal in reconstructing the past." Mutation rates in mtDNA are much higher than nuclear DNA, making it easier to distinguish population groups that have split off from one another. So, where written records quickly lose track of female lines, mtDNA keeps meticulous traces, but only through one line of surviving daughters. If, for example, you were to adopt this relational model through the maternal line, then you would have to discount a grandmother you might have cared for deeply—your father's mother. She simply does not fit into that model of genetic maternal descent. And DNA lines die out. All the people in the world today are products of surviving lines. According to Sykes, virtually any two people will be related through the maternal line; it's just a question of how far back. MtDNA is relational; Y-DNA is differential.

In 2001 Bryan Sykes published *The Seven Daughters of Eve.* The inspiration came from the 1991 discovery of the five-thousand-year-old Iceman in Austria. Sykes was asked to see if he could extract DNA from its ancient bones. Remarkably, he did and, even more remarkably, found a DNA match in the contemporary samples that he had been collecting in his lab. It wasn't difficult to crack the confidentiality code for the sample that matched; it turned out to be one of the women who worked in his lab. When he told her, Marie Moseley, that the Iceman was her relative, Marie began to develop tender ancestral feelings for the desiccated remains. Fascinated by the connection, Sykes imagined that we might all have these traceable DNA connections. "The past is within us all."[19]

In *The Seven Daughters of Eve,* Sykes tells us that he needed DNA from the Cook Islands to work out a puzzle about the origins of the Polynesians and native Hawaiians. With the help of the local government of Rarotonga, "within a few weeks I had collected five hundred samples from [the indigenous populations of] Rarotonga, Atiu, Aitutaki, Magaia, Pukapuka, Rakahangha, Manihiki and even from the tiny atoll of Palmerston (population sixty-six). I packed them carefully in ice and took them back to Oxford."[20]

Using mitochondrial DNA to type large populations of people (migratory patterns are mostly discerned using mtDNA), Sykes determined that almost all 650 million modern Europeans were descendant from seven maternal ancestors. To "bring them to life," he gave them names: Ursula, Xenia, Helena, Velda, Tara, Katrine, and Jasmine. These imaginary mothers who hypothetically lived tens of thousands of years ago—in the case of "Tara," Sykes's DNA mother, 17,000 years ago—became ancestors we could be proud of. Once Sykes's named these clan mothers, they "were no longer theoretical concepts, obscured by statistics and computer algorithms; they were now real women."[21] Lurking behind these seven was the African mother of all, "Mitochondrial Eve." The genealogical sublime has a maternal imaginary, somewhere around 150,000 years old, biblical, even if evolutionary.

Following the publication of *The Seven Daughters of Eve,* public demand for mtDNA tests soon outstripped the capacity of Sykes's laboratory at

Oxford, and Oxford Ancestors, incorporated as a University of Oxford spin-off, moved into a custom-designed lab in Littlemore, just south of Oxford. Sykes went on to establish the relationship between Y chromosomes and surname groups, beginning with his own, and soon the lab started offering tests for both parental lineages but still one genetic family at a time.

A parallel and even more ambitious development was under way in Utah, the nonprofit Sorenson Molecular Genealogy Foundation (SMGF), which had figured out how to combine Y-DNA tests with family trees to create a much more powerful data set. Scott Woodward, the CEO of Sorenson Genealogy, likes to tell the origin story of the database. In the late summer of 1999, Woodward was awakened one night at two in the morning with a phone call. "Are you Scott Woodward?" said the voice on the other end of the line.[22] Woodward was relatively certain he was. "Do you know anything about genetics?" Woodward was a professor of genetics at BYU. "This is Jim Sorenson. Do you know who I am?" One might take that as an existential question in this context, but it wasn't. Sorenson was the second-richest man in Utah; he had made his fortune in medical equipment. "I want you to tell me how much it would cost me to do the DNA of Norway," he demanded of Woodward. Sorenson was in Norway at the time, searching for his roots. Woodward explored that question for a few weeks and realized that it would be a tremendous amount of money. He told Sorenson, "It's going to cost you a half a billion dollars." "I can do that," said Sorenson, and Woodward remembered thinking, "I've set my sights way too low." But, he told Sorenson, "I think there's a more interesting question that we can ask here. I think we can do the DNA of the world, the entire world, for a tenth the cost."

Sorenson's dream, reshaped by Woodward, was to create a database that would allow what would become the Sorenson Molecular Genealogy Foundation to tell any two people in the world not just if they were related to each other but how they were related to each other through common ancestors and their shared DNA. "The idea behind that," Woodward said, "is that if we can make that difference in people's lives it's going to change the way they think about each other and hopefully the way that they act towards each other. This becomes much bigger than just a science project, much bigger than just a genealogy project." Even though Sorenson's motivation for exploring the use of DNA for genealogy came from a lifetime of doing his family history duties as a member of the LDS Church, the foundation was careful not to tie itself to the church in any way. They used the records—they would have been foolish not to, admitted Woodward—but didn't want church interference in their mission.

Woodward thought that if the company had one hundred thousand DNA samples in its database, with their accompanying genealogies to at least four generations—and that was critical—"it would be likely that we could take just about anybody in the world and let them know whether or not they were included within a small population of people, or excluded from that small population of people." They arrived at the figure of one hundred thousand by estimating that it would take about two hundred individuals per cluster to be able to rule in or rule out genetically. If they could find five hundred of those clusters throughout the world, then they thought they could develop a pretty good map of the world.

Woodward's idea participated in the autosomal testing that became the basis for large-scale population and migration studies, again based on generation and mutation modeling, identifying the major haplogroups in the world.

But that process assumed nice packages of populations, and the world isn't organized that way. By combining genetic information with a family tree, they could enlarge the database with fewer samples, creating two powerfully braided databases. DNA sampled from a living person could also be assigned or imputed to that person's parents, four grandparents, eight grandparents, and so on. They were able to build "genetic pictures of populations that existed in the past" by linking the DNA of living people to family trees hundreds of years old. Linking DNA samples with the genealogical information allowed the company to go back hundreds of years to identify many more people than just the original populations they sampled, breaking them up into thousands of clusters. Now these groups are being recast as smaller "genetic communities," offering orientation of both being indigenous and having migrated. Subdividing the clusters led to "real family units": "terminal groups" of people, "family."

"Ten years ago," Woodward told me in 2012, "DNA genealogy didn't exist. . . . It wasn't until we built the data sets, the DNA data set and the genealogical data set, and built the tools that allowed them to be combined that you could really use DNA to do genealogy." In order to do this genealogical research—all geneticists agreed—they needed a critical mass of

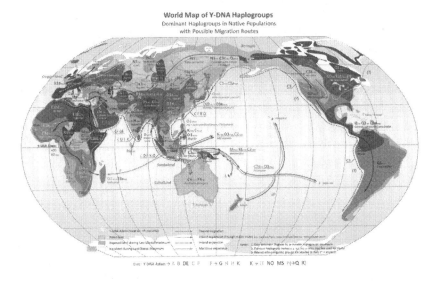

FIGURE 6. World map of Y-DNA haplogroups with possible migration routes (note "Y-chromosome Adam" near Cameroon). Image by Chakazul. This work is licensed for use under a Creative Commons Attribution-Share Alike (CC BY-SA 3.0) License (https://creativecommons.org/licenses/by-sa/3.0/deed.en).

data.[23] And so the Sorenson Molecular Genealogy Foundation was born as a nonprofit genetic genealogy project and began to solicit DNA, collecting its first data sets in March 2000. They patented their method in 2001.

SMGF began with BYU students. From those results Scott Woodward and his colleagues tried to determine how many children Joseph Smith had sired, he of an indeterminate number of "wives." The results were not entirely conclusive.[24] SMGF collected samples (and genealogical histories) from 170 countries, but the most valuable samples were from genetically isolated populations: villages in South and Central America, where the descendants of the Incan, Mayan, Aztec, and Toltec Empires lived; closely knit Mennonite populations in the United States and Mexico; and large sample sets from every African and European country and from China, Singapore, Micronesia, Nepal, Kyrgystan, and the Mongolian steppes. Scott Woodward's breakdown of the Mongolian collection distribution is that 85 percent of the Mongolian DNA was gathered from villages and tribes.

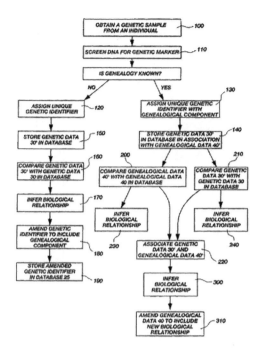

FIGURE 7. Patent: method for molecular genealogical research US7957907 B2. Source: United States Patent and Trademark Office, www.uspto.gov.

The project of genetic genealogy would be built on a gift economy that drew—and continues to draw—on the excitement and appeal of participating in a larger scientific knowledge project with a promise of return in the abstract. And that excitement contributes to the size of the database. Since the data set is only as good as its depth, all of these companies needed new consumers to provide their DNA in order to improve both the science and their sales pitch—the largest database, the most complete database, and so forth. The size of the data set matters, whether it be genetic or on paper. The truth of the matter holds: the data set needs us as much as we need it. SMGF soon realized that people who contributed to the database wanted access, along with other people who didn't contribute to the database. To facilitate that access, they set up GeneTree, which offered DNA tests for a fee. Buyers could then compare their results against the database, the samples that had been collected on a volunteer basis.

From early on in the foundation's history, it had incorporated commercial aims. One of the companies that "sat inside" SMGF was called "GeneTree." Now the story gets a little less altruistic. Woodward explains:

> When the foundation built the database, we essentially went out to the world, and we collected DNA and genealogical information and brought that back to the foundation. When we collected that information, we told the people, and that was the consent, "You are not going to get anything back. This information is going to go into a database that will be available for people to search. You'll be able to come into it, just like everyone else, but you are not going to get any special favors because you are part of the initial database."

Jim Sorenson had a gift for making money, and even his nonprofit venture turned out to be extremely lucrative. Four years after SMGF started collecting data, the profit side was already up and running. Writing for *Forbes*, Matthew Miller published an interview with Sorenson in 2004, "Shrewd, Very Shrewd," in which Miller surveyed Sorenson's hugely successful business ventures. Sorenson was eighty-two by then, with sixty grandchildren and great-grandchildren. "Most intriguing of all, perhaps, is SorensonGenomics, an umbrella company that bundles the old man's best moneymaking impulses with his most expansive DNA dreams. GeneTree does paternity testing, a $1.9-million-a-year business. For $190 RelativeGenetics produces Y-chromosome profiles that identify twenty-six markers on an individual's DNA. (The Y markers are the simplest way to scale a 'family' tree.) That doesn't mean much until you match your markers against the 40,000 DNA samples in the database of Sorenson Molecular Genealogy Foundation, a nonprofit that, paradoxically, holds the most profitmaking potential." The nonprofit database was the secret to the for-profit venture. After Sorenson died in 2008, the nonprofit SMGF continued to be supported by a legacy fund he had established, hitting its target of one hundred thousand DNA samples in 2010.[25]

"And what will the foundation do with all this DNA?" asks Miller—a question I also asked. Sorenson invoked the idea of world peace, exactly as Scott Woodward had answered for me. Miller doesn't quite buy it. "In the next breath he is extolling the frontiers of genetic capitalism: 'Once the database is complete, it will become a gold mine of information,'

Sorenson says. Presumably drug companies will pay lavishly for its secrets," observed a clear-eyed Miller.

I asked Scott Woodward that question directly: "I understand that the foundation is nonprofit, but you are amassing a very valuable database." Woodward didn't quite manage to suppress his smirk. "You are correct," he said, regaining his composure. "I think that the SMGF database is extremely valuable, and there are lots of ways in which it is valuable other than in monetary means, as you can see from the effect that it has on individuals who find something and find it useful. That's a value that's pretty hard to put a dollar figure on." He did admit that Sorenson was talking about collaborating with other companies, but he wasn't at liberty to talk about that. He stressed, however, that SMGF "owned the data," the braided genealogical and genetic information and the biological samples, and that any other company would be able only to license that information.

Shortly after the database was finished, somebody did indeed pay lavishly for its secrets. In 2012, the year that I interviewed Scott Woodward, Ancestry bought GeneTree and all the "DNA-related assets" of SMGF, along with Scott Woodward, outright. This wasn't the first time Ancestry had made a play for SMGF. The Ancestry.com partnership with Sorenson Genomics started in 2002.[26] The first go-round produced wildly inaccurate results and failed, and Ancestry shelved its DNA program. The partnership was relaunched in 2007 and formed the basis of Ancestry's DNA database and testing capabilities. The agreement saw the Generations Network (Ancestry) bring Relative Genetics and its DNA database under Ancestry's wide umbrella. Sorenson Genomics would now provide DNA testing services for the Generations Network, and Ancestry.com would now market DNA testing and database-matching services for genealogy purposes. Relative Genetics' DNA database (remember this is the nonprofit SMGF) would form the basis of Ancestry.com's growing DNA database.

The language of the agreement hedged about the foundation, but without the database and its CEO, SMGF was essentially mothballed. Here's how one blog, *DNAeXplained*, written by a computer scientist and passionate genealogist, reacted: "Those of us who had contributed our DNA to Sorenson for research purposes felt betrayed and exploited. Never did we imagine, in our wildest dreams, that our DNA would wind up with a commercial entity that would use our data, that was never 'released' to us, to profit. Nor were we notified."[27] There was, according to the grapevine, an "opt-out" option, but Ancestry didn't make it obvious.

And then that data set was sold on. In 2015 Ancestry.com agreed to share (for an undisclosed price) all of its braided genetic and genealogical records in partnership with Google-owned Calico research and development for longevity research and associated pharmaceuticals. Katie Palmer reported in *Wired*, "AncestryDNA isn't disclosing the financial terms of its data-sharing, but it stands to reason that it's making a tidy profit off of its customers' data. While a consumer gets a certain amount of information from their genetic test—information about their ancestry, or living relatives who have also gotten sequenced—their genetic data is almost always more valuable in aggregate. And for Calico, a huge genetic database could be worth a lot, especially once data-miners combine it with Ancestry's forest of family trees." A significant proportion of that data set had already been combined, since it was purchased from Sorenson as a braided set. With the sale to Calico, public access to the Sorenson Molecular Genealogy Foundation database of Y and mitochondrial results, complete with pedigree charts, now owned by Ancestry.com, was completely shut down, ostensibly for privacy concerns after a case of a police warrant for Ancestry.com DNA information in an Idaho cold case.[28]

The CEO of Ancestry, Timothy Sullivan (formerly the CEO of the global dating site Match.com), extolled the uplifting information that comes from DNA testing in a January 10, 2017, press release: "Right now, what most people want from a DNA kit is the chance to better understand themselves and get some sense of an answer to the question of 'Who am I?' That's a powerful, emotional thing, and as a company we want to make that experience as rich and rewarding as possible."[29] In the same release, Ancestry.com announced that it had sold 1.4 million AncestryDNA test kits in the fourth quarter of 2016, a record number. The company's blog boasted on the same day, "We are the largest consumer genetic testing company! It took us 11 months to go from 1 million to 2 million customers and just seven months later, we've surpassed 3 million customers in our AncestryDNA database." The next day Sullivan would present an overview of the company's growth and direction at the thirty-fifth annual J. P. Morgan Healthcare Conference. By 2017 the number was up to

4 million; by 2018 the company had amassed more than 7 million DNA samples, by 2019 more than 15 million, winning the database-size battle with 23andMe.[30]

On its corporate pages, Ancestry.com now calls itself a "Science and Technology Company," though you won't see the company advertising itself that way in any of its television or online campaigns.[31] Ancestry has clearly shifted its goals from amassing the records of the world to using the genealogy business to grow its technological assets; its braided genealogical records with its DNA database have turned it into a "medical research juggernaut."[32]

The fourth major player in the popularization of genetic genealogy and perhaps the one that took greatest advantage of a common desire to participate in a "larger knowledge project" was a latecomer to the scene. In 2005 Spencer Wells, the U.S. National Geographic Society, IBM, and the Waitt Family Foundation launched the National Geographic Genographic Project.[33] The Genographic Project was possibly the most controversial of all, yet on the surface the most altruistic and benign. It was a genetic anthropology study whose goal was to map historical human migration patterns by collecting and analyzing DNA samples from indigenous groups as a baseline against which the West could measure its genetic ancestry. The research plan was to collect DNA samples from 100,000 indigenous people, along with a minimum of 100,000 public participants who would pay $99. Paying customers would get a glimpse of their ancestry, based on the genetic information gleaned, some would say "pirated," from indigenous people. The money would be used to fund both the research and the payback projects for the sampled groups. Some 160,000 people ordered their self-testing kit and became "citizen scientists," contributing their DNA to the larger database.

The most controversial of the collection practices were those of the National Geographic Genographic Project. Spencer Wells, the lead in the project, stressed the urgency of this $40 million project: "The world is currently experiencing a cultural mass extinction similar to the biodiversity crisis." He cited statistics that in 1500, before the European "age of exploration," as many as fifteen thousand languages were spoken around the world. After five hundred years, there are fewer than six thousand left.

"We are losing a language every two weeks through the same migration process that is mixing the world's genetic lineages. While we hope that this will lead to a new sense of interconnectedness among the world's peoples, it also means that the genetic trails we follow will become hopelessly intertwined. When this happens we will no longer be able to read the historical document encoded in our DNA."[34] The "we" of this passage is clearly addressed to a European and American audience and not to "vanishing" populations who "have been living in the same place for a long period of time, so-called indigenous people." But the so-called indigenous people were not so keen on providing their DNA so that people from the West could figure out theirs.

Indigenous peoples had been subject to "biopiracy" in the name of Western roots before. In the mid-1990s, the Human Genome Diversity Project (HGDP), the forerunner to the Genographic Project, also proposed to study "isolates of historic interest." Claims that the research would help provide health information for these tribes were rebuffed by the example of the Havasupai of the United States. For the Nuu-chah-nulth First Nation of British Columbia, where samples taken from the tribes were used for research far and wide, years after the samples had been collected and without further consent, there was no benefit for the tribe itself in exposing inherited diseases in the population.[35] Indigenous resistance forced the cancellation of American government and nongovernmental organization funding for the HGDP and resulted in the "Declaration of Indigenous Peoples of the Western Hemisphere Regarding the Human Genome Diversity Project," a collective set of demands from indigenous groups from across South and North Americas. The consortium demanded "an immediate moratorium on collections and/or patenting of genetic materials from indigenous persons and communities by any scientific project, health organization, governments, independent agencies, or individual researchers," whose mission they understood to have been "to appropriate and manipulate the natural order for the purposes of profit, power, and control."[36] They objected not only on the grounds of exploitation but in view of their understanding of natural order as well. "To negate the complexity of any life form by isolating and reducing it to its minute parts, western science and technologies diminished its identity as a precious and unique life form, and alters its relationship to the natural order."

But none of those concerns are reflected in the materials that the National Geographic used to attract its Western paying contributors. Listen to Spencer Wells, the "explorer in residence" for the National Geographic Genographic Project and its leader from 2005 to 2015, in his 2013 video *Beyond Genealogy—Who Are You?* His pitch begins with a familiar story of lack: "Genealogy can only get you back so far." He's a ruddy-faced man with blond hair and green eyes talking against a backdrop of animated genetics.

> Who are you? . . . You can research records, maybe learn more about who your family is, and where they all came from, but if you're lucky the paper trail goes back maybe a couple of hundred years. . . .
>
> But the human lineages go back around two hundred thousand years to one person on your mother's side and also the one person on your father's side that we're all related to. How can you get there? The answer is you can't—unless you look at your DNA. Your DNA contains a road map all the way back through time to those common ancestors. It's as if they were dropping bread crumbs on your DNA to let you find your way back home. . . .[37]

Wells tell us that we will find something close to Adam and Eve, "to one person on your mother's side and also the one person on your father's side that we're all related to," the original parents of all our genetic lineage that at the same time tell the story of "you." The story of "me" is at once mine and everyone else's. We find an individual entry into the family of man, with Adam and Eve of the line as indigenous überparents. In the end, the National Genographic Project, even given its partnership with Walt Disney Studios, could not compete with the larger for-profit companies. It stopped selling tests in May 2019 and announced it would shut down its website as of December 2020, after which those who participated in this alluring science project will no longer have access to their data.[38]

Tribal affiliation is an attractive prospect in settler societies where admixtures are the norm. Autosomal testing offers some sort of ethnic or racial identity that can be quantified and authenticated. As much as larger swaths of genetic inheritance can be confirming (or not), small percentages of something can be a badge of pride. As Catherine Nash, Dorothy Roberts, Alondra Nelson, and Kim TallBear, to name only a few of the better-known critics, all point out, the reinscription of race, ethnic and tribal affiliation, is central to the fantasies, if not the actualities, of genealogical genomics.[39]

Indeed, one American company stands out in this regard, AfricanAncestry.com. Founded in 2003 by geneticist Rick Kittles and entrepreneur Gina Paige, the specialized database has assembled the "world's largest database of African DNA lineages," offering MatriClan tests for women only and PatriClan tests for men.[40] Kittles used the early DNA reference results of the African Burial Ground Study at Howard University to establish his proprietary database, much to the dismay of his research associates.[41] Kittles's work was advertised by Henry Louis Gates Jr.'s popular PBS documentary miniseries *African American Lives* (2006–8), featuring the stories of Oprah Winfrey, Morgan Freeman, Whoopi Goldberg, Maya Angelou, Ben Carson, and other successful African Americans.[42] When Gates tested himself—he and his father were the first father-son combination and the first African Americans to have their genome completely sequenced—he was shocked to find out that he was "half white." Alondra Nelson's *The Social Life of DNA* delves deeply into the complexities and possible reparative findings of DNA testing for African Americans and into Kittles's role in popularizing targeted testing. Gates's more recent PBS series *Faces of America* and *Finding Your Roots* reveal the extent to which all Americans are admixtures, which, Gates believes, will deconstruct the notion of race, while at the same time revealing the family and historical "secrets tantalizing hidden" in the DNA of African Americans.[43]

The paradoxes of DNA testing for admixtures and ethnic inheritance are rife, particularly the paradox of whiteness that likes to claim minority blood. I'll explore this question of what I think of as the "new native" in the next chapter through recent studies of one of the largest and most successful direct-to-consumer genetic heritage databases, 23andMe.

The company 23andMe, a new model of direct-to-consumer genomics combining genealogical and medical genetics, was founded in 2006 by Anne Wojcicki, Linda Avey, and Paul Cusenza with angel-investor funding from Wojcicki's then husband, Sergey Brin, the cofounder of Google. Wojcicki's vision was that consumers with access to their own genetic information would be empowered in the medical system and that the data would lead the way to more personalized medicine, shortcutting the cumbersome clinical studies. The roots half of the business offered a familiar breakdown of global ancestry by percentage, but combining testing for the percentage likelihood of genetically inherited diseases, the company broke new ground. "Welcome to you" is the invitation offered by the company on its sales kits. The pitch that we need to buy information to know ourselves is all too familiar; the implications of amassing biodata in private genome banks turned out to be a new frontier.

Biobanking is the golden egg of the direct-to-consumer genetic genealogy industry. Consider this worrying analysis published in 2016 in the *BMC Medical Ethics*, "23andMe: A New Two-Sided Data-Banking Market Model." The authors, all medical researchers working at French universities, observed that in the United States and Europe in the ten years since the company was founded, demand for DNA and biological samples from research laboratories grew substantially. At the same time, collecting data to meet that demand faced complex and conflicted ethical issues with respect to the ownership of medical information and data. "Given how difficult it is to obtain biological samples from a large cohort with the consent and full history of the patients in a short space of time by the standard route, the idea of creating an interface between individuals and researchers has emerged."[44] The researchers use their analysis of the 23andMe website and scientific literature to highlight how it and other American biotech companies "have specialized in medical genetics so as to become essential intermediaries between researchers and their research subjects, through the generation of DNA banks and biobanks containing hundreds of thousands of different samples provided for DTC genetic testing." The diagram below illustrates the business model of the "two-sided platform" and the ethical questions it raises.

As the tests became cheaper, dropping from $999 in 2007 to $99 for ancestry testing ($199 for combined heath and ancestry) in 2018,[45] demand increased exponentially, accelerating the value of the databank. "DNA banking is becoming a business and there is a rush to acquire DNA sequencing data, which may prove to be the organic and molecular equivalent of a gold mine."[46] We shouldn't be surprised that Google is the repository of that gold mine. Google was one of the principal investors involved in all four rounds of investment in 23andMe. Johnson and Johnson were also major investors in two rounds. So, just to review: Google owns Calico, which now "shares" Ancestry.com's DNA database, into which SMGF disappeared, *and* is the majority investor in 23andMe. The 23andMe biobank is now the world's largest repository of DNA samples that also

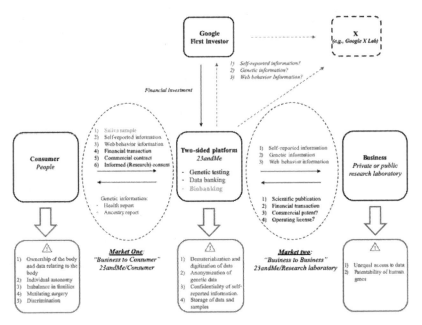

FIGURE 8. 23andMe two-sided market model highlighting ethical aspects of information and biological flows. Image from Henri-Corto Stoeklé, Marie-France Mamzer-Bruneel, Guillaume Vogt, and Christian Hervé, "23andMe: A New Two-Sided Data-Banking Market Model," *BMC Medical Ethics* 17, no. 19 (2016). This work is licensed for use under a Creative Commons Attribution 4.0 International (CC BY 4.0) License (https://creative-commons.org/licenses/by/4.0/) and is being used by permission of the authors. Two figures from the article have been combined into a single image.

contains extensive health information, willingly provided by customers. Our DNA is just another product of us we pay to provide to Google.

In 2013 23andMe ran into trouble with the U.S. Food and Drug Administration for violating the Federal Food and Drug and Cosmetic Act. The company's Personal Genome Service posed significant risk to the public, according to the FDA. "Some of the uses for which PGS is intended are particularly concerning, such as assessments for BRCA-related genetic risk and drug responses . . . because of the potential health consequences that could result from false positive or false negative assessments for high-risk indications such as these."[47] The FDA was particularly concerned that customers were interpreting their results without any medical guidance. The letter makes clear that the FDA and 23andMe had been locking horns since its inception. The company was ordered to "immediately discontinue marketing the PGS until such time as it receives FDA marketing authorization for the device." So 23andMe was left only to market its Ancestry testing, which didn't put much of a dent in its bottom line.

But as Charles Seife argued in *Scientific American* in 2013, even as the FDA was questioning the information that 23andMe was providing to its clients, it was missing the point. "As the FDA frets about the accuracy of 23andMe's tests, it is missing their true function, and consequently the agency has no clue about the real dangers they pose. The Personal Genome Service isn't primarily intended to be a medical device. It is a mechanism meant to be a front end for a massive information-gathering operation against an unwitting public."[48] In January 2015, 23andMe, backed by Facebook billionaire Yuri Milner and Google Ventures, signed a $60 million deal with the California biotechnology company Genentech, a subsidiary of the Swiss drug firm Roche, which gave Genentech access to the genomic and patient-reported data in aid of Parkinson's disease drug research. It was reported to be the first of ten deals with various biotech companies. Once again, observers pointed out, "Such deals, which make use of the database created by customers who have bought 23andMe's DNA test kits and donated their genetic and health data for research, could be a far more significant opportunity than 23andMe's primary business of selling the DNA kits to consumers."[49] The deal was widely reported in the financial and biotech press but seemed to garner little attention elsewhere. A few expressed skepticism: "Likening 23andMe to Google is uncomfortably apt. If you're paying a cut rate to have 23andMe sequence your DNA, you are 23andMe's product."[50]

In February 2015, the FDA cleared 23andMe to provide consumers with information about their "carrier status," genes that might affect their future children. On April 6, 2017, the FDA lifted its ban on 23andMe providing medical information for an additional ten diseases or conditions. Anne Wojcicki, cofounder and chief executive of 23andMe, claimed that this was a win for consumers who didn't need government protection from their own information and had a right to obtain it without a doctor. Indeed, 23andMe cannot sell tests in countries such as France, where, according to French civil law, individuals do not own their own bodies and cannot ask directly for genetic health tests to be performed.[51] In France any genetic tests must be ordered by and discussed with a doctor. Wojcicki is clearly opposed to this kind of protective paternalism. Wojcicki also thinks that 23andMe plays a significant role in promoting science and genetics education, pointing out that 80 percent of people who pay for tests altruistically consent to have their saliva and DNA stored in the company's biobank in order to contribute to the wider research community. The company's sites now do a reasonable job of foregrounding the consumer questions about privacy, consent, and risks, but it would be against their interests to discuss the larger financial and philosophical questions of amassing, selling, and sharing biodata. One example, though, illustrates the potential risks of generous donations of DNA to the pharmaceutical industry.

CODA: BACK TO UTAH

One other population rivals Iceland for the completeness of its genealogical records, the homogeneity of those who belong to it, and their willingness to volunteer DNA: the Mormons. Before deCODE in Iceland started assembling its early databases, and before any of the genealogical databases started testing DNA, researchers at the University of Utah had already embarked on the venture of looking for disease markers via family inheritance. Starting in the 1970s, researchers at the University of Utah were granted access to the church records and began braiding those records with all the available public health and mortality records. That allowed scientists to cross-index family trees with cancer clusters, disease patterns, and death rates. By the 1980s, they began collecting blood samples. It was a family affair. Ken Ward, a geneticist drawn to Utah for its population resources, describes drawing blood from families at family reunions. "We set up a little shade tent and have some orange juice and a phlebotomist. In between softball and hot dogs, people will run by to share family history, sign consent forms, learn about the study and, frequently, roll up their shirt sleeves and give a blood sample."[52]

That heart-warming scenario, which began with fifty big Mormon families, turned into something more proprietary down the road. Although their identities were shielded by the university, their raw data were shared around the world. The Mormon families of Utah were not as pure as Iceland, given the church's propensity for proselytizing and bringing converts into the church and into bloodlines, but it had another historical practice that made it just as valuable for establishing "founders" of genetic mutations. Polygamy, it turns out, is good for genetics. Prominent Mormons from the 1840s to the 1890s took multiple wives, following Joseph Smith's prodigious example, until the church disavowed the practice in order for Utah to gain statehood.[53] Though several sects continued to practice polygamy, in those two or three generations, the genetic contributions of a small number of men were vastly amplified. A genetic mutation could be passed exponentially from a father through multiple wives, who then bore multiple sons, who passed it through multiple wives again to multiple sons. Contemporary Mormon men also tend to be faithful, resulting in less than 1 percent "nonpaternity" surprises, compared to 5 percent in the broader United States, so the genealogical and genetic lines match closely.[54]

Mark Skolnick was also a geneticist at the University of Utah who was involved in early genetic linkage studies involving Mormons. But he felt left behind because as a population geneticist, he found he was laying the statistical groundwork for molecular biologists who then reaped the glory of actually discovering the genetic mutation that caused disease. In 1990, in order to give himself a competitive edge, he formed a company called Myriad Genetics with Peter Meldrum to harness the church records and pedigrees to help map and clone genes, specifically with the goal of isolating the breast cancer susceptibility gene, or BRCA1. Skolnick came up with the idea of "using an industrial answer to the question." He believed that "we then as a company could serve a great social purpose of bringing a diagnostic test, an extremely high quality commercial level diagnostic test, and the education that's required to change doctors' practices, to the world if we were able to discover that gene. And we in fact were able to convince investors that we had a reasonable chance of finding that gene, or other genes if we lost that race, given the resources that I had developed here in Utah."[55]

His fiercest competitor was Mary-Claire King, a geneticist at the University of California, Berkeley, already famous for discovering that human and chimpanzee genes were 99.5 percent identical.[56] She had been searching for the breast cancer gene for seventeen years, recruiting families with high rates of breast cancer, trying to answer the question if some forms of breast cancer might be inherited. She had discovered the BRCA1 locus on Chromosome 17 by studying the linkages in fifteen hundred families with early-onset breast cancer. She published her results in 1990, in part to secure more funding to actually find the gene. Skolnick didn't want to be left behind this time and took advantage of her intellectual generosity (and naïveté). The race was on.[57]

In the end, Myriad and their collaborators announced in 1994 that they located a strong candidate for BRCA1. Their competitive advantage had much to do with the number of collaborators, venture capital funding—and Utah's extraordinary genetic resources: large stable families and the vast genealogical archives of the Mormon Church. What Myriad did next is a lesson—much like that of deCODE and the development of the genetic genealogy industry as a whole—of what happens when venture capital funds health research: the company applied for and received a patent on the breast cancer gene. Their first patent was granted in 1997. And although they were not the first to find the second breast cancer gene, BRCA2, Myriad was the first to isolate it, and they patented that gene in 2001. The patent was challenged by medical researchers and other stakeholders, who mounted legal suits against seven patents owned by or licensed to the Salt Lake City–based biotechnology company Myriad Genetics, Inc. The most egregious patents involved two genes linked to breast and ovarian cancer. In June 2013, the U.S. Supreme Court decided in *Association for Molecular Pathology et al. v. Myriad* that isolated gene sequences were patent ineligible, but synthetic or cDNA—when the gene sequences don't match those occurring in DNA segments in the body—was patent eligible.[58] A number of labs then launched BRCA tests that competed with Myriad's tests. Myriad quickly sued them.[59] The issue of the private ownership of public genes isn't going away, as the U.S. Congress introduced a draft bill reconsidering the question of gene patents in June 2019, much to the dismay of researchers and to the delight of the biomedical and pharmaceutical industries.[60]

This very abbreviated story of the patenting of the BRCA genes and tests offers us an example—as did the story of Iceland—of the other side of the gift economy of genealogical and genetic information. While the potential to save lives is significant (though not without some very complicated decisions about probability and prophylactic treatment),[61] no participant in recreational genealogical genomics will ever realize the value in monetary terms of what they have freely given in exchange for nebulous promises of future cures. That said, many contribute knowing full well the trade-offs.[62]

So what made twenty-six million people buy ancestral DNA tests in spite of knowing that they were the product? Again, it returns to that unanswerable and therefore sublime question: "Who do you think you are?"

CHAPTER 6

....

THE NEW NATIVE
Sublime Percentages of Self and Belonging

If the question "Who do you think you are?" suggests that we have incomplete knowledge about ourselves that we need to be whole, the answers tend to provide exactly the opposite: percentages of the self and origins everywhere. The science fractures us into ever-smaller parts, while the social narratives put us back together in ways that serve to reorient us in the world. That disorientation of the fractional genetic sublime is quickly corrected by the reassuring idea that we are all related. We are all cousins.

One of Ancestry.com's most successful advertising campaigns, in consort with a travel company, Momondo, followed exactly this pattern of disorientation and reorientation. Mounted in 2016, *Momondo—The DNA Journey* is an eight-minute video that has been viewed more than twenty-eight million times on the company's Facebook page.[1] The purpose "of The DNA Journey campaign is to show that we, as people, have more things uniting us than dividing us."[2] Momondo was riding the wave of—and promoting—the phenomenon of heritage or legacy tourism.[3] *The DNA Journey* begins with the tagline "Would you dare to question who you really are?" Dramatic music accompanies slow-motion shock rising on the faces of selected participants. All the participants were proud of who they were and their countries of origin and weren't shy about nations and nationalities they didn't like. Inevitably, these were nations and peoples with whom there had been political conflict in the past or ongoing conflict in the present. (We can assume that the relative homogeneity of attitude was a process of selective auditions.) Then comes the anodyne explanation of how DNA works, delivered by actors playing scientists (some of the subjects were also revealed as actors after the fact). The DNA expert is actually Brad Argent, the international commercial development director and spokesperson for Ancestry.com, who has a graduate diploma in counseling. He is neither a scientist nor a geneticist. He is the primary pitchman for AncestryDNA. "Do you know how DNA works?" he asks a neophyte consumer. "You get half from Mom and half from Dad, 50 percent from each of them. And they get 50 percent from their parents, and back, and back, and back. And all those little bits of your ancestors, they filter down to make you you."

After spitting a tube full of spit, the participants are told, "The story of you is in that tube." Of course, all the subjects were sure that they were pure whatever—a notion that few people in the world actually hold and that we know is scientific nonsense. On the one hand, the Momondo pitch promises a one-world message; on the other, it confirms the genetic fallacy of measurable populations of pure stock. As Anders Johannes Hansen, a professor at the National History Museum of Denmark, explains it, "Whatever you measure the DNA up against, how do you decide what is 100 percent Danish, or German or English DNA? It's impossible—because we're part of a genetically multicultural story."[4] Kim Tallbear, writing about Native American DNA and recreational genomics testing, makes exactly the same point more bluntly: "Mixture is predicated on purity."[5] Two weeks later, the participants file back to be told their results. They are, predictably, as we all are, mongrels, some of them with percentages of DNA from nationalities they don't like—which was the whole point of the exercise. The British nationalist finds out he is 5 percent German, a nationality he intensely dislikes. He is thus shamed for his nationalism. "There would be no such thing as extremism in the world if people knew their heritage like that," said the Frenchwoman who found out she was significantly English. The most dramatic moment is when two of the participants are told they are cousins, though not how far removed. In individual segments devoted to each participant, it turns out their shared common ancestor was somewhere between 150 and 200 years ago, but they embrace as if they are indeed long-lost relations. It is a heartwarming message: "In a way we are all kind of cousins, in a broad sense," says Argent, sincerely. But cousin results are highly context dependent. Parent-child relationships are very clear. For anything beyond that, laterally, even siblings or, historically, aunts and uncles, we need genealogical information to confirm the nature of the relationship, since all of our genes recombine in every generation.

Cousin is a very relative word when you consider that your third cousin shares less than 1 percent of your DNA. Given the standard generational computation of twenty-five years, their closest ancestor was at least six generations or more. Shared DNA declines at a rate of 25 percent per generation, which means sixth cousins share (very approximately) 0.01 percent of their DNA. The red boxes in the diagram below show just how much or little DNA we share with close cousins, never mind ones removed by centuries.

Ultimately, this video is a pitch for a travel company and for DNA testing. Travel to the places from whence some part of your DNA has migrated (along with vast snippets of other DNA) is the antidote to a closed mind. One of the closing takeaway title cards reads: "You have much more in common with the world than you think." Human geographer Catherine Nash, who studies geographies of relatedness and the way we think about ourselves and our relationships to others through bonds of biological connections and place, set up the problem this way: "What these tests are

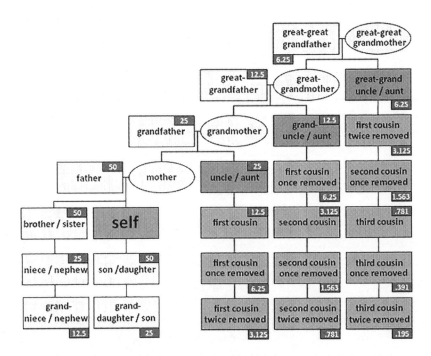

FIGURE 9. "Cousin Kinship Chart": the percentage of genetic relationship (gene share) of cousins to a "Self." Image by Dimario, Wikimedia Commons.

actually offering you is a place within a global geography of genetic difference. What you're being sold is a model of genetic distinction and a model of genetic connection. But the genetic connection is to particular other people in the world. Not the whole world. You're not told you're related to the whole world, because it doesn't make sense really to produce a test that will tell you that." How does the genetic genealogy testing grapple with that problem? "The idea that global families are all related frames an industry that is selling models of difference . . . These markers are meaningless alone. They only make sense in terms of comparisons."[6] 23andMe would launch a very similar campaign in 2019, pairing up with AirBnB to encourage heritage tourism, marketing cultural identities derived from consumer testing.[7] An industry selling relatedness relies on a notion of difference located in our bodies and in the world. With what percentage of ourselves do we identify? And how do we figure out what part of us is what?

As much as genetic genealogy loves the promise of its recurring tagline, "We are all related," the stakes of those relations vary intensely by contemporary categories of race, indigeneity, and cultural context. Here I want to talk, albeit briefly, about these very different stakes in "recreational genomics" and the infinitely smaller numbers that become part of our genealogical sublime. We cannot think about these questions without thinking about admixtures and racial identification, a mathematical computation that "proves" and "disproves" who we think we are. In 2014 23andMe published a study in the *American Journal of Human Genetics* titled "The Genetic Ancestry of African Americans, Latinos, and European Americans across the United States." The company analyzed samples of 23andMe customers in the following proportions: "We studied the genetic ancestry of 5,269 self-described African Americans, 8,663 Latinos, and 148,789 European Americans." Reviewing the study in the *Atlantic*, Rose Eveleth pointed out that the sample sizes corresponded to groups that were less likely to have their DNA tested for various social and historical reasons. "Out of more than 160,000 genomes, only 3 percent of 23andMe customers who authorized their data for the study were black, compared with the approximately 14 percent of the United States population who identifies as such. And while the paper traced what percent of white, black, and Latino customers' ancestry led back to Native Americans, there were few users, as far as the paper reported, 'who self-identified as native people.'"[8]

The study was to prove just to what extent 23andMe users, as a cross-section of the United States, were admixtures of all kinds, yet "The Genetic Ancestry" questioned at length the self-reported ethnic or racial identities of its subjects. "Self-reported survey data was used to generate cohorts of African Americans, Latinos, and European Americans. Out of 35,524 self-reported 'European' individuals, 35,279 selected 'white' on the ethnicity survey, yielding a per-survey error estimate of 0.2%. Out of 1,560 self-reported 'Latino' individuals, 1,540 selected 'Hispanic,' giving a per-survey error estimate of 0.7%. Lastly, out of 1,327 self-reported 'African American' individuals, 1,287 selected 'black,' resulting in a per-survey error rate estimate of 1.1%."[9]

We are clearly back to the problem of purity of racial categories even in studies that purport to prove the opposite—that ethnic categories are widely varying combinations rather than genetic consistencies. What constituted an "error" of identification? I couldn't find the answer to that question anywhere in this study, though this statistic suggests a cutoff of sorts: "Most individuals who have less than 28% African ancestry identify as European American, rather than as African American."[10] Counter to that statistic, the bioethicist Françoise Baylis asks the question, "What can it mean, in the face of pigmentation to the contrary, for me to assert with confidence that I am Black?" Baylis, who looks white, must assert her black identity in the face of being perceived as white. The statistics above have none of the nuance of identity formation. "We are both who we say we are (based on our own interpretation and reconstruction of personal stories) and who others will let us be (as mediated through historical, social, cultural, political, religious and other contexts)," including, now, genetic genealogy.[11]

The general results of the study show that a large proportion of participants had "ancestral compositions" that matched much of what we already know about U.S. history (pace Jefferson and Hemings). Roughly 5 percent of African Americans had a maternal European inheritance, whereas 19 percent had a paternal European line. It puzzles me a bit that European "ethnicities" were not further probed, particularly since all genetic genealogy tests identify proportions of other white ethnicities, such as Jewish or Irish, but it really seems that this was a study about skin color, rather than ethnicity, and the relative genetic contributions of light-skinned (read: Europeans) versus dark-skinned (African American, Native

American, and Latino) ancestors to various contemporary American ethnic identifications.

The observation that we might make about the respondents to the ethnicity survey that accompanied this study is that 92 percent of them were "white." The industry knows and promotes its products to its racial base. It also, somewhat cynically, understands itself in that light. In a July 2012 interview on the radio show *BusinessMakers*, Bennett Greenspan (the founder of FamilyTreeDNA) said, "Genealogy is a, so to speak, Western European sport. Most of our customers are either from America, Canada, Australia or the British Isles." In *Roots Too: White Ethnic Revival in Post–Civil Rights America*, Matthew Jacobson (and as Elizabeth Hirschman and Donald Panther-Yates highlight) cogently describes the emergence of white roots discourse out of the melting pot in reaction to identity politics of all stripes in the 1970s and '80s, much as the genealogy boom in the late nineteenth century was a reaction to "nonwhite" European immigration. But now, paradoxically, those markers serve as a point of pride. As Jacobson writes, "After decades of striving to conform to the Anglo-Saxon standard, descendants of earlier European immigrants quit the melting pot. Italianness, Jewishness, Greekness, and Irishness had become badges of pride, not shame." Wendy Roth reports in her study of one hundred Americans across the racial and ethnic categories who had themselves tested for genetic admixtures that white interviewees were drawn to the distinctiveness "of a nonwhite or multiracial identity as a corrective to their view of whiteness as boring or plain," while hanging on to the belonging afforded by being white. The surge in Jewish identity stems, in part, from a similar need to reassert difference after generations of assimilation into whiteness.[12]

Jacobson points out that millions of people did not become "newly absorbed in their ethnic heritage at the same moment" without "support and direction from the key institutions that engaged their lives," including television, film, government-sponsored heritage projects, school curriculum (in Canada), identification with Old World conflicts, and political leadership. We can now add the messages of the heritage industry to this list. Out of this evolved the "hyphen nation," one enthusiastically embraced by white (North) Americans, as a way of countering black nationalism, gender and gay identity politics, and indigenous rights—in a word, multiculturalism. People are apt now to call themselves Irish American, African American, Ukrainian Canadian, Asian Canadian, etc., while still claiming the prize of early or late arrivals. Time in the genetic genealogical world tends to be undifferentiated, as long as the bloodlines are clear.

Kim TallBear's *Native American DNA: Tribal Belonging and False Promise of Genetic Science* provides a historically detailed and nuanced account of the genetics industry and direct-to-consumer tests with respect to the science and narratives of having Native blood. As TallBear points out, the federal policy in the United States in the nineteenth century (and in Canada right through the twentieth with the residential school system) was to "*de*tribalize." Genetic genealogy has "*re*articulated trivialization of Native Americans in blood fractions and through bloodlines."[13] TallBear's discussion of her own "blood-quantum designations" on the reverse of her tribal identity card issued by the Sisseton Wahpeton Oyate of the Lake Traverse Reservation in South Dakota makes clear the strangely arcane complexity of tribal genealogical inheritance and its cultural and the material stakes:

> Degree of SWO Indian Blood: $\frac{1}{32}$ (my maternal great-grandfather was classified as $\frac{1}{4}$ Sisseton-Wahpeton).
>
> Other Sioux Blood: $\frac{1}{16}$ Flandreau Santee (my maternal great-grandfather was also classified as $\frac{1}{2}$ Flandreau Santee).
>
> Other Indian Blood: $\frac{1}{16}$ Turtle Mountain Chippewa (my maternal great-grandmother was classified as $\frac{1}{2}$ Chippewa); and $\frac{1}{4}$ Cheyenne and Arapaho (my maternal grandfather was classified as "full-blood" Cheyenne and Arapaho).[14]

Citing those fractions, writes Tallbear, makes her "think of my grandparents and great-grandparents. I remember their names and their parents' and grandparents' names. I remember how, through both dispossession and restricted choices, they came to be on the particular reservations now denoted in my blood-quantum fractions." And, as Daryl Leroux in his work in white settlers claiming indigenous blood, there are stakes in making genetic claims—particularly in Quebec and Nova Scotia—where the category of Métis has expanded exponentially as a way of making claims to lands. Beyond that, the entire question of the accuracy of these results was exposed by a simple ruse when dog samples submitted to a company that tests specifically for indigenous DNA came back with human percentages of indigenous blood.[15]

As Nash observes, "Genetic genealogy is so strongly framed by the idea that it will erode race, it will overcome race, and it will promote global harmony." The industry sells the idea that "we're all part of this global genetic human family" and "insists and repeatedly suggests that it's on the side of progressive anti-racism." But, Nash continues, we are "not being sold an answer that says we're all related, because you wouldn't need to buy the test. There's no market for being told we're all related."[16]

Alondra Nelson at Columbia University is the author of *The Social Life of DNA: Race, Reparations, and Reconciliation after the Genome* and one of the author and editors of *Genetics and the Unsettled Past*, about the "collision of DNA, race, and history." "The purpose of genealogy is to make stories," said Nelson—exactly what Kory Meyerink of ProGenealogists said to me at the very beginning of my research project: "We are stories. We've been stories since our ur-ancestors were scrawling on cave walls and learning to write, and I think that is what fuels the interest in genealogy today." So what's changed in the twenty-first century, said Nelson, "is that there is a different relationship to the story making." With conventional genealogy, "genealogists were involved in the story making because they would be doing the archival work, they'd been collecting oral histories from members of their families. What's different about genetic story making is that data or the evidence has scientific authority. You have scientists, capital *S* Science, capital *G* Genetics telling you who you are." Nash calls it the "technology-assisted extension of ordinary family history" that comes "with the expectation that the results can be incorporated into a usable narrative, that the science will make sense in an everyday context." Basically, as Nelson points out, "the companies are creating identity categories out of probability and statistics."[17]

Admixture testing shows us the limit case (which always matters for the sublime). Admixture testing, as Nelson explains,

> gives one a proportion of Subsaharan African, East Asian or European ancestry, to create these categories and give people percentages of their composite whole is also to make assumptions about what human history has been. And the assumption that admixture scientists make often is that at one time we were 100 percent. So there were populations that were 100 percent Subsaharan African, purely so, 100 percent East Asian, purely so, and that we can give contemporary people proportions of who they are

today. And that really flies in the face of everything we know about human behavior and also what we know in anthropology about human migration. We've been mixtures for a very long time.[18]

Bryan Sykes also refutes the idea that people once existed in racially pure groupings. "They never did," Sykes said. "We're just a temporary state of a huge swirling cloud of genes coming from all over the place."[19]

In the course of making my documentary, *Data Mining the Deceased,* I worked with Kevin and Lisa Winston, an interracial couple from Salt Lake City, to try to discover if several stories about Kevin's ancestry were true. For lack of any better language—and because no matter how much we talk about race as a social construct we still identify ourselves and others by skin color—Kevin is black and Lisa white. Lisa had a pretty good sense of family history, but Kevin could go back only a couple of generations on either side of his family. He had, however, stories that framed his concept of origins. The first was that his African ancestors had come from Ethiopia. "That's been the story," said Kevin, "brought down through the years on my mother's side of the family. And on my father's side of the family, Choctaw Indian. My grandmother . . . my father's mother, was Choctaw Indian, and they were from Austin, Texas. And then they moved to Oklahoma. Muskogee and Orchid, Oklahoma."[20] He had been to Africa once. "I actually got a taste of knowing who I am and where I came from when I went to Africa. But I still felt lost when I was in Africa, because it was like going to a family reunion and you knew none of your cousins." But, even so, he felt "at home." "It was a feeling that I never could get anywhere in the United States. It was a feeling that I don't think I could get anywhere in the world, except in Africa."

Another story about his family history was less uplifting. Kevin and Lisa had done a bit of research before I came to interview them, and the story they found and its burden seemed to be primarily carried by Lisa. "Well, what we found out on his mother's side was, back to the slave owner, if the information is accurate. We found it back to John Collette, who was the white slave owner, and those families originated from Knoxville after they were brought here under slavery conditions to live on his plantation. And that is how his mother's side of the family started here in America." The information had made Lisa mad.

Yeah, I was pissed. I was mad because he had actually impregnated their female family member with a mulatto child. It's my opinion that it was not a consensual sexual relationship because of the terms of slavery and everything they had to endure. . . . And so for me, being a white woman, having half African American children, it's very upsetting. I never thought I would have to explain to one of my kids that their family started from a white slave owner that raped their many ancestors' great-ago-grandmother.

We took Kevin to the Family History Library, where they had already prepared material for him. He was able to confirm a few generations back, basically what he already knew. No sign of a Collette. The Sorenson Molecular Genealogy Foundation agreed to test Kevin's DNA and let me film Scott Woodward telling Kevin his results. "We looked at your mtDNA," explained Woodward. "This is DNA that you inherited from your mother, who got it from her mother, who got it from her mother, who got it from her mother and her mother. Gwendolyn. Ella. Matilda. So when we looked at that DNA, we found that the type of DNA that you have there is probably not really surprising to you. It comes from Africa." They had identified his DNA as haplogroup "L3" with a subgroup of E3. The researchers at SMGF looked at more than seventy-seven thousand people in their database and found four people who were pretty closely related to Kevin in that they shared a common grandmother at some point in the near past. They then asked a question: Where were the terminal ancestors of these people? They found two people in their database who were genetic "cousins," one from Benin and one from Ghana. "Really," said Kevin, expressing surprise. "Ethiopia is out of it." Woodward confirmed: "We haven't seen anybody in Ethiopia so far." Kevin's Y-chromosome DNA told a different story.

"And this is where maybe you'll be a little surprised," said Woodward, preparing Kevin. "It's not African."

"Really . . . It is . . . ?"

"European." Kevin laughs, "Okay."

"Are you okay with that?" Scott checks in.

"I'm fine with that," says Kevin, though clearly bemused.

"It's fact now. It's real."

"Are there stories?"

"There are stories. We've been talking about the stories."

"It's pretty clear that it came out of Europe someplace. It's called I2B1M223."

"That's on my father's side! I'm white! I've got it on both sides."

"We're cousins," says Scott, holding up his hand for a slap.

Unusually, SMGF had found one other person in the database who was a very close match to Kevin with a common ancestor, probably within the last three generations, but with a different last name, which Woodward disclosed. The lab could act as the go-between if Kevin wanted to contact this relative. Also on that line was some suggestion of Native American DNA. Kevin had thought that he had Choctaw Indian blood on his mother's side through his grandmother, but now it seems that it came from his father's line, or perhaps both. "We shocked you with some European stuff," Woodward acknowledged, "but if you saw these people walking down the street, you would say African American. The European DNA is at least a couple of more steps back." In the end, Kevin was a bit confused about how he felt but joked that he had been called white since he came to Utah. "But we were having a discussion in my family about a white slave owner going back to the Colletes on my mother's side, and to hear that it's on my father's side." "Nothing is absolute," admitted Woodward, "but we are 99 percent sure."

In order to find out if Kevin had European blood on his mother's side, they would have to test his cousins, descendants of the siblings of his grandmother. The Native American line was a few steps removed. A lot of discussion followed about how to connect the lines and how to find cousins to test. Kevin and Lisa remembered meeting Colletes at a funeral; maybe that was the line that started with a white slave owner.

Kevin felt strongly that the information was really important to him, but went straight to the restroom to look in the mirror. After he'd thought about it for a while, he didn't feel quite so jocular. "I feel a disconnect kind of, from what I'd known and what I'd kind of been going with."[21] Lisa, however, was reassured by the DNA. "I'm not reassured any more based on paper, because all the stories that were told on paper or through word of mouth through the generations are obviously not true, because they are nowhere in the DNA." That said, the near-exact match in the database led to a young man whose father turned out to be a half brother, the first son of Kevin's father, whom he'd met once as a "cousin." He's a doctor in Los Angeles. Kevin finally found a doctor in the family. Kevin's son now has the flag of Ghana tattooed on his shoulder.

The stakes of having admixtures identified along racial lines are quite different for people who belong to visible racial groups and those that primarily present as white. In April 2019, Ancestry.com was forced to pull a commercial called "Inseparable," an ad that turned the history of interracial relations in the United States into a romance. "Inseparable," in which a white man pleads with a black woman to flee to "a place" with him so that they can marry, suggesting by costume and setting that they are secret lovers in the slave-owning South, unleashed a "torrent of backlash from people who accused the company of whitewashing the violent history of slavery."[22] While Kevin and Lisa struggled with the relationship between Kevin's sources of European blood and the historical realities of sex and slavery, for people who don't carry histories of oppression, a bit of another's blood can be exciting and exotic.

In Boston I interviewed Brenton Simons, president and CEO of the New England Historical Genealogical Society, the oldest genealogical society not only in North America but also, according Simons, in the Western world. I also had interviews arranged with the Harvard professor Henry Louis Gates, the host of several series of family history television shows, *African American Lives, Faces of America,* and *Finding Your Roots;* unfortunately, Gates canceled twice, perhaps because I had, in the questions I had provided before the interview, made it clear that I had some doubts about the industry. I also arranged to talk to Harvard neurolinguist Steven Pinker. I wanted to ask all three, among other things, about genetic genealogy and its relationship to more conventional forms of genealogical interest, and its racial implications.

The New England Historical and Genealogical Society, founded in 1845—one of the parallel societies to the Mormon Utah Genealogical Society—was a legacy of the work of John Farmer, who was convinced, and succeeded in convincing others, that genealogy, unlike the decidedly unrepublican pursuit of a pedigree, was central to the understanding of American history and the American family. The French historian François Weil credits John Farmer and his peer group of first-generation genealogists with "inventing and legitimating ideological acceptable forms of genealogical interest."[23] Simons is proud to be an inheritor of that history and a progenitor of the next revolutionary step in genealogy: genetic inheritance. The New England society prides itself on the accuracy of its records and the histories it produces, in contrast to the easy, but sometimes not all that accurate, information on Ancestry.com and in the Mormon database. But a few years ago, much against its historical methodology, the New England society began to publish studies by families who were engaged in genetic testing, recognizing that genetic proofs could support established pedigrees. The ramifications of genetic testing for genealogical research were huge, "because now," as Simons pointed out, "the proverbial story of the three brothers who came to Salem in 1645, who left descendants, can be tested." The society became very involved in trying to integrate DNA work into genealogy. As the cost of individual genetic genealogy testing dropped significantly, more and more people had themselves tested, including Simons. At first his reaction was "So what?" It didn't answer any questions for him. It does for many people who have genealogical questions that need resolution by a genetics test, but Simons didn't happen to have one of these questions, or so he thought, until he worked with Bryan Sykes, the author of *The Seven Daughters of Eve,* who was conducting a study on American DNA patterns for his next book, *DNA USA: A Genetic Biography of America.*[24]

Simons had documented his ancestry to a Mohawk woman but didn't have any physical proof until Sykes explained his results. "What Bryan Sykes did for me was to really open up that ancestry in a whole new way, because he, on hearing this story, said, 'Well, you've got to be tested.' And I was tested, and a small portion of my makeup identifies as Asian, which is where the Native American lineage presented." Sykes wrote Simons's story into his book. "For me," said Simons,

> that was a revelatory experience, because I certainly believed this lineage was there. But having a test to establish it made it all the more concrete. And so then I began to ask myself, well, what does it feel like to have a Native American line? What does it feel like to connect to an origin of a very different ethnic identity? So now, 20+ years into doing genealogy, something new and revelatory occurred to me that I wasn't expecting. One percent or less of my make-up has this Asian marker. So, it's a tiny percent. But it shows. . . . [I]t is in the results. It's there. And that's not Caucasian. That's not European. So, while I consider myself to be a Caucasian, and I am, I have something else in my ancestry that is very different, and so a scientific test that illustrates this is powerful to me.[25]

Though Brenton had heard through family tradition that there was a Native American line, and had been able to find that lineage through primary records, establishing a trail of evidence, the most dramatic layer of this genealogical trace, was the scientific testing, because it confirmed the truth of the narrative. The genetic test was at the top of a ladder of proof. The genetic test made him examine his feelings about that less than 1 percent Native blood. It made him feel "special."

I was struck by several things in this story. The first, which is an idea I would hear repeated by many people, though few as sophisticated about genealogy as Brenton Simons, was that the genetic genealogy provided some kind of absolute scientific "proof" of who they were. After twenty years of searching, Simons now knew he had Native American blood, which made him something other than descended from Caucasian immigrants. In other words, some small part of him was from "here." Simons declared, "I'm not going to change when I apply for something and I have to put my race. I'm still Caucasian. It hasn't changed my public identity. But, for me, it's an internal thing. It's something that makes me feel different. Maybe it makes me feel a little special, that I have something that not everyone has, or that a lot of people think they may have, and tests show they don't. That's often the case."[26] In Simons's example, European American or Caucasian American identification with these fractions and bloodlines as something "special" eradicates a history of Native American genocide in the name of identification and recreational genomics. Simons's 1 percent in no way resembles the genealogical genetics of those who have actual affinity to indigenous life.

The appeal of being indigenous drives the genealogy in two ways, as Nash told me. "There's a growing recognition of the rights of indigenous people, but also sort of sets of cultural associations about being indigenous that makes being indigenous very attractive, a model of identity. The entire question of 'Where do I come from?' is predicated on the notion of being indigenous to a place, not in the sense of first peoples, but of that place, belonging to it." Simons's identification with his Native American line acts exactly in this fashion, tying him to place in a way that makes him from "here." "I think, for one thing, it connected me to this continent in a new and unique way, that not all of my ancestors came on ships from Europe. That there were some that were here long before that who lived in a completely different way. And what part of my makeup now relates to that very different experience? It's just a question."[27]

That question, it turns out, has many political facets. Elizabeth Warren's reveal of her DNA tests in the face of President Donald Trump's taunts about her Native American ancestry was a case that really cut two ways. The taunts were undeniably racist, but the tests followed the same mathematical logic that suggests we can measure ethnicity in percentages of blood. Warren's indigenous or part-indigenous ancestor lived somewhere in the range of six to ten generations previously, giving her a range of between 1/32nd and 1/1,024th Native American.[28] Warren was careful to make the distinction between blood and culture, but the debate highlighted the political nature of any claim to indigenous identity based on DNA tests that indigenous people themselves refuse, and Warren's claim to indigenous blood gave her the moral high ground, linking slight genetic associations with indigenous affinity.

Kim TallBear's press release (after repeated requests for a statement about Warren's results) was pointed. "She and much of the US American public privilege the voices of (mostly white) genome scientists and implicitly cede to them the power to define Indigenous identity. . . . [I]t is one of the privileges of whiteness to define and control everyone else's identity." Interestingly, while European Americans are quick to embrace small percentages of "others," a study that looked at the stories people told about their "race" after they had taken a DNA test revealed that even though the predominant response was "surprise" at the results, "Europeans/whites picked a single ethnicity twice as often as they used multiple ethnicities, whereas non-Europeans never described themselves using a single ethnicity."[29]

Perhaps the most telling study of all about genealogy and race was a huge population study built on publicly available online family trees. The study harvested eighty-six million profiles on Geni.com, a public site owned by MyHeritage.com, which gave permission to the project. Data from the pedigrees of thirteen million people were organized into population-scale family trees. The trees were matched with genetic information also available on public databases (therefore requiring no further consent), scrubbed of identifiers (de-identified), providing a high-quality population database.[30] One of the things that jumps out at me from the research is that the geography of the assembled trees and genetic samples reveals the extent to which the genealogy is primarily motivated by migration from western Europe to eastern North America, in keeping with everything else we know about the racial skew of genetic genealogy.

The racial distribution of the databases has turned out to be a problem for the companies, given that the ethnic percentages reflect the samples in the database. Controversially, 23andMe has launched several plans to entice underrepresented groups, primarily African, to submit their DNA for free, raising again the specter of genetic colonialism and biopiracy.[31] Not surprisingly, given issues of DNA appropriation and reluctant communities, DNA testing services dedicated to specific racial and ethnic groups also play a role in the market. AfricanAncestors, started by Rick Kittles and Gina Paige in 2003, promotes pride through "MatriClan" and "PatriClan" lineages, distinguishing their database in comparison to what the big companies lack. They insist, however, that there "is no test for racial identification. Race is a social construct, not genetically determined. Similarly, ethnicity is more cultural than biological."[32]

It's a hard line to define, though, given our shifting allegiances to blood percentages. Are they national, tribal, essential, scientific, metaphysical, a parlor game? All of these. The indeterminate nature of the exercise itself is part of the sublime appeal of narrative, certainly in the face of statistical reevaluation. We decide what the mathematics mean in a conceptual maneuver that creates a measurable certainty out of the manifest uncertainty of the idea of an "estimate." The best example of the crisis created by raising the specter of very contingent calculations came when Ancestry.com updated their ethnicity estimates in September 2018. Genealogy blogs were flooded with discussions of what the new percentages meant.[33] Some people, particularly professional genealogists, took it all with a grain of salt, knowing that serious genealogists test with multiple companies and compare the results, but consumers were angry and shocked. The company issued a detailed white paper with all of the methods, calculations, and assumptions, including the insistence that "by definition" the people in their "reference panel" were ethnically 100 percent "single origin" and thus representative of their group.[34] The detailed statistical analysis emphasized that the company's estimates were just that, but consumers haggled with the results. Two sets of comments from Roberta Estes's *DNAeXplained—Genetic Genealogy* blog reveal the faith that consumers place in ethnicity testing and the dismay when the numbers run counter to the narrative:

> I can't believe the results from my new updated Ancestry.com DNA estimate!! The results are ridiculous. They show that I'm supposed to now be 46% French even though I have NO ancestors nor family from France. My

Spanish ancestry went down to 9% even though 2 of my grandparents are from Spain. It shows 2% Native American Andean even though we have NO ancestors nor family from Peru.

I know my folks have always told me I'm Scotch-Irish: I'm red-headed with green/hazel eyes. And yet with ancestryDNA, I've now got only 19% Ireland and Scotland on ancestry's new DNA Story, with the rest (81%) England, Wales, and NW Europe. But just today I received an email from 23andMe, "13 New Populations Added to Ancestry Composition Report." So I went over there to look, and they have got me with NA and Sub-Saharan African. Oh my goodness! But tiny amounts, like: .2% Congolese, .2% Nigerian, .1% Southern East Africa. Native American .2%. They aren't saying whether those estimates are speculative, or if they are, to what extent. But it's working, if it's marketing. I think many of us actually do want to have interesting ancestors! Wow, do you think the 23andMe update is a response to the ancestryDNA updates??[35]

Of course, the numbers will change and change again as more and more people test, and the stories that people tell about those numbers will reflect the changes in cultural capital that we ascribe to particular identities.

Even in 2010, Dan Taggart was prescient about the future of genetic genealogy and its aspirations:

Right now, one of the biggest problems in genetic genealogy is that there's just not enough data. We only have a very small sampling of the Earth's population in that database. So, imagine if you had a sample from every person that lives on this planet, that you actually had all of the gene pool to analyze. Eventually, that's what'll happen. They'll have the entire gene pool to analyze. When that happens, they can reconstruct all of the lines from the information that exists in our DNA. All the way back to our, you know, whoever our first ancestors were. Adam and Eve. We can reconstruct all of those lines absolutely perfectly all the way back, because the data is all there. It just has to be mapped back.[36]

Taggard perfectly expresses the genealogical sublime, that one day with complete databases we will know ourselves and our origins perfectly.

CHAPTER 7

THE GENEALOGICAL SUBLIME
We Are All Related

The year 2018 was a watershed for our understanding of relatedness, but it came in a very unexpected form. In April of that year, a story broke about the police helping themselves to DNA data that had been uploaded by genealogy enthusiasts to GEDmatch, a public database that had much fewer privacy provisions—and therefore a much higher likelihood of identifying relatives and ancestors—than private company databases.[1] Using DNA from a cold case and the services of Barbara Rae-Venter (a retired patent attorney with a PhD in biology and the former wife of Craig Venter, one of the first geneticists to sequence the human genome), the police solved the case of a brutal string of California murders and rapes from the 1980s.[2] That case quickly spawned a new industry, a collaboration between law enforcement and genetic genealogists that produced a genetic genealogy arm of Parabon, a DNA engineering company, that promised to "solve your toughest cases—FAST."[3] Parabon hired celebrity genealogist CeCe Moore, founder of the DNA Detectives and a producer of *Finding Your Roots with Henry Louis Gates, Jr.* as their "chief genetic genealogist." Within a year, more than forty cases had been solved, with the count running higher daily.[4]

This breakthrough for law enforcement provoked an intense new discussion on the question of relatedness and privacy. No one could argue against the social benefits of solving decades-old cases, bringing relief to families and success to police forces; at the same time, though, the generosity and drive of the genealogical community in its search for ever-growing trees had revealed a frightening aspect of "we are all related"—a complete loss of privacy. All privacy agreements are made with individual consumers who decide to give away the family strands. When you send off or upload your DNA, you are also sharing the DNA of everyone in your family, near and far. One of the sublime paradoxes of DNA is that the thing that is most individual about us belongs to everyone else as well. The communal nature of the genealogical sublime was revealed for better and for worse.

FamilyTreeDNA, the first commercial direct-to-consumer genetic genealogy company, started by Bennett Greenspan, turned out to be at the center of the privacy-versus-police controversy. In February 2019, *BuzzFeed News,* an online magazine with a record of investigating the genealogy industry, reported that FamilyTreeDNA had been actively cooperating with the Federal Bureau of Investigation for two years without informing any of its customers. Earlier in the year, it had been ranked as one of the best sites for protecting privacy. Greenspan apologized, though he claimed he was only "enabling his customers to crowdsource the catching of criminals."[5] The company tacked several times, first telling consumers they could opt out of sharing altogether, then changing the privacy policy to allow users to opt out of sharing information with the FBI, then taking a new approach altogether, releasing an ad campaign with Ed Smart, the father of Elizabeth Smart, who was abducted in 2002 and held captive for nine months, calling on their consumers to recognize their moral obligation to share their DNA for families "who want answers." It's not clear how DNA matching would have helped solve Elizabeth Smart's case, but the moral implications are clear, and most people who have submitted DNA samples seem to be onside.[6] Sarah Zhang, writing for the *Atlantic,* made a disturbing argument about who matters in these cases, mostly white young women.[7] On the other hand, given that the databases are primarily European, racialized communities who are overrepresented in the criminal system are somewhat protected for now.

The moral aspects of genealogy are never far from the surface, as we have seen in just about every chapter in this book. Here the moral implications of sharing DNA results extend well beyond the goods associated with having more family, or a clearer pedigree, to the communal good of exposing violent criminals. Is law enforcement likely to stop there? Almost everyone who works in this area of privacy is calling for restrictions on police use of genetic genealogy databases, and each case tests the limits of the kind of privacy incursions we will accept in the hunt for criminals. Cold cases seem acceptable, while recent cases pose greater moral and privacy quandaries. Resistance may be futile in the end, given that police may override consumers' choices to opt out by pursuing warrants for entire data sets.[8]

The genealogy industry has, in effect, created an almost complete form of "surveillance capitalism." As Shoshana Zuboff writes in her explosive criticism of the digital giants, "Surveillance capitalism feeds on every aspect of every human's experience." I am perhaps taking her notion of "surveillance" a bit too literally, since digital surveillance is used to sell predicative behavior, but it's not too difficult to imagine a world in which criminality is predicted on DNA inheritance. "A movement that aims to impose a new collective order based on total certainty," the seventh postulate in her definition of "surveillance capitalism," echoes weirdly with my idea of the all-identifying databases of the genealogical sublime. As she argues in her introduction, "The sense of home slipping away provokes an unbearable yearning. The Portuguese have a name for this feeling: *saudade*, a word said to capture the homesickness and longing of separation from the homeland among emigrants across the centuries. Now the disruptions of the twenty-first century have turned these exquisite anxieties and longings of dislocation into a universal story that engulfs each one of us."[9] Surely, the genealogy industry has exploited that longing more than any other.

As we have seen, those longings are both external and internal. Returning to the sublime pleasures and displeasures of finding the hidden truths of self, perhaps nowhere are those feelings revealed more deeply than adoptees from closed adoptions looking for birth parents. DNA testing turned up more surprises than anyone anticipated. Stories of "nonpaternity events" and finding half siblings flood genealogy blogs and Facebook sites. The stories run the gambit of deeply healing to disastrous, but few who discover these hidden parts of the self are the same. Discovery comes at the price of destruction. The unmitigated good of the reunion of blood family turns out also to have extensive privacy implications, pitting the rights of parents who had given children up for adoption against their children's need to know and children conceived with donated sperm against the privacy of their donors, or revealing the extent to which donors have played out their own versions of the genealogical sublime.

AncestryDNA does warn on its site, buried in the fine print of its terms and conditions, that you may discover "unanticipated facts about yourself or your family" that "you may not have the ability to change (e.g. you may discover an unknown genetic sibling or parent, surprising facts about your ethnicity, or unexpected information in public records)."[10] But consumers have been so unprepared for these results that the genetic genealogy customer service reps have become de facto counselors who are trained to listen empathetically to people bewildered by their results and steer them toward the science and the data.[11]

One extraordinary case is that of "Louis," a man who doesn't want to be identified publicly, who, motivated by profound anxiety about mortality, fathered as many children as he could through anonymous sperm donation, hoping that one day they would track him down. "I had started to think, 'Who will remember me when I'm gone? Who will talk about me? Who will be my heir?'" he says. "I think our biggest fear in life is not to die, but to be forgotten."[12] He fathered somewhere between two hundred and one thousand children and has now met more than forty of the fifty-seven children with whom he has been matched. Their reactions have run the gambit from hostility to love, but he has beyond a doubt written himself into the eternal genome of the future.

Most stories of discovery are less prolific but just as profound. Katharine Wall, founder of Adopted.com—"Where people come to reunite instantly!"—a website that has 850,000 members and helps adoptees and biological parents connect, observed, "Technology can really change things overnight."[13] The site keeps a counter of how many people have registered in the last month (as of the end of April 2019, 7,632), the past day (223), and the past hour (14). All of the major testing companies—23andMe, FamilyTreeDNA, AncestryDNA, MyHeritageDNA, and Whitepages—are sponsors. The site has a constant scroll of life-changing testimonies, eschewing the displeasures of sublime reunions.[14] Family secrets are secret no longer, and those crushed by those revelations have found consolation in NPE (Not Parent Expected) support groups.[15] Curiously, the homepage of the "NPE Friends Fellowship" shows a lonely human dwarfed by a sublime landscape, instinctively evoking the confusion of hidden knowledge revealed in an internal landscape larger than we can comprehend.[16]

The stunning privacy implications of genetic genealogy were revealed by the chief science officer of MyHeritage, an Israeli genealogy company with thirty-five million family trees, in a paper published in the fall of 2018 in *Science* under the rather innocuous title "Identity Inference of Genomic Data Using Long-Range Familial Searches." In it Yaniv Erlich (also a professor of computer science at Columbia as well as being the chief security officer of MyHeritage)[17] and his research associates responded to the exploitation of consumer genomic database by law enforcement. Using the genomic data of 1.28 million consumers who had tested commercial companies, they investigated the power of the police technique to identify criminals via distant relatives. The results were shocking: "We project that about 60% of the searches for individuals of European-descent will result in a third cousin or closer match, which can allow their identification using demographic identifiers. Moreover, the technique could implicate nearly any US-individual of European-descent in the near future." Perhaps most astonishing was the broader statistic that "a genetic database needs to cover only 2% of the target population to provide a 3rd cousin match to nearly any person." Apparently, the United States is almost at that threshold. As the *New York Times* reported, "Within two or three years, 90 percent of Americans of European descent will be identifiable from their DNA, researchers found. The science-fiction future, in which everyone is known whether or not they want to be, is nigh."[18] We are reaching our database destiny.

"With the exponential growth of consumer genomics," Erlich and his colleagues warned, "we posit that such database scale is foreseeable for some 3rd party websites in the near future." So, GEDmatch or MyHeritage or some other company that allows users to upload their results from testing companies with stronger privacy provisions would become the sites where everyone can be discovered. Erlich and his team proposed a potential encryption strategy and clear legislation to mitigate the ease with which de-identified profiles can be reidentified and the potential for the misuses of genetic genealogy. The report pointed out that law enforcement had already moved from solving cold cases to solving active ones. MyHeritage was perhaps sensitized to privacy issues since the company was hacked in October 2017, which was not discovered until June 2018, exposing 92 million user accounts (though not their DNA).[19]

The MyHeritage hack and Erlich's report garnered headlines, but didn't appear to slow the intensity of interest in genetic genealogy or police use of GEDmatch, even as most corporate databases voluntarily tightened their privacy provisions.[20]

Dan Taggart's prediction is coming to pass. "In the future they'll have the DNA of everyone, and then we'll be able to trace the lines back to Adam and Eve, or whoever."[21] Except that the database will be owned by a private company, and Adam and Eve will be trademarked. Indeed, the church is moving toward incorporating DNA into its FamilyTree, bringing genetic science to its purpose of tracking the genealogy of humanity to our godly beginnings.

In 2018, under the rubric of "Big Data," a group of geneticists and analysts published the world's largest analysis of genealogical data to date, "Quantitative Analysis of Population-Scale Family Trees with Millions of Relatives." They collected eighty-six million profiles from publicly available online data from Geni.com, "the world's leading collaborative

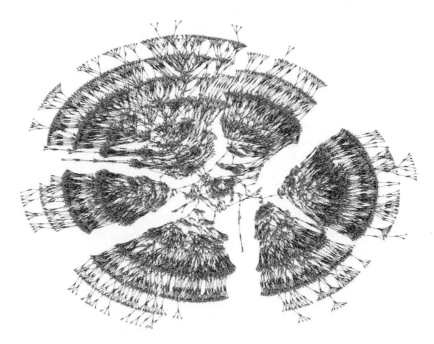

FIGURE 10.   A six-thousand-person family tree, showing individuals spanning seven generations and their marital links. Courtesy of Yaniv Erlich, Columbia University.

genealogy site," a site owned by MyHeritage.com, a study on a "massive scale that covers nearly every country in the Western world."[22] The authors write that "after extensive cleaning and validation, we obtained population-scale family trees, including a single pedigree of 13 million individuals."[23] The illustration of one of the family trees is very beautiful. This one, with approximately six thousand members, spans about seven generations. The circular layout of the model seems less dependent on the age-old figure of the tree and closer to a circular model of connectivity that will soon blur the lines even further between family groups. It's hard to imagine the individuality of every single green dot on the chart, that every dot is a person, a life, a death.

The purpose of the study is revealing: "By harnessing our resource, we sought to build a model for the sources of genetic variance in longevity." In other words, the data of the dead became a source for figuring out which genes will help us to live longer. The authors admit that the study proved the opposite: "On the basis of a large number of data points and study designs, we measured an additive component ($h2 \sim 16\%$) that is considerably smaller than the 25% figure that is generally cited in the literature. These results indicate that previous studies are likely to have overestimated the heritability of longevity. As such, we should lower our expectations about our ability to predict longevity from genomic data and presumably to identify causal genetic variants."[24]

The search for ancestors, heeding the sublime narrative pleasures of inner knowledge, in the end, coalesces into an effort to fend off mortality itself. An observation like this points to the structure of pleasure and displeasure in the sublime: the sense of awe of being connected is haunted by the specter of death, of ancestors whose DNA we have inherited and whose DNA will ultimately cause us to die as well. The displeasures of inheritance become clearer when we consider this statistical proposition about our most recent common ancestor (MRCA): "As genealogical ancestry is traced back beyond the MRCA, a growing percentage of people in earlier generations are revealed to be common ancestors of the present-day population. Tracing further back in time, there was a threshold, let us say U_n generations ago, before which ancestry of the present-day population was an all or nothing affair. That is, each individual living at least U_n generations ago was either a common ancestor of all of today's humans or an ancestor of no human alive today."[25]

Unlike studies that search for "Mitochondrial Eve" that might find a MRCA one hundred thousand years ago or Y-chromosome studies of single surnames, these researchers assumed a more natural and necessary form of two-parent families, predicting an MRCA in a much more recent past, "that all modern individuals have identical ancestors by about 3,000 BC."[26] Though they admit that such estimates are "extremely tentative," the study's "main message is that substantial forms of population subdivision can still be compatible with very recent common ancestors." What is perhaps harder to grasp is that we have no evidence in us of lines that have died out completely. Here in the databases that promise eternal life, we must contemplate the possibility that we too will disappear entirely.

As this genealogy of genealogy shows, the search for ancestors is an exercise in continuity and discontinuity. Never before have we been able to trace the history of humans—all humans, not just groups of noble citizens—with such a democratic and expanded notion of relatedness. The desire to know our genealogies seems almost universally human. Never has it been more scientific or more mythic. The largest genealogical project in the world, that of the Church of Jesus Christ of Latter-day Saints, promises that the records, combined with saving ordinances, will liberate us from our earthly spirits and turn us into gods, reversing the trend in human history that provided our mythic descent from the gods.

Combinations of technology, capital (cultural and monetary), religious doctrine, and curiosity have driven our interest in ancestors across cultures and for millennia. What is completely different in this particular moment of the early twentieth century is the sublime desire to capture *all* of the world's records and *all* of humanity. The idea of completeness expands in digital archives and DNA, around us and inside us everywhere. The past is not at all foreign; it lives on in every one of us, extracted from our cells. This collapse of deep time, mythic origins, and contemporary science of us in the world and the world in us is an entirely new combination, an emergent phenomenon of descent. Enraptured as we are in the idea that we are all related, that pernicious question "Who do you think you are?" has led us to the brink of a dangerous place. We are, indeed, all related, and relatedness is a product unlike any other. It offers a sense of connectedness lost over time and dislocation, disasters and mass deaths, restitution to bucolic origins (premigratory and Paleolithic), and promises of longevity in life and in memory by revealing the records of us, in ever-growing archives and secreted in our genes. Family history is compelling emotionally and culturally and just for sheer historical pleasure, but genealogy has expanded far beyond heraldic emblems, noble pedigree charts, and lines of famous or infamous primogenitors. We are willing to pay handsomely for relatives, giving away treasures of information in return.

Genealogy is the largest historical project in the world (I think we can safely say), extending relatedness of humans mathematically and mythically, a vast inheritance dominated by the institutions, industries, and technologies that spawned it. Genealogical curiosity seems to have no limits. Few human endeavors are so sublime in their pursuit of completeness—and the consequences of that desire. The answer to "Who do you think you are?" turns out to be answerable along so many lines, primarily narrative, built out of rumor, religion, history, statistics and probability (the mathematical foundations of genetics), and, above all, it seems, relatives. We are singular in an ever-growing body of relatedness, but I'm not at all sure that all that connectedness has solved the question.

NOTES

INTRODUCTION

1. Jacques Derrida, *Archive Fever: A Freudian Impression* (Chicago: University of Chicago Press, 1998).

2. Danilo Kiš, *The Encyclopedia of the Dead* (Evanston, IL: Northwestern University Press, 1997), 39–65. See Julia Creet, "The Archive and the Uncanny: Danilo Kiš's 'Encyclopedia of the Dead' and the Fantasy of Hypermnesia," in *Lost in the Archives,* ed. Rebecca Comay (Toronto: Alphabet City, 2002), 8:265–75.

3. Kiš, *Encyclopedia of the Dead,* 41.

4. Ibid., 43.

5. Ibid., 65.

6. *Duga,* May 19–23, 1981, quoted in Kiš, *Encyclopedia of the Dead,* 193–94.

7. Immanuel Kant, *Critique of Judgement,* rev. ed. (Oxford: Oxford University Press, 2008); David E. Nye, *American Technological Sublime* (Cambridge, MA: MIT Press, 1994).

8. "Ancestry.com Invests in Future of Genetic Genealogy by Offering DNA Testing for Only $79," January 27, 2009, http://blogs.ancestry.com; "Database Sizes—September 2018 Update," *The DNA Geek* (blog), September 4, 2018, https://the dnageek.com; "Interview with David Sacks, Geni and Yammer," September 30, 2008, www.socaltech.com.

9. Kevin Meethan, "Remaking Time and Space: The Internet, Digital Archives and Genealogy," in *Geography and Genealogy: Locating Personal Pasts,* ed. J. Timothy Dallen and Jeanne Kay Guelke (New York: Routledge, 2016). As Meethan writes, the "development of information technologies has created the means by which people can now reclaim their lost kin, and by so doing provide a tangible and proven connection between the immediate here and now and the more abstract temporal scale of history and collective memory" (108).

10. One of the most elegant recent histories of genealogy is Susan Tucker's visually rich *City of Remembering: A History of Genealogy in New Orleans* (Jackson: University Press of Mississippi, 2016). Tucker is curator of books and records for the Newcomb

Archives and Vorhoff Library at Tulane University and an archivist who has been working with genealogy and genealogists for thirty years. She provides a good overview of how the United States became the "nation of genealogy," arguing that "family history becomes a gift of remarkable generosity, not just to one's immediate kin but also a wider world, to cousins across time and space" (3). Similarly, Peter Benes and Jeremy Dupertuis Bangs's book *The Art of Family Genealogical Artifacts in New England* (Boston: New England Historic Genealogical Society, 2002) collects the artifacts, family Bibles, pedigrees, painting, embroidery, woodworking, carved stone, engraved silver, and photographs of the New England Genealogical Historical Society—some of which I filmed in my documentary being delicately handled by the white-gloved society archivist—illustrating the profound aesthetic appeal of the material culture of kinship.

11. Fredric Jameson, *Postmodernism; or, The Cultural Logic of Late Capitalism* (Durham, NC: Duke University Press, 1992), 36.

12. Casper C. de Jonge, "Dionysius and Longinus on the Sublime: Rhetoric and Religious Language," *American Journal of Philology* 133, no. 2 (2012): 272–73.

13. Kant, *Critique of Judgement*, 187–88.

14. Nye, *American Technological Sublime*, xiii. Nye credits Perry Miller in *The Life of the Mind in America from the Revolution to the Civil War* (New York: Harcourt Brace, 1965) as the first to coin the term as well as subsequent interpreters, but says that none had produced a sustained discussion of its meanings (xv).

15. Jos de Mul, "The (Bio)Technological Sublime," *Diogenes* 59, nos. 1–2 (2012): 34.

16. Ilan Stavans, "Danilo Kiš in Buenos Aires," *Review of Contemporary Fiction* 14, no. 1 (1994): 174; Gabriel Motola, "Danilo Kiš: Death and the Mirror," *Antioch Review* 51, no. 4 (1993): 605–21.

17. de Mul, "The (Bio)Technological Sublime," 37.

18. Sigrid Weigel, "Genealogy: On the Iconography and Rhetorics of an Epistemological Topos," *Encicilopedia e Hipertexto*, www.educ.fc.ul.pt/hyper/resources/sweigel/.

19. Alex Shoumatoff, *The Mountain of Names: A History of the Human Family* (New York: Kodansha Amer, 1995), 233.

20. Christiane Klapisch-Zuber, "The Genesis of the Family Tree," *I Tatti Studies in the Italian Renaissance* 4 (1991): 105–29; Mary Bouquet, "Family Trees and Their Affinities: The Visual Imperative of the Genealogical Diagram," *Journal of the Royal Anthropological Institute* 2 (1996): 43–66. These two exceptional essays provide detailed visual and discursive histories of the iconography and logic of the family tree.

21. Carlo Ginzburg, "Family Resemblances and Family Trees: Two Cognitive Metaphors," *Critical Inquiry* 30, no. 3 (2004): 537–56; Klapisch-Zuber, "Genesis of the Family Tree"; Sigrid Weigel, "'Generation' as a Symbolic Form: On the Genealogical Discourse of Memory since 1945," *Germanic Review: Literature, Culture, Theory* 77, no. 4 (2002): 264–77; Weigel, "Genealogy: On the Iconography and Rhetorics of an Epistemological Topos"; Bouquet, "Family Trees and Their Affinities."

22. Weigel, "Genealogy."

23. Klapisch-Zuber, "Genesis of the Family Tree."

24. Eric Ketelaar, "The Genealogical Gaze: Family Identities and Family Archives in the Fourteenth to Seventeenth Centuries," *Libraries and the Cultural Record* 44, no. 1 (2009).

25. Jost Eickmeyer, Markus Friedrich, and Volker Bauer, eds., *Genealogical Knowledge in the Making: Tools, Practices, and Evidence in Early Modern Europe* (Boston: Walter de Gruyter, 2019), 2.

26. Bouquet, "Family Trees and Their Affinities," 57, 44; Weigel, "Genealogy."

27. Nye, *American Technological Sublime*, 25.

28. Daniel Gasman, "Haeckel's Scientific Monism as Theory of History," *Theory in Biosciences* 121, no. 3 (2002): 260–79.

29. François Weil, "John Farmer and the Making of American Genealogy," *New England Quarterly* 80, no. 3 (2007): 408–34.

30. Francesca Morgan, "Lineage as Capital: Genealogy in Antebellum New England," *New England Quarterly* 83, no. 2 (2010): 250–82.

31. François Weil, *Family Trees: A History of Genealogy in America* (Cambridge, MA: Harvard University Press, 2013), 5, 2.

32. Alex Haley, *Roots: The Saga of an American Family,* annotated ed. (New York: Vanguard Press, 2007). See, for example, Erica L. Ball and Kellie Carter Jackson, eds., *Reconsidering "Roots": Race, Politics, and Memory* (Athens: University of Georgia Press, 2017); Matthew F. Delmont, *Making "Roots": A Nation Captivated* (Berkeley: University of California Press, 2016); Helen Taylor, "'The Griot from Tennessee': The Saga of Alex Haley's *Roots,*" *Critical Quarterly* 37, no. 2 (1995): 46–62; David Chioni Moore, "Routes," *Transition,* no. 64 (1994): 4–21; and Elizabeth Shown Mills and Gary B. Mills, eds., "'Roots' and the New 'Faction': A Legitimate Tool for Clio?," *Virginia Magazine of History and Biography* 89, no. 1 (1981): 3–26.

33. Morgan, "Lineage as Capital."

34. Lloyd DeWitt Bockstruck, "Four Centuries of Genealogy: A Historical Overview," *RQ* 23, no. 2 (1983): 162–70.

35. Susan Tucker, "Doors Opening Wider: Library and Archival Services to Family History," *Archivaria* 62 (2006): 130. Recent ballpark statistics provided for me by Library and Archives Canada (LAC) and the Ontario Archives were dramatically lower, where only 10–15 percent of registered researchers noted genealogy as their primary interest. One can reasonably hypothesize that the growth of online databases has reduced the need for genealogists to visit physical archives.

36. See Susan Tucker, "Archivists and Genealogical Researchers: A Bibliography," n.d., www.tulane.edu. See also, for example, Anne Billeter, "Why Don't Librarians Like Genealogists? Beginning Genealogy for Librarians," *Oregon Library Association* 7, no. 4 (2001): 2–6; Charles Bryan, "What Should We Do about the 'Genies'?," *History News* 41, no. 1 (1986): 31–33; Allen Gardiner, "Genealogy and the Librarian: Hope and

Help for the Librarian's Frayed Nerves," *Show Me Libraries* (1984): 25–32; and Hannah Little, "Archive Fever as Genealogical Fever: Coming Home to Scottish Archives," *Archivaria* 64 (Fall 2007): 89–112.

37. The National Archives of Canada, for example, responding to a growing demand in the 1980s and concurrent with the shift away from a "total archive" of national significance, opened a genealogy wing in 2003, which soon saw 50 percent of the research traffic in its amalgamated successor, the Library and Archives Canada. Laura Millar, "Discharging Our Debt: The Evolution of the Total Archives Concept in English Canada," *Archivaria* 46 (1998): 103–46; Myron Momryk, "'National Significance': The Evolution and Development of Acquisition Strategies in the Manuscript Division, National Archives Canada," *Archivaria* 52 (2001): 151–74; Hugh A. Taylor, "The Collective Memory: Archives and Libraries as Heritage," *Archivaria* 15 (1982–1983): 118–30.

38. This rearrangement of priorities from the representation of groups to the accessibility of public records for individual use was not without bureaucratic resistance, particularly with respect to important issues of privacy. In 2003 LAC and the Alberta Family Histories Society took legal action against Canada's chief statistician and the federal government to obtain the 1911 census records, winning online access through LAC in 2005. See Heather MacNeil, "Defining the Limits of Freedom of Inquiry: The Ethics of Disclosing Personal Information Held in Government Archives," *Archivaria* 32 (January 1, 1991); Tucker, "Doors Opening Wider," 132; and "Bill S-18: An Act to Amend the Statistics Act (LS-493E)," https://lop.parl.ca/About/Parliament/ LegislativeSummaries/bills_.

39. Julia Creet, "How Cops Used a Public Genealogy Database in the Golden State Killer Case," http://theconversation.com; Yaniv Erlich et al., "Identity Inference of Genomic Data Using Long-Range Familial Searches," *Science,* October 11, 2018.

40. Tucker, "Doors Opening Wider," 129.

41. Spencer Wells, *Deep Ancestry: The Landmark DNA Quest to Decipher Our Distant Past* (Washington, DC: National Geographic, 2007), 11. Wells's claim—he provides no evidence to back it up—has entered popular discourse to the extent that he is no longer cited as the source of this information. I can find no contemporary sources that back these claims, though Wells might have derived his information from a Marist poll, which is also cited by multiple sources. I checked with Marist, and they have no record of ever conducting this poll or, of course, ever providing the information that would substantiate this claim.

42. Bernard Cova, Robert Kozinets, and Avi Shankar, eds., *Consumer Tribes* (Oxford: Butterworth Heinemann, 2007).

43. Derrida, *Archive Fever;* Francis X. Blouin and William G. Rosenberg, eds., *Archives, Documentation, and Institutions of Social Memory: Essays from the Sawyer Seminar* (Ann Arbor: University of Michigan Press, 2006); Antoinette M. Burton, ed., *Archive Stories: Facts, Fictions, and the Writing of History* (Durham, NC: Duke University

Press, 2005); Luciana Duranti, *Diplomatics: New Uses for an Old Science* (Lanham, MD: Scarecrow Press, 1998); Carolyn Steedman, *Dust: The Archive and Cultural History* (New Brunswick, NJ: Rutgers University Press, 2002); Rebecca Comay, ed., *Lost in the Archives* (Toronto: Alphabet City, 2002); Kate Eichhorn, *The Archival Turn in Feminism: Outrage in Order* (Philadelphia: Temple University Press, 2014); Charles Merewether, *The Archive* (London: Whitechapel, 2006); Pierre Nora, "Between Memory and History: *Les lieux de mémoire*," *Representations*, no. 26 (Spring 1989): 7–24. See also the journals *Archivaria, Archival Science,* and *American Archivist.*

44. Derrida, *Archive Fever,* 90, 91.

45. Jerome de Groot, *Consuming History: Historians and Heritage in Contemporary Popular Culture* (New York: Routledge, 2008), 60, 75; Carla Almeida Santos and Grace Yan, "Genealogical Tourism: A Phenomenological Examination," *Journal of Travel Research* 49, no. 1 (2010): 56–67; Anne-Marie Kramer, interview, November 2010. See also Kramer, "Mediatizing Memory: History, Affect and Identity in Who Do You Think You Are?," *European Journal of Cultural Studies* 14, no. 4 (2011): 428–45.

46. Catherine Nash, *Genetic Geographies: The Trouble with Ancestry* (Minneapolis: University of Minnesota Press, 2015); Nash, *Of Irish Descent: Origin Stories, Genealogy & the Politics of Belonging* (Syracuse, NY: Syracuse University Press, 2008); Nash, "Geographies of Relatedness," *Transactions of the Institute of British Geographers* 30, no. 4 (2005): 449–62; Nash, "Genetic Kinship," *Cultural Studies* 18, no. 1 (2004): 1–34; Nash, "Genealogical Identities," *Environment and Planning D: Society and Space* 20, no. 1 (2002): 27–52.

47. Eviatar Zerubavel, *Time Maps: Collective Memory and the Social Shape of the Past* (Chicago: University of Chicago Press, 2004); Zerubavel, *Ancestors and Relatives: Genealogy, Identity, and Community* (New York: Oxford University Press, 2012), 26.

48. Gilles Deleuze and Félix Guattari, *A Thousand Plateaus* (Minneapolis: University of Minnesota Press, 1987); Pierre Bourdieu, *Outline of a Theory of Practice* (Cambridge: Cambridge University Press, 1977); Anne McClintock, *Imperial Leather: Race, Gender, and Sexuality in the Colonial Contest* (New York: Routledge, 1995); Marilyn Strathern, *Kinship, Law and the Unexpected* (New York: Cambridge University Press, 2005).

49. Bouquet, "Family Trees and Their Affinities," 44.

50. An intriguing use of this turn of phrase is by David G. Kendall in "The Genealogy of Genealogy Branching Processes before (and after) 1873," *Bulletin of the London Mathematical Society* 7, no. 3 (1975): 225–53. Kendall's essay rehearses a set of mathematical proofs about the rate of surname extinction of men from privileged lines. "Backward" genealogy is much simpler than "forward," in which "we expect to observe extinction."

51. Michel Foucault, "Nietzsche, Genealogy, History," in *Language, Counter-memory, Practice: Selected Essays and Interviews* (Ithaca, NY: Cornell University Press, 1977), 144.

52. Ibid., 145.

53. Ibid., 147–48; Weigel, "Genealogy."
54. Friedrich Nietzsche, "On the Genealogy of Morals" (1887), section 5.
55. Ibid., section 6.
56. Foucault, "Nietzsche, Genealogy, History," 150, 162.
57. There is something of Neil Hertz's notion of "blockage," "a play between confusion and assurance," in these discoveries of new selves that must then be incorporated into stories of our becoming. Hertz, *The End of the Line* (Aurora, CO: Davies Group, 2008), 41.
58. Nye, *American Technological Sublime*, xx.
59. "Family Family Tree," www.familytree.ru/en/help/worktree.htm.

CHAPTER 1: CONFUCIUS

1. *The Guinness Book of World Records* affirmed this record in 2015 after reviewing the 2009 revision of the *Confucius Genealogy*. It's unclear if Confucius may have displaced a 1999 record accorded to the "Lurie Legacy," a Jewish lineage descendant from King David. See Neil Rosenstein, *The Lurie Legacy: The House of Davidic Royal Descent* (Bergenfield, NJ: Avotaynu, 2004).
2. Qingjie James Wang, "Genealogical Self and a Confucian Way of Self-Making," *International Philosophical Quarterly* 42, no. 1 (2002): 108.
3. Genealogical pedigrees can be organized in many ways. If one starts with the self and works historically toward one's ancestors, the chart ascends. This is the most common form of charting for amateur genealogists. The chart can be organized vertically or horizontally. Charts also come in bow ties or circles, again fanning outward from the self. A descendant pedigree chart usually starts with a famous figure and charts all the descendants. This site provides a good overview: "Are There Different Types of Genealogy Pedigree Chart?," *My Family History—Genealogy* (blog), August 11, 2016, http://myfamilyhistorygenealogy.com.
4. Christiane Klapisch-Zuber, "The Genesis of the Family Tree," *I Tatti Studies in the Italian Renaissance* 4 (1991): 112.
5. Anning Hu, "Ancestor Worship in Contemporary China: An Empirical Investigation," *China Review* 16, no. 1 (2016): 169–86.
6. Ibid., 178.
7. Francis Fukuyama, "Mao's Battle with Confucius for China's Soul," *Financial Times*, July 12, 2011, www.fullertreacymoney.com.
8. Michael Schuman, *Confucius: And the World He Created* (New York: Basic Books, 2015), 5.
9. "New *Confucius Genealogy* Out Next Year," www.china.org.cn.
10. Jane Qui, "Inheriting Confucius," http://seedmagazine.com/content/article/inheriting_confucius/.
11. "Updated Confucius Family Tree Has Two Million Members," *Xinhua*, February 16, 2008, www.chinadaily.com.cn.

12. "Confucius' Family Tree Goes Digital," *People's Daily Online*, November 15, 2012, http://en.people.cn/90782/8020528.html.

13. Chen Na, "Dreams of Imperial Descent Drive Chinese to DNA Testing," *Sixth Tone*, April 25, 2018, www.sixthtone.com.

14. On a similar theme, see David Lowenthal, "On Arraigning Ancestors: A Critique of Historical Contrition," *North Carolina Law Review* 87 (2008–9): 901.

15. Qui, "Inheriting Confucius."

16. "Confucius Descendents Say DNA Testing Plan Lacks Wisdom," *Qingdao News*, August 21, 2007, http://web.archive.org/web/20110707013208/eng.bandao.cn/news detail.asp?id=4644.

17. Ibid.

18. Qui, "Inheriting Confucius."

19. "Confucius Descendents Say DNA Testing Plan Lacks Wisdom."

20. Stephen Chen, "Study Finds Single Bloodline among Self-Claimed Confucius Descendants," *South China Morning Post*, November 13, 2013, www.scmp.com.

21. Bryan Sykes and Catherine Irven, "Surnames and the Y Chromosome," *American Journal of Human Genetics* 66, no. 4 (2000): 1417, https://doi.org/10.1086/302850.

22. Carl Elliott and Paul Brodwin, "Identity and Genetic Ancestry Tracing," *BMJ: British Medical Journal* 325, no. 7378 (2002): 1470.

23. Francesc Calafell and Maarten H. D. Larmuseau, "The Y Chromosome as the Most Popular Marker in Genetic Genealogy Benefits Interdisciplinary Research," *Human Genetics* 136, no. 5 (2017): 559–73.

24. Mark Liberman, email to the author, March 9, 2017; Mark Liberman, "Being Descended from Confucius," *Language Log* (blog), February 9, 2012, https://language log.ldc.upenn.edu/nll/?p=3755.

25. R. L. Cann, "DNA and Human Origins," *Annual Review of Anthropology* 17, no. 1 (1988): 127–43; M. J. McGuffin and R. Balakrishnan, "Interactive Visualization of Genealogical Graphs," paper presented at the IEEE Symposium on Information Visualization, Minneapolis, October 23–25, 2005, 16–23.

26. Liberman, email.

27. Qui, "Inheriting Confucius."

CHAPTER 2: THE MORMONS

1. On August 16, 2018, President Russell M. Nelson decreed, "The Lord has impressed upon my mind the importance of the name He has revealed for His Church, even The Church of Jesus Christ of Latter-day Saints." The directive emphasized that the name of Jesus Christ should be included in every mention of "The Church," which poses significant stylistic problems for this book. I will use all of the shorter forms, keeping in mind that Jesus Christ is the Lord God of Mormonism.

2. See, for example, Donald Akenson, *Some Family: The Mormons and How Humanity Keeps Track of Itself* (Montreal and Kingston: McGill-Queen's University Press, 2007);

Dallen J. Timothy and Jeanne Kay Guelke, *Geography and Genealogy: Locating Personal Pasts* (Burlington, VT: Ashgate, 2008); James B. Allen, *The Story of the Latter-day Saints* (Salt Lake City: Deseret Book, 1992); James B. Allen, Jessie L. Embry, and Kahlile B. Mehr, *Hearts Turned to the Fathers: A History of the Genealogical Society of Utah, 1894–1994* (Provo, UT: Brigham Young University Studies, 1995); Claudia L. Bushman, *Contemporary Mormonism: Latter-day Saints in Modern America* (Westport, CT: Greenwood, 2006); Jerome de Groot, *Consuming History: Historians and Heritage in Contemporary Popular Culture* (New York: Routledge, 2008).

3. Akenson, *Some Family*, 3.

4. Ibid., 125.

5. Ibid., 28.

6. Alan Taylor, "The Free Seekers: Religious Culture in Upstate New York, 1790–1835," in *From the Outside Looking In: Essays on Mormon History, Theology, and Culture*, ed. Reid Larkin Neilson and Matthew J. Grow (New York: Oxford University Press, 2015), 13. The history of Joseph Smith and the early Mormon Church deserves a much deeper and wider discussion than I can afford it here. Some of the most influential histories include Fawn McKay Brodie, *No Man Knows My History: The Life of Joseph Smith, the Mormon Prophet* (New York: Vintage Books, 1945), a book for which she was excommunicated the year after its publication, and Richard L. Bushman's correctives, *Joseph Smith and the Beginnings of Mormonism* (Urbana: University of Illinois Press, 1984) and *Joseph Smith: Rough Stone Rolling* (New York: Knopf Doubleday, 2007).

7. Taylor, "Free Seekers," 17, 19.

8. Akenson, *Some Family*, 51. See also Gary James Bergera, "The Earliest Eternal Sealings for Civilly Married Couples Living and Dead," *Dialogue: A Journal of Mormon Thought* 35, no. 3 (2002): 41–66; D. Michael Quinn, "The Practice of Rebaptism at Nauvoo," *Brigham Young University Studies* 18, no. 2 (1978): 226–32.

9. Kory Meyerink, interview by the author, Salt Lake City, May 2010.

10. "The prototype for American state-based registration was created after a cholera epidemic engulfed England and Wales prompting British reforms such as the maintenance of vital records through a single office in 1836. This stimulated the first American State registration law enacted in Massachusetts in 1842." John B. Blake in "The Early History of Vital Statistics in Massachusetts," *Bulletin of the History of Medicine; Baltimore, Md.* 29 (January 1, 1955): 46–68, argues that the earliest efforts at establishing vital statistics in the United States occurred two centuries before British efforts when the General Court of Massachusetts established the civil registration of marriages, births, and deaths in 1639. The success of this law was spotty, though outbreaks of disease often spurred a renewed urgency.

11. See Margo J. Anderson, *The American Census: A Social History* (New Haven, CT: Yale University Press, 1990), for the fascinating details of the six schedules of the 1850 U.S. Census.

12. David A. Worton, *Dominion Bureau of Statistics: A History of Canada's Central Statistical Office and Its Antecedents, 1841–1972* (Montreal and Kingston: McGill-Queen's University Press, 1998).

13. Akenson, *Some Family*, 50.

14. Samuel M. Otterstrom, "Genealogy as Religious Ritual: The Doctrine and Practice of Family History in the Church of Jesus Christ of Latter-day Saints," in *Geography and Genealogy: Locating Personal Pasts*, ed. Jeanne Kay Guelke (New York: Routledge, 2016), 144.

15. Roger Minert, interview by the author, Salt Lake City, May 2010.

16. Joseph Smith, *History of the Church of Jesus Christ of Latter-day Saints*, ed. B. H. Roberts (Salt Lake City: Deseret News, 1908), 4:231.

17. Alexander L. Baugh, "'For This Ordinance Belongeth to My House': The Practice of Baptism for the Dead Outside the Nauvoo Temple," *Mormon Historical Studies* 3, no. 1 (2002): 47.

18. Quinn, "Practice of Rebaptism at Nauvoo," 228.

19. R. Bushman, *Joseph Smith*.

20. Shipley Munson, interview by the author, Salt Lake City, May 2010.

21. "The Doctrine and Covenants of the Church of Jesus Christ of Latter-day Saints," 127, www.lds.org/scriptures/dc-testament?lang=eng.

22. Ibid.

23. "Plural Marriage in Kirtland and Nauvoo," ChurchofJesusChrist.org.

24. François Weil, *Family Trees: A History of Genealogy in America* (Cambridge, MA: Harvard University Press, 2013), 174.

25. Allen, Embry, and Mehr, *Hearts Turned to the Fathers*, 40.

26. François Weil, "John Farmer and the Making of American Genealogy," *New England Quarterly* 80, no. 3 (2007): 409, 411, 417.

27. Ibid., 423.

28. Appleton Prentiss Clark Griffin, *Bibliography of American Historical Societies (the United States and the Dominion of Canada)* (Washington, DC: American Historical Association, 1896).

29. Robert M. Taylor and Ralph J. Crandall, *Generations and Change: Genealogical Perspectives in Social History* (Macon, GA: Mercer University Press, 1986), 8. Taylor and Crandall's essay collection provides an excellent overview of the waves of interest in genealogy from the 1840s through the 1980s.

30. Quoted in Weil, *Family Trees*, 174.

31. Allen, Embry, and Mehr, *Hearts Turned to the Fathers*, 40–44.

32. R. Taylor and Crandall, *Generations and Change*, 7.

33. Allen, Embry, and Mehr, *Hearts Turned to the Fathers*, 53.

34. Susa Young Gates and Church of Jesus Christ of Latter-day Saints, General Board of the Relief Society, *Surname Book and Racial History? A Compilation and Arrangement*

of Genealogical and Historical Data for Use by the Students and Members of the Relief Society of the Church of Jesus Christ of Latter-day Saints. Prepared and Published under the Auspices of the General Board of the Relief Society with the Approval of the Board of the Genealogical Society of Utah (Salt Lake City: Board of the Genealogical Society of Utah, 1918), http://archive.org/details/surnamebookracia00gate.

35. Max Perry Mueller, *Race and the Making of the Mormon People* (Chapel Hill: University of North Carolina Press, 2017). Further, Mueller makes the argument that the Mormons created "a new, distinctly white Mormon race to which even other white Americans did not belong" (11).

36. Gates and Church of Jesus Christ of Latter-day Saints, General Board of the Relief Society, *Surname Book and Racial History,* vi.

37. *Proceedings International Congress of Genealogy, San Francisco, July 28–31, 1915,* 3, http://hdl.handle.net/2027/nyp.33433034017032.

38. Allen, Embry, and Mehr, *Hearts Turned to the Fathers,* 99. See also Otterstrom, "Genealogy as Religious Ritual."

39. There have been many other additions to the Family History library, including in Logan, St. George, and smaller centers dotted all along the Wasatch front and more than forty-seven hundred branch libraries worldwide.

40. Ernie Smith, "The Strange History of Microfilm, Which Will Be with Us for Centuries," June 20, 2016, www.atlasobscura.com; Lester K. Born, "History of Microform Activity," *Library Trends* 8, no. 3 (1960): 348–58.

41. Allen, Embry, and Mehr, *Hearts Turned to the Fathers,* 215–17. Even as an early institutional adopter, the church is rarely mentioned in histories of microfilm use.

42. A "stake" is a group of at least five wards or branches (congregations) that operates as an intermediate level in the Mormon Church hierarchy.

43. Ibid., 217.

44. David Conley Nelson, *Moroni and the Swastika: Mormons in Nazi Germany* (Norman: University of Oklahoma Press, 2015), 4–5.

45. Fawn McKay Brodie, quoted ibid., 114–15.

46. Allen, Embry, and Mehr, *Hearts Turned to the Fathers,* 225–27.

47. See Gary Mokotoff, "The Mormon/Jewish Controversy: What Really Happened," www.avotaynu.com/mormon.htm; and Bernard Kouchel, "A Chronicle of the Mormon/Jewish Controversy: The LDS Agreement," www.jewishgen.org/info Files/ldsagree.html. Kouchel provides a link to the full text of the agreement. "LDS Church and Jewish Group Reach Agreement," *Deseret News,* April 28, 1995, www .deseretnews.com; Gustav Niebuhr, "Mormons to End Holocaust Victim Baptism," *New York Times,* April 29, 1995, www.nytimes.com.

48. Don Casias, telephone interview with the author, June 21, 2019.

49. Allen, Embry, and Mehr, *Hearts Turned to the Fathers,* 141.

50. Ibid., 222, 230, 103.

51. Ibid., 175.

52. Scott Taylor, "Mormon Church's Storied Granite Mountain Vault Opened for Virtual Tour," *Deseret News,* April 29, 2010, www.deseretnews.com; "Granite Mountain Records Vault," October 1, 2012, www.mormonnewsroom.ca.

53. Allen, Embry, and Mehr, *Hearts Turned to the Fathers,* 175.

54. Ibid., 304.

55. Ibid., 184.

56. Minutes of the General Council Executive Committee of the United Church of Canada, "Guidelines and Policy for Access to Baptism, Marriage, or Burial Registers," November 1992, 1993, draft provided courtesy of Nicole Vonk, United Church archivist, email to the author, June 28, 2017.

57. Allen, Embry, and Mehr, *Hearts Turned to the Fathers,* 267.

58. "An Insider's View of Mormon Genealogy and Temple Work," Don Anderson (Casias), interviewed by John Delhin, *Mormon Stories* (blog), March 6, 2019, www .mormonstories.org/podcast/don-anderson-casias/.

59. Christine Kenneally, "The Mormon Church Is Building a Family Tree of the Entire Human Race," *New Republic,* October 14, 2014, https://newrepublic.com. I haven't seen this figure confirmed elsewhere, and even the Library of Congress has trouble assessing the size of its holdings. Susan Manus, "The Immeasurable Library of Congress," August 6, 2012, https://blogs.loc.gov.

60. "What Is the Four-Generation Program?," www.churchofjesuschrist.org; Casias, telephone interview.

61. "Insider's View of Mormon Genealogy and Temple Work."

62. Casias, telephone interview.

63. "Statement by the Catholic Church on the LDS Mormon Church," www.truth andgrace.com; "Vatican Rules LDS Baptisms 'Invalid,'" *Deseret News,* July 18, 2001.

64. Tom Heneghan, "Catholic-Mormon Tension over LDS Baptism of the Dead," *Reuters Blogs* (blog), May 8, 2008, http://blogs.reuters.com/faithworld/2008/05/08/ catholic-mormon-tension-over-lds-baptism-of-the-dead/.

65. Jason Horowitz, "In Mormon Files, Researcher Helen Radkey Seeks to Cause a Headache for Romney," *Washington Post,* February 16, 2012; Peggy Fletcher Stack, "Who Is Helen Radkey and Why Is She Out to Get the LDS Church?," *Salt Lake Tribune,* December 4, 2009.

66. Amy Davidson Sorkin, "Romney, Wiesel, and the Baptism of the Dead," *New Yorker,* February 15, 2012; Peter Wallsten and Jason Horowitz, "Elie Wiesel Calls on Mitt Romney to Make Mormon Church Stop Proxy Baptisms of Jews," *Washington Post,* February 14, 2012.

67. Howard Berkes, "Mormon Church Limits Access to Controversial Baptism Records," March 9, 2012, www.npr.org.

68. Jay Verkler, interview by the author, Salt Lake City, May 2010.

69. Munson, interview.

70. Dick Eastman, "The Death of Microfilm," *Eastman's Online Genealogy Newsletter* (blog), May 29, 2014, https://blog.eogn.com.

71. Casias, telephone interview.

72. Munson, interview.

73. Casias, telephone interview.

CHAPTER 3: ANCESTRY.INC

1. Dan Taggart, interview by the author, Provo, UT, May 2010.

2. Ibid.

3. Ibid.

4. Paul B. Allen, interview by the author, Provo, UT, May 2010.

5. Taggart, interview.

6. Web crawlers are virtual tools designed to "crawl the Web" on a regular basis to find new material to index.

7. Brian Leverich, "An (Almost) Unexpurgated History of Rootsweb," http://home pages.rootsweb.ancestry.com/~socgen/history.html#leverich.

8. Karen Isaacson, "RootsWeb and USGenWeb: Working Together for Genealogy on the Internet," http://homepages.rootsweb.ancestry.com; Leverich, "An (Almost) Unexpurgated History of Rootsweb."

9. Allen, interview.

10. "Broderbund," https://en.wikipedia.org.

11. Patricia McMorrow, "Mattel Spins Off FTM," *Family Tree* (blog), www.family treemagazine.com/premium/mattel-spins-off-ftm/.

12. Taggart, interview.

13. "MyFamily.com, Inc. Acquires Genealogy.com," http://news.genealogytoday.com.

14. Allen, interview; Taggart, interview.

15. Anne-Marie Kramer, interview by the author, Nottingham, 2010.

16. Taggart, interview.

17. Ancestry, Inc., "Editor's Note," *Ancestry Magazine,* February 1997; Loretto Dennis Szucs, "Editor's Note," *Ancestry Magazine,* August 1997.

18. Doug Bremner, *The Fastest Growing Religion on Earth: How Genealogy Captured the Brains and Imaginations of Americans* (Atlanta: Laughing Cow Books, 2013). Bremner tries to answer the question of his own addiction and those of other genealogists he encounters, including Cindy Howells, writer of one of the most widely influential genealogical blogs, "cyndislist." www.cyndislist.com.

19. Quincy LeNear, "I Have a DNAddiction," *Huffington Post* (blog), August 9, 2016, www.huffingtonpost.com; Roberta Estes, "The Stages of Genetic Genealogy Addiction," *DNAeXplained—Genetic Genealogy* (blog), July 6, 2016, https://dna

-explained.com; Amanda, "Signs You Might Be Addicted to Genealogy," *Fun with Genealogy* (blog), www.geni.com.

20. Neal Ungerleider, "Ancestors, Inc.: Inside the Remarkable Rise of the Genealogy Industry," *Fast Company*, July 15, 2015, www.fastcompany.com; "Free Family Tree, Genealogy and Family History," www.myheritage.com.

21. Taggart, interview.

22. "Ancestry.com Pulls in Another $33.2 Million," www.ecommercetimes.com.

23. Allen, interview.

24. Taggart, interview; Saul Hansell, "CMGI Can Defy Gravity Only So Long," *New York Times*, December 10, 2000, www.nytimes.com.

25. "Orem's MyFamily.Com Inc. Collects $30 Million in New Round of Financing," *Deseret News*, March 28, 2000, www.deseretnews.com.

26. "CMGI—MyFamily.com Partners with Onebox.com to Deliver Email, Voice Mail and Fax in a Single, Free Electronic Inbox," www.wallstreet-online.de; "MyFamily.com Brings Families Together—Courtesy of the Net," *Deseret News*, June 25, 2000, www.deseretnews.com.

27. Karen Aden, "Good News, Bad News, Good News: The Merger of RootsWeb and MyFamily.com," www.garycaden.com.

28. Taggart, interview.

29. "MyFamily.com to Buy Web Site ThirdAge," *Los Angeles Times*, October 31, 2000, http://articles.latimes.com; "CMGI—MyFamily.Com Partners with Onebox.Com."

30. Allen, interview.

31. "Broderbund Teams with MyFamily.Com to Launch Family Tree Maker® Version 11—the #1 Selling Genealogy Software Program," www.thefreelibrary.com.

32. "MyFamily Growing in Utah," April 13, 2004, www.deseretnews.com.

33. "TGN and Ancestry.com Sold," www.ancestryinsider.org.

34. Rafat Ali, "Ancestry.com Files for $75 Million IPO," *Washington Post*, August 4, 2009, www.washingtonpost.com.

35. "Ancestry.com Inc. (Form: S-1, Received: 08/03/2009 16:10:09)," www.nasdaq.com.

36. "Ancestry.com Buying Spree," www.tamurajones.net.

37. "Ancestry Ups Affiliate Commissions," *Paul Allen: Keynote Speaker, Tech Visionary* (blog), July 26, 2006, http://paulallen.net/2006/07/26/ancestry-ups-affiliate-commissions/.

38. Neil Genzlinger, "*Who Do You Think You Are?* Lisa Kudrow and Family Trees," *New York Times*, March 3, 2010, www.nytimes.com.

39. David Lieberman, "NBC Cancellation of *Who Do You Think You Are?* Uproots Ancestry.com Investors," *Deadline Hollywood*, May 14, 2012, https://deadline.com.

40. Graeme Davison, "Speed-Relating," *History Australia* 6, no. 2 (2009): 7–8.

41. Allen, interview.

42. Lieberman, "NBC Cancellation of *Who Do You Think You Are?*"

43. Allen, interview; "Ancestry.com Agrees to $1.6 Billion Buyout, Making Multi-millionaires of Its Execs," www.dailymail.co.uk.

44. Taggart, interview.

45. Erik Davis, "Databases of the Dead," *Wired,* July 1, 1999, www.wired.com; Taggart, interview.

46. "Uncharitable Doings at the Family History Library," May 7, 2007, http://voice ofutah.livejournal.com/34556.html; "Ancestry.com Message on APG Regarding Use at LDS Libraries," www.ancestryinsider.org.

47. "Concerns in FamilySearch/NARA Partnership," www.ancestryinsider.org.

48. "The Generations Network Reiterates, 'We Absolutely Do Not View the Church as a Competitor,'" www.ancestryinsider.org; Peggy Fletcher Stack, "Online Genealogy Just Got Easier," *Salt Lake Tribune,* May 19, 2007, http://archive.sltrib .com/story.php?ref=/search/ci_5934059.

49. Chris Paton, "FamilySearch and Ancestry Announce Partnership over US Census Records," July 21, 2008, http://scottishancestry.blogspot.com.

50. Shipley Munson, interview by the author, Salt Lake City, May 2010.

51. Shane Bauer, "Did an Inmate Digitize Your Genealogical Records?," *Mother Jones,* August 13, 2015, www.motherjones.com; Megan Smolenyak, "Inmates Indexing Genealogy Records," *Huffington Post* (blog), August 13, 2015, www.huffingtonpost .com.

52. Don Casias, telephone interview with the author, June 21, 2019.

53. "Exploitation and Spin: How the LDS Church Is Making Millions by Driving Members to Do Genealogy Work, and Selling the Results Back to Them and Others," *r/exmormon* Reddit (blog), August . 2, 2015, www.reddit.com; Dennis Brimhall, "FamilySearch Partnerships: Some Questions and Answers," *FamilySearch Blog* (blog), February 26, 2014, www.familysearch.org; "Concerns in FamilySearch/ NARA Partnership."

54. Casias, telephone interview.

55. Taggart, interview.

56. Susan D. Young, email to the author, March 3, 2017.

57. "Terms and Conditions," www.ancestry.com.

58. Allen, interview.

59. "Canceling a Subscription," support.ancestry.com; "How to Close an Ancestry. com Account When Someone Dies," Everplans, www.everplans.com.

60. Allen, interview.

61. Jon Christian and Alex Barasch, "Deleting the Family Tree," *Slate,* April 23, 2015, www.slate.com; "Ancestry.com Announces Retirement of Several Websites," www .ancestryinsider.org; "Most Popular Genealogy Application," www.tamurajones .net; "Ancestry to Retire Family Tree Maker Software," https://blogs.ancestry.com.

62. Family Tree Editors, "Opinions on the MyFamily-RootsWeb Merger," *Family Tree* (blog), August 20, 2008, www.familytreemagazine.com.

63. RootsWeb.com home page, http://home.rootsweb.ancestry.com/.

64. Taggart, interview.

CHAPTER 4: ICELAND

1. "New App Helps Icelanders Avoid Accidental Incest," *USA Today,* April 18, 2013, www.usatoday.com; Rose Eveleth, "Some Icelanders Are Accidentally Dating a Relative and Now There's an App for That," April 18, 2013, www.smithsonianmag .com.

2. Gunnar Karlsson, *The History of Iceland* (Minnesota: University of Minnesota Press, 2000), 11.

3. Arnar Árnason and Bob Simpson, "Refractions through Culture: The New Genomics in Iceland," *Ethnos* 68, no. 4 (2003): 545; Ben Myers, "The Icelandic Sagas: Europe's Most Important Book?," *Guardian,* October 3, 2008.

4. Axel Kristinsson, "Lords and Literature: The Icelandic Sagas as Political and Social Instruments," *Scandinavian Journal of History* 28, no. 1 (2003): 1.

5. Theodore Murdock Andersson, *The Growth of the Medieval Icelandic Sagas (1180–1280)* (Ithaca, NY: Cornell University Press, 2006), 17, 16.

6. Siân Grønlie, trans., *Íslendingabók—Kristni Saga / The Book of the Icelanders—the Story of the Conversion,* Viking Society for Northern Research Text Series (University College London, 2006), 3, www.vsnrweb-publications.org.uk/Text%20Series/IslKr .pdf.

7. Herman Palsson and Paul Edwards, *The Book of Settlements: Landnámabók* (Winnipeg: University of Manitoba Press, 2014), 8.

8. Jenny M. Jochens, "The Church and Sexuality in Medieval Iceland," *Journal of Medieval History* 6, no. 4 (1980): 377–92, https://doi.org/10.1016/0304-4181(80)90039-1.

9. Tom de Castella, "The Eruption That Changed Iceland Forever," April 16, 2010, http://news.bbc.co.uk/2/hi/8624791.stm.

10. Jamaica Potts, "At Least Give the Natives Glass Beads: An Examination of the Bargain Made between Iceland and deCODE Genetics with Implications for Global Bioprospecting," *Virginia Journal of Law Technology* 7 (2002): 5.

11. Michael Specter, "Decoding Iceland," *New Yorker,* January 18, 1999, 43–51.

12. Interestingly, one of the religious influences in Iceland were the Mormons. Icelanders were among the Mormons who migrated to Utah in the 1850s, and Icelandic Mormon converts began to practice in Iceland around the same time. The journal of *Mormon Historical Studies* devotes a special section of its 2016 volume 17 issue to the study of Mormons in Iceland and Icelanders in Utah.

13. The first significant infusion of new blood did not occur until the Second World War, when the Allies occupied the island, and afterward, when the disliked U.S.

troops stationed in Reykjavik in a Cold War defensive outpost against the Russians fathered many unclaimed children. There were forty thousand soldiers stationed in Iceland at the height of the war, more than the numbers of Icelandic men. These were occupation forces, but nonetheless the war brought prosperity and sovereignty to Iceland, leading to some profoundly ambivalent emotions about Americans. One of the women I interviewed in Reykjavik, Asa, was the likely child of such a union, but her mother, more ashamed of having had a child with an American than having had a child out of wedlock, lied and said the father was an Icelander. Asa forced the man's children to have a DNA test and then another American family. Bloodlines matter greatly in tightly knit communities.

14. Gunnar "Viking" Olafsson, interview by the author, Reykjavik, June 2012.

15. Friðrik Skúlason, interview by the author, Reykjavik, June 2012.

16. Gísli Pálsson, *Anthropology and the New Genetics* (Cambridge: Cambridge University Press, 2007), 83.

17. This "added-value" argument was exactly the same as the justification given to me by the Mormon Church, the Ancestry founders, and Scott Woodward at SMGF for copywriting public information.

18. *Maorgunblaðið* (2002), quoted ibid., 84n1.

19. Gísli Pálsson, "The Wen of Kin: An Online Genealogical Machine," in *Kinship and Beyond: The Genealogical Model Reconsidered* (New York: Berghahn Books, 2009), 96.

20. Christina von Nolcken, "Egil Skallagrimsson and the Viking Ideal," Fathom Archive, n.d., http://fathom.lib.uchicago.edu.

21. Jeffrey R. Gulcher and Kári Stefánsson, "deCODE: A Genealogical Approach to Human Genetics in Iceland," *ELS* (September 15, 2006): 2.

22. Árnason and Simpson, "Refractions through Culture," 544.

23. Specter, "Decoding Iceland."

24. Gulcher and Stefánsson, "deCODE"; H. A. Arnarson, *Decoding Iceland: The DNA of Greed* (documentary, 2013), http://decodingiceland.com/; Specter, "Decoding Iceland."

25. Jon F. Merz, "'Iceland Inc.'? On the Ethics of Commercial Population Genomics," *Social Science and Medicine* 58, no. 6 (2004): 1202–3.

26. Potts, "At Least Give the Natives Glass Beads," 9–10; Einar Árnason and Bogi Andersen, "deCODE and Iceland: A Critique," *ELS* (February 15, 2013): 2.

27. Potts, "At Least Give the Natives Glass Beads," 13; Vilhjálmur Árnason, "Coding and Consent: Moral Challenges of the Database Project in Iceland," *Bioethics* 18, no. 1 (2004): 33; Jeffrey R. Gulcher and Kári Stefánsson, "The Icelandic Healthcare Database and Informed Consent," *New England Journal of Medicine* 342, no. 24 (2000): 1827–30.

28. Specter, "Decoding Iceland," 49.

29. Skúli Sigurdsson, "Yin-Yang Genetics; or, The HSD deCODE Controversy," *New Genetics and Society* 20, no. 2 (2001): 110.

30. Potts, "At Least Give the Natives Glass Beads," 18.

31. Richard Lewontin, "People Are Not Commodities," *New York Times*, January 23, 1999.

32. Tina Piper, "The Collusion of Law and Science in the Piracy of Human Genes," *Dalhousie Journal of Legal Studies* 9 (2000): 237–77; Gísli Pálsson and Paul Rabinow, "The Icelandic Genome Debate," *TRENDS in Biotechnology* 19, no. 5 (2001): 169.

33. Specter, "Decoding Iceland," 45; David Oddsson quoted in Simon Mawer, "Iceland, the Nation of Clones," *New York Times*, January 23, 1999.

34. Árnason and Andersen, "deCODE and Iceland," 4.

35. Arnarson, *Decoding Iceland*.

36. James Meek, "Decode Was Meant to Save Lives . . . Now It's Destroying Them," *Guardian*, October 11, 2002, www.theguardian.com.

37. Matthew Herper, "Choppy IPO for deCode Genetics," *Forbes*, July 19, 2000, www.forbes.com.

38. "DECODE GENETICS INC (Form: 424B4, Received: 07/18/2000 11:52:42)," www.nasdaq.com/markets/ipos/filing.ashx?filingid=1223935.

39. The Association of Icelanders for Ethics in Science and Medicine, or Mannvernd, and a group of physicians and other citizens intended to file lawsuits against the state of Iceland and any other relevant parties, including deCODE, to test the constitutionality of the act.

40. "DECODE GENETICS INC (Form: 424B4, Received: 07/18/2000 11:52:42)."

41. Ibid., 15; Árnason and Simpson, "Refractions through Culture," 545–46.

42. Potts, "At Least Give the Natives Glass Beads," 6.

43. "Act on Biobanks," Persónu Vernd, May 13, 2000, www.personuvernd.is/information-in-english/greinar/nr/439.

44. Potts, "At Least Give the Natives Glass Beads"; Gulcher and Stefánsson, "Icelandic Healthcare Database and Informed Consent"; Gísli Pálsson and Paul Rabinow, "Iceland: The Case of a National Human Genome Project," *Anthropology Today* 15, no. 5 (1999): 14–18; Árnason and Andersen, "deCODE and Iceland."

45. Potts, "At Least Give the Natives Glass Beads."

46. Sigurdsson, "Yin-Yang Genetics," 113.

47. Michael Fortun, *Promising Genomics: Iceland and deCODE Genetics in a World of Speculation* (Berkeley: University of California Press, 2008).

48. Meek, "Decode Was Meant to Save Lives"; Herper, "Choppy IPO for deCode Genetics."

49. Potts, "At Least Give the Natives Glass Beads."

50. Meek, "Decode Was Meant to Save Lives."

51. See Merz, "'Iceland Inc.'?," 1203, for a simplified diagram of the encryption process.

52. Christian Lenk, Nils Hoppe, and Roberto Andorno, eds., *Ethics and Law of Intellectual Property: Current Problems in Politics, Science and Technology* (New York: Routledge, 2016), 30; Alison Abbott, "Icelandic Database Shelved as Court Judges Privacy in Peril," *Nature* 429, no. 118 (2004).

53. James Butcher, "Profile, Kári Stefánsson: A General of Genetics," *Lancet* 369 (January 27, 2007): 267.

54. James Gallagher, "DNA of 'an Entire Nation' Assessed," *BBC News,* March 26, 2015, www.bbc.com.

55. Samantha Bresnahan, "The Isolated Island That Could Reveal New Medicines," CNN, March 16, 2017, www.cnn.com.

56. Masha Gessen, *Blood Matters: From BRCA1 to Designer Babies, How the World and I Found Ourselves in the Future of the Gene* (Boston: Houghton Mifflin Harcourt, 2009).

57. George F. Will, "The Real Down Syndrome Problem: Accepting Genocide," March 14, 2018, www.washingtonpost.com; Julian Quinones et al., "'What Kind of Society Do You Want to Live in?': Inside the Country Where Down Syndrome Is Disappearing," August 14, 2017, www.cbsnews.com; Patricia Heaton, "'Iceland Isn't Eliminating Down Syndrome—They Are Just Killing Everyone Who Has It,'" *America Magazine,* December 4, 2017, www.americamagazine.org.

58. Michael D. Lemonick, "The Iceland Experiment," *Time,* February 12, 2006, content.time.com.

59. Meg Tirrell, "Iceland's Genetic Goldmine, and the Man behind It," April 6, 2017, www.cnbc.com.

60. Kevin Davies, "Kari Stefansson on deCODE's Alzheimer's Discovery, Future Plans," July 11, 2012, www.bio-itworld.com.

61. Ibid.

62. "Ancel Keys," *Seven Countries Study: The First Study to Relate Diet with Cardiovascular Disease* (blog), www.sevencountriesstudy.com.

63. Stephen T. Sinatra et al., "The Saturated Fat, Cholesterol, and Statin Controversy: A Commentary," *Journal of the American College of Nutrition* 33, no. 1 (2014): 79–88.

64. Anne Georget, *Cholesterol, the Great Bluff* (Andana Films, 2016), www.andana films.com.

65. Cristin E. Kearns, Laura A. Schmidt, and Stanton A. Glantz, "Sugar Industry and Coronary Heart Disease Research," *JAMA Internal Medicine* 176, no. 11 (2016): 1680–85.

66. Michel de Lorgeril, *Cholesterol and Statins: Sham Science and Bad Medicine,* trans. Anne Pietrasik (France: Thierry Souccar, 2014), 67; Michel de Lorgeril and Mikael Rabaeus, "Beyond Confusion and Controversy, Can We Evaluate the Real Efficacy and Safety of Cholesterol-Lowering with Statins?," *Journal of Controversies in Biomedical Research* 1, no. 1 (2016): 67–92.

67. Erika Check Hayden, "Icelandic Genomics Firm Goes Bankrupt," *Nature* 462, no. 7272 (2009): 401.

68. Dan Vorhaus, "Meet the New deCODE, Same as the Old deCODE?," January 25, 2010, www.genomicslawreport.com.

69. Monya Baker, "Big Biotech Buys Iconic Genetics Firm," *Nature,* 492, no. 7429 (2012): 321.

70. Hayden, "Icelandic Genomics Firm Goes Bankrupt."

71. Dan Vorhaus and Lawrence Moore, "What Happens If a DTC Genomics Company Goes Belly Up?," Privacy Report, September 18, 2009, https://theprivacy report.com.

72. Matt O'Brien, "The Miraculous Story of Iceland," *Washington Post,* June 17, 2015, www.washingtonpost.com.

73. Baker, "Big Biotech Buys Iconic Genetics Firm."

74. Henry T. Greely, "Amgen Buys deCODE—Reflections Backwards, Forwards, and on DTC Genomics," *Stanford Law School* (blog), https://law.stanford.edu.

75. Árnason, "Coding and Consent."

76. www.decode.com/publications/.

77. Davies, "Stefansson on deCODE's Alzheimer's Discovery"; Gallagher, "DNA of 'an Entire Nation' Assessed."

78. Bresnahan, "Isolated Island That Could Reveal New Medicines."

79. Benjamin Capps, "Models of Biobanks and Implications for Reproductive Health Innovation," *Monash Bioethics Review* 33, no. 4 (2015): 238–57; Einar Árnason, "Commentary on Models of Biobanks and Implications for Reproductive Health Innovation," *Monash Bioethics Review* 33, no. 4 (2015): 258–64.

80. "Behind the NextCode Spinout | Amgen Business Development," www.amgen bd.com.

81. Ben Fidler, "Second Exit for DeCode Investors as Spinout NextCODE Sold to WuXi," https://xconomy.com.

82. Yian Q. Mui, "China's $9 Billion Effort to Beat the U.S. in Genetic Testing," *Washington Post,* December 30, 2016, www.washingtonpost.com.

83. Reuters, "China to Tighten Rules on Foreigners Using Genetic Material," www .reuters.com.

CHAPTER 5: GENETIC GENEALOGY

1. "Ancestry CEO Tim Sullivan Stepping Down," September 12, 2017, www.ancestry .com.

2. Mark G. Thomas et al., "Origins of Old Testament Priests," *Nature* 394, no. 6689 (1998): 138–40; Eugene A. Foster et al., "Jefferson Fathered Slave's Last Child," *Nature* 396, no. 6706 (1998): 27–28.

3. Thomas et al., "Origins of Old Testament Priests," 139. One of the most prolific contributors to the field of Jewish genetic genealogy is Jeffrey Mark Paull, whose research, most of it self-published, now claims to have identified the Y-DNA genetic signatures of "the world's most esteemed and historically significant rabbinical lineages and dynasties." See Academia.edu.

4. Ian Vincent McGonigle, "'Jewish Genetics' and the 'Nature' of Israeli Citizenship," *De Gguyter* 13, no. 2 (2015): 97, 98.

5. Foster et al., "Jefferson Fathered Slave's Last Child."

6. E. A. Foster et al., "Reply: The Thomas Jefferson Paternity Case," *Nature* 397, no. 6714 (1999): 32.

7. One of the earliest biographers to argue for Jefferson's paternity of Hemings's children was Fawn McKay Brodie in *Thomas Jefferson: An Intimate History* (New York: W. W. Norton, 1974) (Brodie was used to controversy, given her earlier biography of Joseph Smith). Annette Gordon-Reed, *Thomas Jefferson and Sally Hemings: An American Controversy* (Charlottesville: University of Virginia Press, 1998) updated her book based on the DNA results. See also a very small selection of the response: Joseph J. Ellis, "Jefferson: Post-DNA," *William and Mary Quarterly* 57, no. 1 (2000): 125–38; Thomas Jefferson Foundation, "Report of the Research Committee on Thomas Jefferson and Sally Hemings," January 2000, www.monticello.org; and Annette Gordon-Reed, *The Hemingses of Monticello: An American Family* (New York: W. W. Norton, 2009).

8. Dead ends or "brick walls" in genealogy are usually anomalies in record keeping produced by all kinds of dis-orderly conduct: children being disowned, bigamy, adoption (formal or informal), name changes, sex changes, race changes. Added to these regular occurrences are the major traumatic breaks of the past three hundred years: the Atlantic slave trade, the Irish exodus, and the Holocaust, all of which destroyed family lines and records.

9. Bennett Greenspan, "An Insider's Look at the Genealogy DNA Field," *Texas Jewish Historical Society* (November 2010).

10. Karl Skorecki et al., "Y Chromosomes of Jewish Priests," *Nature* 385, no. 6611 (1997): 32.

11. Bennett Greenspan, "Bennett Greenspan—FamilyTreeDNA.com," *HighDrive Network* (blog), December 2, 2012, www.highdrive.tv.

12. Nurit Kirsh, "Population Genetics in Israel in the 1950s: The Unconscious Internalization of Ideology," *Isis* 94, no. 4 (2003): 631–55; Esther Kahana et al., "Creutzfeldt-Jakob Disease: Focus among Libyan Jews in Israel," *Science* 183, no. 4120 (1974): 90–91.

13. Raphael Falk, "Genetic Markers Cannot Determine Jewish Descent," *Frontiers in Genetics* 5 (January 21, 2015): 7.

14. Sheila Jasanoff, ed., *States of Knowledge: The Co-production of Science and the Social Order* (London: Routledge, 2004).

15. McGonigle, "'Jewish Genetics,'" 98–99; Jeremy Sharon, "'Who Is a Jew?' Can Now Be Answered by Genetic Testing," *Jerusalem Post,* October 3, 2017, www.jpost.com.

16. McGonigle, "'Jewish Genetics,'" 90.

17. Falk, "Genetic Markers Cannot Determine Jewish Descent," 9; Raphael Falk, *Zionism and the Biology of Jews* (New York: Springer International, 2017); Eran Elhaik, "In Search of the Jüdische Typus: A Proposed Benchmark to Test the Genetic Basis of Jewishness Challenges Notions of 'Jewish Biomarkers,'" *Frontiers in Genetics* 7 (August 5, 2016).

18. Bryan Sykes, *The Seven Daughters of Eve: The Science That Reveals Our Genetic Ancestry* (New York: W. W. Norton, 2001), 16.

19. Ibid., 8.

20. Ibid., 95.

21. Ibid., 197.

22. Scott Woodward, interview by the author, Salt Lake City, 2012. Unless otherwise noted, all subsequent quotes are taken from this interview.

23. Spencer Wells, *Deep Ancestry: The Landmark DNA Quest to Decipher Our Distant Past* (Washington, DC: National Geographic, 2007). As Wells explains, the sequencing of the human genome in 2000 ushered in the genomic era. The hard science was in place, but not the human subjects.

24. Ugo A. Perego, Natalie M. Myres, and Scott R. Woodward, "Reconstructing the Y-Chromosome of Joseph Smith: Genealogical Applications," *Journal of Mormon History* 31, no. 2 (2005): 42–60.

25. Matthew Miller, "Shrewd, Very Shrewd," *Forbes,* March 1, 2004, www.forbes.com; "Sorenson Molecular Genealogy Foundation's Genetic Genealogy Database Crosses Historic Milestone with 100,000 DNA Samples, Aided by Multi-million Dollar Gift from Founder," EON: Enhanced Online News, April 28, 2010, www.businesswire.com.

26. Roberta Estes, "Is History Repeating Itself at Ancestry?," *DNAeXplained—Genetic Genealogy* (blog), August 30, 2012, https://dna-explained.com.

27. Ibid.

28. www.calicolabs.com/; Katie Palmer, "Another Personal Genetics Company Is Sharing Client Data," *Wired,* July 2015, www.wired.com; Jennifer Lynch, "How Private DNA Data Led Idaho Cops on a Wild Goose Chase and Linked an Innocent Man to a 20-Year-Old Murder Case," Electronic Frontier Foundation, May 1, 2015, www.eff.org.

29. "MyFamily.com (Ancestry.com) Names New Chief Executive Officer," Spectrum Equity, September 2005, www.spectrumequity.com; "Ancestry Sets AncestryDNA Sales Record Over Holiday Period and Fourth Quarter," Ancestry Corporate, January 10, 2017, www.ancestry.com.

30. Antonio Regalado, "2017 Was the Year Consumer DNA Testing Blew Up," *MIT Technology Review* (February 12, 2018), www.technologyreview.com.

31. "Our Story," Ancestry Corporate, March 27, 2018, www.ancestry.com.

32. Daniela Hernandez, "Ancestry.com Is Quietly Transforming Itself into a Medical Research Juggernaut," Splinter, April 3, 2015, https://splinternews.com.

33. https://genographic.nationalgeographic.com/. Just an aside, but IBM played a significant role in the Nazi project of Jewish genocide by generating and tabulating punch cards of national census data.

34. Wells, *Deep Ancestry*, 4, 5.

35. Adam Muller, "Asking Too Much, Receiving Too Little: Indigenous Identity and the Aims of Science," *Topia* 22 (2009): 5–34.

36. "Declaration of Indigenous Peoples of the Western Hemisphere Regarding the Human Genome Diversity Project," February 19, 1995, www.ipcb.org.

37. http://video.nationalgeographic.com/video/genographic/beyond-genealogy -who-are-you?source=relatedvideo.

38. Justine Petrone, "NatGeo Discontinues Genographic Ancestry Kit Sales, Will Shutter Service by End of 2020," *GenomeWeb*, June 7, 2019, www.genomeweb.com; https://genographic.nationalgeographic.com/.

39. Catherine Nash, *Genetic Geographies: The Trouble with Ancestry* (Minneapolis: University of Minnesota Press, 2015); Dorothy Roberts, *Fatal Invention: How Science, Politics, and Big Business Re-create Race in the Twenty-First Century* (New York: New Press, 2012); Alondra Nelson, *The Social Life of DNA: Race, Reparations, and Reconciliation after the Genome* (Boston: Beacon Press, 2016); Kimberly TallBear, *Native American DNA: Tribal Belonging and the False Promise of Genetic Science* (Minneapolis: University of Minnesota Press, 2013).

40. AfricanAncestry.com.

41. Nelson, *The Social Life of DNA*.

42. Henry Louis Gates Jr., *Finding Oprah's Roots: Finding Your Own* (New York: Crown, 2007); Henry Louis Gates Jr., *In Search of Our Roots: How 19 Extraordinary African Americans Reclaimed Their Past* (New York: Crown, 2009). Gates, a distinguished literary scholar from Harvard University, also turned his subjects' stories into reparative celebrations of finding themselves and their families, a process that "we might think of as 'reversing the middle passage'" (*Oprah's Roots*, 29).

43. Henry Louis Gates Jr., "African American Lives: The Past Is Another Country 2," PBS, February 6, 2008.

44. Henri-Corto Stoeklé et al., "23andMe: A New Two-Sided Data-Banking Market Model," *BMC Medical Ethics* 17, no. 19 (2016): 2.

45. "About Us," *23andMe Media Center* (blog), https://mediacenter.23andme.com/ company/about-us/.

46. Stoeklé et al., "23andMe," 5.

47. "Warning Letters—23andMe, Inc. 11/22/13," WebContent, 2013, www.fda.gov; Ruth Macklin, "The FDA and 23andMe: Regulating Direct-to-Consumer Genetic Tests," *Huffington Post*, December 17, 2013, www.huffingtonpost.com.

48. Charles Seife, "23andMe Is Terrifying, but Not for the Reasons the FDA Thinks," *Scientific American,* November 27, 2013, www.scientificamerican.com.

49. Matthew Herper, "Surprise! With $60 Million Genentech Deal, 23andMe Has a Business Plan," *Forbes,* January 6, 2015, www.forbes.com.

50. Sarah Zhang, "Of Course 23andMe's Plan Has Been to Sell Your Genetic Data All Along," Gizmodo, January 6, 2015, http://gizmodo.com.

51. L. Kalokairinou et al., "Legislation of Direct-to-Consumer Genetic Testing in Europe: A Fragmented Regulatory Landscape," *Journal of Community Genetics* 9, no. 2 (2018): 117–32.

52. Kristen Moulton, "Large Families Make Utah Fertile Ground for Genetics Researchers," *Los Angeles Times,* October 25, 1998, http://articles.latimes.com.

53. Richard S. Van Wagoner, *Mormon Polygamy: A History,* 2nd ed. (Salt Lake City: Signature Books, 1989).

54. Kirk Johnson, "By Accident, Utah Is Proving an Ideal Genetic Laboratory," *New York Times,* July 31, 2004, www.nytimes.com.

55. Mark Skolnick, "Why He Formed Myriad," DNA Learning Center, n.d., www.dnalc.org.

56. Mary-Claire King and A. C. Wilson, "Evolution at Two Levels in Humans and Chimpanzees," *Science* 188, no. 4184 (1975): 107–16.

57. E. Richard Gold and Julia Carbone, "Myriad Genetics: In the Eye of the Policy Storm," *Genetics in Medicine* 12, no. 1s (2010): S39–S70.

58. Tobin Klusty and Richard Weinmeyer, "Supreme Court to Myriad Genetics: Synthetic DNA Is Patentable but Isolated Genes Are Not," *AMA Journal of Ethics* 17, no. 9 (2015): 849.

59. "Myriad, Fresh Off Supreme Court Loss, Keeps on Suing over Gene Patents," Ars Technica, November 17, 2013, https://arstechnica.com.

60. Kelly Servick, "Controversial U.S. Bill Would Lift Supreme Court Ban on Patenting Human Genes," *Science,* June 4, 2019, www.sciencemag.org; Megan Molteni, "Congress Is Debating—Again—Whether Genes Can Be Patented," *Wired,* June 5, 2019, www.wired.com; Fay Flam, "Corporations Shouldn't Be Able to Patent Your DNA," June 14, 2019, www.bloomberg.com.

61. Masha Gessen, *Blood Matters: From BRCA1 to Designer Babies, How the World and I Found Ourselves in the Future of the Gene* (Boston: Houghton Mifflin Harcourt, 2009).

62. Meredith Salisbury, "Are 23andMe Customers Suckers or Empowered Consumers?," Techonomy, January 28, 2015, https://techonomy.com.

CHAPTER 6: THE NEW NATIVE

1. "Let's Open Our World," *Momondo—The DNA Journey,* June 1, 2016, www.youtube.com.

2. AeroMexico produced a brilliant spoof of this idea of connectedness and travel in Mexico by offering discounted flights to Americans from a Texas town who disliked

Mexico—after testing for their percentage of Mexican blood. It just happened to coincide, not coincidentally, with President Trump's bellicose border-wall threats against Mexican immigration to the United States. Both ads selected people who were not shy about being nationalistic and disliking other nationalities and races.

3. Paul Basu, *Route Metaphors of "Roots Tourism" in the Scottish Highland Diaspora* (London: Routledge, 2004); Kalyan Bhandari, "Imagining the Scottish Nation: Tourism and Homeland Nationalism in Scotland," *Current Issues in Tourism* 19, no. 9 (2016): 913–29; Tim Coles and Dallen J. Timothy, eds., *Tourism, Diasporas and Space* (London: Routledge, 2004); Gregory Higginbotham, "Seeking Roots and Tracing Lineages: Constructing a Framework of Reference for Roots and Genealogical Tourism," *Journal of Heritage Tourism* 7, no. 3 (2012): 189–203; Sabine Marschall, "'Homesick Tourism': Memory, Identity and (Be) Longing," *Current Issues in Tourism* 18, no. 9 (2015): 876–92; Gary McCain and Nina M. Ray, "Legacy Tourism: The Search for Personal Meaning in Heritage Travel," *Tourism Management* 24, no. 6 (2003): 713–17; Nina M. Ray and Gary McCain, "Personal Identity and Nostalgia for the Distant Land of Past: Legacy Tourism," *International Business & Economics Research Journal* (2012); Dallen J. Timothy, "Genealogical Mobility: Tourism and the Search for a Personal Past," in *Geography and Genealogy: Locating Personal Pasts,* ed. Dallen J. Timothy and Jeanne Kay Guelke (Burlington, VT: Ashgate, 2008), 115.

4. Shifa Rahaman, "Experts Claim Viral Momondo DNA Advert Isn't All It's Cracked Up to Be," June 7, 2016, http://cphpost.dk.

5. Kimberly TallBear, *Native American DNA: Tribal Belonging and the False Promise of Genetic Science* (Minneapolis: University of Minnesota Press, 2013), 75. Alondra Nelson will tell me the same thing.

6. Catherine Nash, interview by the author, London, November 2010. See also Catherine Nash, "Genetic Kinship," *Cultural Studies* 18, no. 1 (2004): 1–34. In this article, Nash studies "the cultural work entailed in converting the highly technical and inaccessible language of population genetics into meaningful concepts and valuable commodities" (4).

7. Maxine Mackintosh, "23andMe and AirBnB: Is Cultural Identity a Market for Consumer Genetic-Testing Companies?," *Forbes,* June 1, 2019, www.forbes.com.

8. Katarzyna Bryc et al., "The Genetic Ancestry of African Americans, Latinos, and European Americans across the United States," *American Journal of Human Genetics* 96, no. 1 (2015): 37; Rose Eveleth, "Genetic Testing and Tribal Identity," *Atlantic,* January 26, 2015, www.theatlantic.com.

9. Bryc et al., "Genetic Ancestry," 42.

10. Ibid., 44.

11. Françoise Baylis, "Black as Me: Narrative Identity," *Developing World Bioethics* 3, no. 2 (2003): 143, 148–49.

12. Bennett Greenspan, "Bennett Greenspan—FamilyTreeDNA.com," www.highdrive.tv/businessmakers/bennett-greenspan-familytreedna-com-2/; Matthew Frye

Jacobson, *Roots Too* (Cambridge, MA: Harvard University Press, 2006); Elizabeth C. Hirschman and Donald Panther-Yates, "Peering Inward for Ethnic Identity: Consumer Interpretation of DNA Test Results," *Identity* 8, no. 1 (2008): 47–66; Jacobson, *Roots Too*, 2; Wendy D. Roth and Biorn Ivemark, "Genetic Options: The Impact of Genetic Ancestry Testing on Consumers' Racial and Ethnic Identities," *American Journal of Sociology* 124, no. 1 (2018): 150–84; Natasha Golbeck and Wendy D. Roth, "Aboriginal Claims: DNA Testing and Changing Concepts of Indigeneity," in *Biomapping Indigenous Peoples: Towards an Understanding of the Issues,* ed. Susanne Berthier-Foglar, Sheila Collingwood-Whittick, and Sandrine Tolazzi (Amsterdam: Rodopi, 2012), 415–32; Dory Fox, "'We Are in the First Temple': Fact and Affect in American Jews' Emergent Genetic Narrative," *Shofar* 36, no. 1 (2018): 74–107.

13. TallBear, *Native American DNA,* 47.

14. Ibid., 62.

15. Ibid., 64; Darryl Leroux, "'A Genealogist's Paradise': France, Québec and the Genealogics of Race," *Ethnic and Racial Studies* 38, no. 5 (2015): 718–33; Darryl Leroux, "We've Been Here for 2,000 Years: White Settlers, Native American DNA and the Phenomenon of Indigenization," *Social Studies of Science* 48, no. 1 (2018): 80–100; Jorge Barrera and Tiffany Foxcroft, "Lab's DNA Results Say This Chihuahua Has 20% Indigenous Ancestry," June 13, 2018, https://newsinteractives.cbc.ca.

16. Nash, interview. See also Catherine Nash, "Geographies of Relatedness," *Transactions of the Institute of British Geographers* 30, no. 4 (2005): 449–62.

17. Alondra Nelson, interview by the author, New York, July 2014; Nash, interview; Meyerink, interview; Nelson, interview.

18. Nelson, interview.

19. Howard Wolinsky, "Genetic Genealogy Goes Global," *EMBO Reports* 7, no. 11 (2006): 1072–74.

20. Kevin and Lisa Winston, interview by the author, Salt Lake City, October 2010.

21. For a discussion of "genealogical disorientation," see Alondra Nelson, "Bio Science: Genetic Genealogy Testing and the Pursuit of African Ancestry," *Social Studies of Science* 38, no. 5 (2008): 759–83.

22. "Ancestry TV Commercial, 'Inseparable,'" iSpot.tv, http://www.ispot.tv; Salvador Hernandez, "Ancestry.com Has Pulled an Ad Amid Backlash That It Whitewashed the Violent History of Slavery," *BuzzFeed News,* April 18, 2019, www.buzzfeednews.com.

23. François Weil, "John Farmer and the Making of American Genealogy," *New England Quarterly* 80, no. 3 (2007): 408–34.

24. Brenton Simons, interview by the author, Boston, May 2011; Bryan Sykes, *DNA USA: A Genetic Portrait of America* (New York: Liveright, 2012). For a scientific critique of Sykes's book, see Charles C. Mann, "The Making of Americans," *Wall Street Journal,* July 6, 2012.

25. Simons, interview.

26. Ibid.

27. Nash, interview; Simons, interview.

28. Annie Linskey, "Elizabeth Warren Releases DNA Test on Native American Ancestry," *Boston Globe,* October 15, 2018, www.bostonglobe.com.

29. Anita Foeman, Bessie Lee Lawton, and Randall Rieger, "Questioning Race: Ancestry DNA and Dialog on Race," *Communication Monographs* 82, no. 2 (2015): 280.

30. Joanna Kaplanis et al., "Quantitative Analysis of Population-Scale Family Trees with Millions of Relatives," *Science,* April 12, 2018, 171–75.

31. Dieter Holger, "DNA Testing for Ancestry Is More Detailed for White People. Here's Why, and How It's Changing," *PC World,* December 4, 2018, www.pcworld.com; "The Real Issue: Diversity in Genetics Research," *23andMe Blog* (blog), September 12, 2016, https://blog.23andme.com; "23andMe Populations Collaborations Program," *23andMe for Scientists* (blog), https://research.23andme.com; "23andMe Launches the Global Genetics Project," *23andMe Blog* (blog), February 8, 2018, https://blog.23andme.com; Euny Hong, "23andMe Has a Problem When It Comes to Ancestry Reports for People of Color," *Quartz,* https://qz.com; Sarah Zhang, "23andMe Wants Its DNA Data to Be Less White," *Atlantic,* April 23, 2018, www.theatlantic.com.

32. "AfricanAncestry.com—Trace Your DNA. Find Your Roots. Today," http://africanancestry.com/faq/. For a history of the development of the DNA industry directly targeted African Americans, see Alondra Nelson, *The Social Life of DNA: Race, Reparations, and Reconciliation after the Genome* (Boston: Beacon Press, 2016).

33. Roberta Estes, "Ancestry 2018 Ethnicity Update," *DNAeXplained—Genetic Genealogy* (blog), September 13, 2018, https://dna-explained.com; "Major Enhancement to AncestryDNA's Ethnicity Estimates," *The DNA Geek* (blog), September 12, 2018, https://thednageek.com; "It's Time to Stop Giving Attention to 'Ethnicity' and Genetic Admixture," *An American Genealogy* (blog), September 24, 2018, https://anamericangenealogy.com.

34. Keith Noto et al., "Ethnicity Estimate 2018 White Paper," 2018, www.ancestry.com.

35. Estes, "Ancestry 2018 Ethnicity Update." See also "Major Enhancement to AncestryDNA's Ethnicity Estimates"; and "It's Time to Stop Giving Attention to 'Ethnicity' and Genetic Admixture."

36. Dan Taggart, interview by the author, Provo, UT, May 2010.

CHAPTER 7: THE GENEALOGICAL SUBLIME

1. Julia Creet, "How Cops Used a Public Genealogy Database in the Golden State Killer Case," http://theconversation.com.

2. Heather Murphy, "She Helped Crack the Golden State Killer Case. Here's What She's Going to Do Next," *New York Times,* September 10, 2018, www.nytimes.com.

3. "Parabon® Snapshot® DNA Analysis Service—Powered by Parabon NanoLabs," https://snapshot.parabon-nanolabs.com/.

4. Ellen M. Greytak, CeCe Moore, and Steven L. Armentrout, "Genetic Genealogy for Cold Case and Active Investigations," *Forensic Science International* 299 (June 1, 2019): 103–13.

5. Salvador Hernandez, "One of the Biggest at-Home DNA Testing Companies Is Working with the FBI," *BuzzFeed News*, January 31, 2019, www.buzzfeednews .com; Brad Berman, "Best DNA Testing Kits," *U.S. News & World Report*, January 7, 2019, https://health.usnews.com; Bennett Greenspan, "Press Release: Connecting Families and Saving Lives," *FamilyTreeDNA Blog* (blog), February 1, 2019, https://blog .familytreedna.com/press-release-connecting-families-and-saving-lives/.

6. Christi J. Guerrini et al., "Should Police Have Access to Genetic Genealogy Databases? Capturing the Golden State Killer and Other Criminals Using a Controversial New Forensic Technique," *PLOS Biology* 16, no. 10 (2018).

7. Sarah Zhang, "A DNA Company Wants You to Help Catch Criminals," *Atlantic*, March 29, 2019, www.theatlantic.com.

8. Tina Hesman Saey, "Genealogy Companies Could Struggle to Keep Clients' Data from Police," *Science News*, June 10, 2019, www.sciencenews.org.

9. Shoshana Zuboff, *The Age of Surveillance Capitalism: The Fight for a Human Future at the New Frontier of Power* (New York: PublicAffairs, 2019), 4, 5.

10. "Terms and Conditions," www.ancestry.com.

11. Kristen V. Brown, "Surprise DNA Results Are Turning Customer-Service Reps into Therapists," *BNN Bloomberg*, December 19, 2018, www.bnnbloomberg.ca.

12. Simon Usborne, "'I Thought—Who Will Remember Me?': The Man Who Fathered 200 Children," *Guardian*, November 24, 2018, www.theguardian.com.

13. "Finding My Parents | Find Birth Parents Now | We Are Here to Help in Finding Birth Parents," www.adopted.com/; Alison Bowen, "Genealogy Sites Are Helping Birth Parents Find Children They Placed for Adoption—but Not Everyone Wants to Be Found," *Chicago Tribune*, April 18, 2019, www.chicagotribune.com; Thomas Brewster, "Why Sperm Donor Privacy Is under Threat from DNA Sites—Is There Anything They Can Do about It?," *Forbes*, April 23, 2019, www.forbes.com; Mark Bridge, "Ban DNA Family Searches to Protect Sperm Donors," *Times*, April 23, 2019, www.thetimes.co.uk.

14. Amy Dockser Marcus, "Two Sisters Bought DNA Kits. The Results Blew Apart Their Family," *Wall Street Journal*, February 1, 2019, www.wsj.com.

15. Sarah Zhang, "When a DNA Test Shatters Your Identity," *Atlantic*, July 17, 2018, www.theatlantic.com.

16. "NPE Friends Fellowship," www.npefellowship.org/.

17. This wasn't the first time Erlich had published on the problem of genetic privacy. See also Erika Check Hayden, "Privacy Protections: The Genome Hacker," *Nature News* 497, no. 7448 (2013): 172.

18. Yaniv Erlich et al., "Identity Inference of Genomic Data Using Long-Range Familial Searches," *Science*, October 11, 2018, 690; Heather Murphy, "Most White

Americans' DNA Can Be Identified through Genealogy Databases," *New York Times,* October 11, 2018, www.nytimes.com.

19. Erlich et al., "Identity Inference of Genomic Data"; "MyHeritage Statement about a Cybersecurity Incident," *MyHeritage Blog* (blog), June 4, 2018, https://blog .myheritage.com/2018/06/myheritage-statement-about-a-cybersecurity-incident/; Kari Paul, "MyHeritage Hack Affects 92 Million Customers, Reveals More Risks with Genealogy Sites," www.marketwatch.com.

20. Carson Martinez, "Privacy Best Practices for Consumer Genetic Testing Services," *Future of Privacy Forum* (blog), July 31, 2018, https://fpf.org/2018/07/31/ privacy-best-practices-for-consumer-genetic-testing-services/. In 2019 the major genetic genealogy companies, Ancestry, 23andMe, and Helix, spent significant money lobbying Congress in order to influence privacy legislation to their advantage. Garrett Gangitano, "DNA Testing Companies Launch New Privacy Coalition," *Hill,* June 25, 2019, https://thehill.com.

21. Dan Taggart, interview by the author, Provo, UT, May 2010. See also the website of FamilyTreeDNA where paternal and maternal ancestry tests explicitly invoke "Adam" and "Eve" as our parents. www.familytreedna.com/.

22. Greenspan, "Connecting Families and Saving Lives."

23. Joanna Kaplanis et al., "Quantitative Analysis of Population-Scale Family Trees with Millions of Relatives," *Science,* April 12, 2018, 171.

24. Ibid., 173.

25. Douglas L. T. Rohde, Steve Olson, and Joseph T. Chang, "Modelling the Recent Common Ancestry of All Living Humans," *Nature* 431, no. 7008 (2004): 562. Joseph T. Chang, a Yale statistician and one of the authors of this study, had previously worked out "the high probability" that for a large population, "all individuals who have any descendants among the present-day individuals are actually ancestors of all present-day individuals." Joseph T. Chang, "Recent Common Ancestors of All Present-Day Individuals," *Advances in Applied Probability* 31, no. 4 (1999): 1002–26.

26. Rohde, Olson, and Chang, "Modelling the Recent Common Ancestry," 563.

INDEX

··